Translating Global Ideas

SUNY series, Education in Global Perspectives

Published in cooperation with the

CIES

COMPARATIVE &
INTERNATIONAL
EDUCATION
SOCIETY

Series Editors:
Laura C. Engel, Claire Maxwell, and Miri Yemini (2022–)
Lesley Bartlett, Jun Li, M. Najeeb Shafiq,
and Frances Vavrus (2018–2022)

Translating Global Ideas

How Policy Legacies and Domestic Politics Shape Education Governance in Latin America

CLAUDIA DIAZ-RIOS

SUNY
PRESS

Cover illustration: city lights at night of South America from outer space. Earth map texture provided by Nasa. Shutterstock

Published by State University of New York Press, Albany

For information, contact State University of New York Press, Albany, NY www.sunypress.edu

Library of Congress Cataloging-in-Publication Data

Name: Díaz-Ríos, Claudia, author.
Title: Translating global ideas : how policy legacies and domestic politics
    shape education governance in Latin America / Claudia Diaz-Rios.
Description: Albany : State University of New York Press, [2024]. | Series:
    SUNY series, Education in global perspectives | Includes bibliographical
    references and index.
Identifiers: LCCN 2023036251 | ISBN 9781438497266 (hardcover : alk. paper) |
    ISBN 9781438497273 (ebook) | ISBN 9781438497259 (pbk. : alk. paper)
Subjects: LCSH: Education and state—Chile. | Education and state—
    Argentina. | Education and state—Colombia. | Educational change—
    Chile. | Educational change—Argentina. | Educational change—Colombia.
Classification: LCC LC92.C5 D53 2024 | DDC 379.83—dc23/eng/20230925
LC record available at https://lccn.loc.gov/2023036251

To Sebastián, Violeta, Tomás, Jesús, and María.

Contents

List of Illustrations   ix

Preface and Acknowledgments   xiii

Acronyms and Abbreviations   xv

Introduction: Global Ideas, Policy Variation, and the Governance
of Secondary Education in Latin America   1

Chapter 1   Policy Legacies and Domestic Conflict in the
            Translation of Global Ideas   29

Chapter 2   Translation of Manpower Education Planning Ideas   43

Chapter 3   Varieties of State Retrenchment: Market-Based
            and Active-State Ideas   81

Chapter 4   The Translation of Education for All in the Era
            of Accountability   129

Paths of Translation: Implications for Future Research and Reforms   171

Appendix   187

Notes   193

References   197

Index   235

Illustrations

Figures

I.1 Gross Enrollment Ratio in Latin America and the
     Caribbean, Secondary Education   9

I.2 Gross Enrollment Ratio in Secondary Education in
     Argentina, Chile, and Colombia   19

I.3 Percentage of Enrollment in Private Schools out of
     Total Enrollment in Argentina, Chile, and Colombia,
     Secondary Education   20

Tables

I.1 Policy Alternatives in Education Governance   8

I.2 Changes in Secondary Education Governance in Chile,
     Argentina, and Colombia Between the 1960s and 2010s   21

1.1 Outline of Translation Mechanism   31

1.2 Translation Outcomes According to the Interaction
     Between Global Ideas, Policy Legacies, and Domestic
     Coalitions   39

2.1 Changes in Global Education Ideas in the 1950s   45

2.2   Compatibility Between Chilean Policy Legacies and
       MEP Ideas   49

2.3   Coalitions' Actors and Activities During MEP-Inspired
       Frei-Montalva's Reform by Policy Area (1964–1970)   52

2.4   Coalitions' Actors and Activities During MEP-Inspired
       Allende's Reform by Policy Area (1970–1973)   54

2.5   Translation of MEP Ideas in Chile   55

2.6   Ambiguous Compatibility Between Argentinean Policy
       Legacies and MEP Ideas   60

2.7   Coalitions' Actors and Activities During MEP Ideas in
       Argentina by Policy Area   63

2.8   Translation of MEP Ideas in Argentina   66

2.9   Incompatibility of Colombian Policy Legacies with
       MEP Ideas   70

2.10   Coalitions' Actors and Activities During MEP Ideas in
       Colombia by Policy Area   73

2.11   Translation of MEP Ideas in Colombia   77

2.12   Summary of Translation Outcomes by Country and
       Policy Area During MEP Ideas   79

3.1   Varieties of State Retrenchment in Education   87

3.2   Diffusion Channels and Timing of State-Retrenchment
       Ideas in Chile, Argentina, and Colombia   88

3.3   Relative Incompatibility of Chilean Policy Legacies with
       Market-Oriented Ideas in the mid-1970s   91

3.4   Coalitions' Actors and Activities During Pinochet's
       Regime   94

3.5   Coalitions' Actors and Activities After the Transition
       to Democracy in Chile   97

3.6   Translation of State-Retrenchment Ideas in Chile   104

3.7   Incompatibility of Policy Legacies with State
       Retrenchment at the Time of Democratic Transition
       in Argentina   107

3.8   Coalitions' Actors and Activities in Argentina in the
       1990s   112

3.9   Translation of State-Retrenchment Ideas in Argentina   115

3.10   Compatibility of Policy Legacies with Market-Oriented
       Ideas by the End of the National Front (mid-1970s)   118

3.11   Coalitions' Actors and Activities in Colombia in the
       1990s   122

3.12   Translation of State-Retrenchment Ideas in Colombia   125

3.13   Summary of Translation Outcomes by Country and
       Policy Area During State-Retrenchment Ideas   127

4.1   Changes in Global Ideas Between the 1980s and the
       2010s   132

4.2   Compatibility of Policy Legacies with EFA and
       Accountability Ideas in Chilean Education   137

4.3   Coalitions' Actors and Activities for the 2010s Chilean
       Education Reforms   143

4.4   Translation of EFA and Accountability Ideas in the
       Chilean Education   146

4.5   Compatibility of Policy Legacies with Ideas on a
       Stronger Role of the State in Argentinean Education   149

4.6   Dominance and Compromises of a Stronger State
       Coalition   153

4.7   Translation of EFA and Accountability Ideas in
       Argentina   156

4.8   Compatibility of Policy Legacies with EFA and
       Accountability Ideas in Colombia   160

4.9   Coalitions' Actors and Activities by Policy Area in
       Colombia (2000–2015)   164

4.10   Translation of EFA and Accountability Ideas in Colombia   168

4.11   Summary of Translation Outcomes by Country and
       Policy Area During EFA and Accountability Ideas   169

Preface and Acknowledgments

Over the past few decades, the globalization of education policy has captivated scholars who contribute invaluable insights into the impact of international actors and the prevalence of similar education policies worldwide. However, they often overlook the significance of domestic actors in this process, leading to an excessive emphasis on policy convergence. Drawing on my dual background in political science and sociology, this book integrates methodologies and perspectives from comparative politics and comparative education through a historical analysis of education policymaking in three Latin American countries. The book explains how prior domestic decisions shape the positions, power resources, and strategies of local actors in embracing, modifying, or rejecting global ideas propagated by influential transnational organizations. In essence, this book elucidates the critical role of domestic politics in the process of globalizing education policy.

This book would not have been possible without the support of many people. Foremost, I am profoundly grateful to Michelle Dion, whose guidance and mentorship played an indispensable role in refining my research and comparative skills. Her encouragement served as the catalyst for undertaking this book. I also extend my sincere appreciation to Scott Davies, who helped me stay connected to the field of education and fueled my passion while I navigated a political science community with contrasting interests. Shafiqul Huque's valuable insights from a development perspective enriched my work. Additionally, I am indebted to the invaluable feedback, advice, and engaging discussions with esteemed colleagues, including D. Brent Edwards, Lesley Bartlett, Mauro Moschetti, Mariano Narodowski, and Veronica Gottau, as well as the participants in the panels of multiple CIES conferences where I shared aspects of this project. I also extend my gratitude to the three anonymous referees whose thorough reviews contributed significantly to the final version of this book.

Several individuals helped ensure that my field research in each country was successful. I am particularly grateful to Pamela Ried, Daniel Contreras, Rossana Castiglioni, Felipe Rivera, Marcela Bautista, and Daniela Ataíro for helping me organize numerous interviews, giving me access to primary documents, and teaching me a great deal about education politics in their respective countries. I am thankful for every one of the officials, politicians, education policymakers and administrators, representatives of civil society organizations, and education experts who accepted to be interviewed and generously shared their time, insights, and experiences with me. Some of the data included here was previously discussed in Díaz-Ríos, 2019, 2020; and Díaz-Ríos & Urbano-Canal, 2023. The Social Science and Humanities Research Council of Canada and the McMaster Grant in Aid of Travel Research & Field Study Fund provided financial support for the field research.

I am also thankful for my mentors in the early stages of my career: Víctor M. Gómez, who guided me through my first explorations of sociology of education; and Luz Gabriela Arango, whose early departure took away from me thoughtful sociological, feminist, and personal conversations. I wish she could have seen this book. Lastly, I am profoundly indebted to my family. My husband, Sebastián, made significant sacrifices, granting me the time to travel, conduct fieldwork, and dedicate myself to writing. To Violeta and Tomás, my children, I express deep gratitude for their patience and understanding during the countless moments when I was unable to assist with homework, attend games, or just spend time with them. A mis padres les debo una gran parte de todas mis metas profesionales y personales ya que a pesar de sus pocos privilegios me dieron la mejor educación posible y me enseñaron a creer en mí. In heartfelt appreciation of their unconditional love and support, I dedicate this book to my family.

Acronyms and Abbreviations

ACES: Coordination Assembly of Secondary Students—Chile

ANDERCOP: National Association of Private School Principals—Colombia

CDP: Christian Democratic Party—Chile

CEPAL: United Nations' Economic Commission for Latin America

CIDE: Catholic Centre for Educational Research and Development—Chile

COLEGIO: Colegio de Profesores—Chilean Teacher Union

CONACED: National Confederation of Teaching Centres—Colombia

CONACEP: Association of Chilean Private Schools

CONADE: National Development Council—Argentina

CONES: National Committee for Secondary Students—Chile

CONET: National Council for Technical Education—Argentina

CPEIP: Center for Improvement, Experimentation and Pedagogical Research—Chile

CTERA: Confederation of Education Workers of Argentina

DNP: National Planning Department—Colombia

EFA: Education for All

ENU: Unified National School—Chile

ETS: Educational Testing Service

FECODE: Colombian Federation of Teachers

FEL: Federal Education Law—Argentina

FESES: Santiago's Federation of Secondary Students—Chile

FIDE: Federation of Secondary Schools—Chile

FIEL: Foundation for Latin American Economic Research—Argentina

FLACSO: Latin American Faculty of Social Sciences

GEL: General Education Law—Chile

IADB: Inter-American Development Bank

ICFES: Colombian Institute for the Promotion of Higher Education / Colombian Institute for Education Assessment

ICOLPE: Colombian Pedagogical Institute

IIEP-UNESCO: International Institute for Educational Planning in Buenos Aires—Argentina

ILARI: Latin American Institute for International Relations—Argentina

IMF: International Monetary Fund

LEN: National Education Law—Argentina

LETP: Vocational Education Law—Argentina

LFE: Education Budget Law—Argentina

LLECE: Latin American Laboratory for Assessment of Education Quality

LOCE: Organic Constitutional Education Law—Chile

MAPU: Popular Unitary Action Movement—Chile

MECE-Media: Program for the Improvement of Quality and Equity in Secondary Education—Chile

MEP: Manpower Educational Planning

NAP: Priority Learning Cores—Argentina

NM: New Majority—Chile

NPC: National Pedagogical Congress—Argentina

NPM: New Public Management

OAS: Organization of American States

ODEPLAN: Planning Office—Chile

OECD: Organization for Economic Cooperation and Development

PISA: Programme for International Student Assessment

PPP: Public-Private Partnerships

SENA: National Agency for Job Training—Colombia

SIMCE: System for Measurement of Education Quality—Chile

SINEC: National System for Education Quality Assessment

SNED: National System for Performance Assessment—Chile

TIMMS: Trends in International Mathematics and Science Study

UNDP: United Nations Development Program

UNESCO: United Nations Educational Scientific and Cultural Organization

UP: Popular Unity—Chile

USAID: United States Agency for International Development

VOCSED: Vocational Secondary School

WB: World Bank

Introduction

Global Ideas, Policy Variation, and the Governance of Secondary Education in Latin America

Since the 1980s, Latin American education policy has been influenced by policy proposals advocating for the delegation of education decision-making authority; the introduction of private actors through market-oriented mechanisms; the provision of curriculum autonomy to subnational units, communities, and schools; and the implementation of large-scale standardized assessments to improve school performance. These proposals signal a shift from previous recommendations that advocated for the state's responsibility in educational planning, delivery, and definition of learning contents. These changes also run parallel with enrollment expansion in secondary schools and significant growth in the educational systems.

These dynamics prompted diverse sequences of events and policy outcomes across Latin American countries. In 1979, the authoritarian regime of Augusto Pinochet (1973–1990) in Chile initiated school transfers from central government to municipalities as well as the implementation of a voucher system that made public and private schools compete for students to receive funding. Large-scale standardized exams were later implemented in 1988, but curriculum decisions were never decentralized. After the transition to democracy in 1990, successive center-left governments retained and further consolidated the governance model inherited from the authoritarian regime. These governments delegated more responsibility to nonstate actors by allowing private schools to charge extra fees beyond vouchers (shared payment) and by refining the system of performance-based incentives and sanctions to schools

1

and teachers. It was not until 2015 that the Socialist government of Michelle Bachelet (2014–2018) reversed various market-oriented policy instruments, including student selection by schools and shared payments. Nevertheless, the governance model kept the main features of the system implemented in the late 1970s that arguably fueled educational inequality and segregation.

At the same time, the Argentinean military regime (1976–1983) transferred the fiscal responsibility for primary schools to provinces in 1978 without delegating secondary schools or learning contents. Only after the transition to democracy did the Peronist government of Carlos Menem (1989–1999) decentralize curriculum and fiscal responsibility for secondary schools. This government also implemented standardized exams in 1993, although their use as an accountability tool was quickly dismissed. More recently—due to the unpopularity of Menem's reforms—the Peronist government of Nestor Kirchner (2003–2007) partially recentralized fiscal responsibilities and curriculum decisions in 2005, and the subsequent government of Cristina Fernández (2007–2015) also continued to reject test-based accountability. Even though power changed to a right-wing party in 2015, the right-wing government of Mauricio Macri (2019) was not able to implement significant changes in the governance of secondary education. Thus, while secondary schools were decentralized, the federal government regained significant authority, and schools never achieved substantial autonomy.

In the mid-1970s, Colombia was still trying to advance a centralization process for a poorly coordinated education system. Funding and provision responsibilities were dispersed among municipal, department (similar to state or province), and national levels, and curriculum decisions for secondary schools were nobody's land. Without consolidating this centralization, the Liberal government of Cesar Gaviria (1990–1994) undertook the transfer of national schools to departments and large municipalities, and it increased curriculum autonomy of these units and schools in 1993. Yet, the government failed to implement a voucher system and test-based accountability while it was forced to increase government education expenditure. Unsatisfactory education results pushed a new reform in 2001 under the Conservative government of Andres Pastrana (1998–2002). This reform finally transferred the administration of schools to municipalities, although funding responsibilities remained centralized. Decisions in 2001 also recentralized curriculum choices through national standards and expanded large-scale assessments, although they were not used to award incentives or sanctions for school performance. While these reforms increased state control on secondary schools, the central government's educational investments decreased.

These sequences of reforms in Chile, Argentina, and Colombia raise several baffling questions: Why did these three countries—with comparable levels of development and under the influence of similar globally disseminated policy ideas—pursue different education governance reforms? Why did the Chilean authoritarian regime follow global recommendations more closely, compared to the Argentinean dictatorship? Why did Colombia manage to initiate these reforms during democracy? Why did democratic and ideologically different governments in Chile and Argentina retain and continue reforms inherited from dictatorships? Why did Colombia implement reforms that did not respond to problems rooted in the country's educational system? More generally, what do these reforms tell us about the influence of global forces on education policy decisions?

This book answers these questions by specifying the mechanisms through which domestic dynamics shape the (non)acceptance and reinterpretation of globally diffused education policy ideas. Scholars have provided multiple understandings of mechanism in the social sciences without reaching a consensus (Bengtsson & Hertting, 2014; Falleti & Lynch, 2009; Mahoney, 2001). While settling this debate goes beyond the scope of this book, two tensions inform the work presented here. The first tension refers to whether mechanisms can be defined as chains of intervening variables (G. King et al., 1994) or as a causal pathway in which relations between entities and their activities produce specific outcomes (Beach, 2016; Gerring, 2008; Hedström, 2010). Unraveling chains of intervening variables identifies factors that covariate with other factors and are therefore assumed to prevent or facilitate an outcome. For instance, cultural legacies of a strong state role in education may prevent the adoption of or modify substantially global market-oriented ideas. Nevertheless, this identification does not tell us sufficiently about the process through which factors lead to particular effects; for example, how legacies of a strong state shape the influence of foreign prescriptions. For that, we need to look not only at the characteristics of cultural legacies but also at the activities that these legacies trigger in actors modifying global ideas. More generally, in order to identify the mechanisms that reinterpret global ideas, we need to focus on the causal pathway through the identification of entities (e.g., actors, organizations, structures) that engage in activities and produce changes in the adoption of foreign recommendations (Beach, 2016).

The second tension relates to the discussion about whether mechanisms found in a single or small set of cases are portable and can explain other cases (Falleti & Lynch, 2009). Some consider mechanisms as deterministic, producing the same outcome whenever they are present (Bengtsson & Hertting, 2014; Mahoney, 2001). Yet, continuing with our example, not all countries with a strong state tradition in education significantly modify or reject ideas of education markets (e.g., Chile, Sweden). More convincingly, other scholars rather regard mechanisms as probabilistic, which means that their presence increases the chances of an effect to happen but that the actual outcome may vary due to its interaction with the context or other mechanisms (Danermark, 2012; Elster, 1998; Hedström, 2010). Thus, mechanism-based explanations need to "define both the mechanism at work and the context in which it operates" (Falleti & Lynch, 2009, p. 1151) in order to pinpoint the conditions under which a mechanism is more likely to produce a particular outcome.

Building on these assumptions, I argue that the reinterpretation of a global idea occurs when groups of multiple domestic actors (e.g., political parties, teacher unions, bureaucrats, social movements) engage in supporting or opposing the adoption of the foreign recommendation. Their support or opposition depends on whether the global idea favors their interests and matches their beliefs about how the governance of education should look. The result of this conflict depends not only on what group is more influential but also on the context created by the encounter between global ideas and existing domestic governance arrangements. When these two are compatible, supporters of global ideas have more leverage to facilitate the adoption and emulation of external recommendations. Incompatibility between these entities fuels domestic conflict and gives greater chances to opponents to reinterpret or even reject a global idea. The theoretical framework presented in chapter 1 further unpacks this argument, explains the different outcomes that the modification of global ideas can have under different circumstances, and ultimately illuminates the question of why and how comparable countries under the influence of similar global policy ideas adopt different secondary education governance models. The book, therefore, complements and qualifies theories of education policy globalization by combining institutionalist perspectives from comparative politics and organizational theories.

Education Governance in Latin America

Although there is no consensus about the meaning of governance, different definitions attempt to describe the growing complexity of societal coordination that shifts away from the hierarchical regulation of the state and increasingly involves other non-state actors (Rizvi & Lingard, 2010; Windzio et al., 2005). This book builds on Rosenau's definition of governance as the combination of formal and informal steering mechanisms to make demands, frame goals, issue directives, pursue policies, and generate compliance (2004, p. 31). Thus, the notion of governance entails at least four aspects: (1) who has the power to make decisions, (2) over what matters these decision-makers have authority, (3) how other actors participate in these decisions, and (4) how an account of these matters is rendered. This definition raises several questions in the field of education, such as who the new actors involved in steering education are, what the politics involved in these new ways of coordination are, and, more broadly, who controls different education matters and how (Jakobi et al., 2009).

This book is particularly concerned with the changes in the governance of provision, curriculum, and evaluation in secondary education. The governance of education provision has two dimensions. The first dimension refers to what actors are authorized to deliver education; for example, the central state through national schools, subnational units through provincial or municipal schools, nongovernment actors through community schools, or private actors through private establishments (McGinn & Welsh, 1999). The second dimension refers to the degree to which families can select their children's school. The level of school choice can be limited by state exams or geographic location, determined by schools selecting students, or opened to parental decisions (Herbst, 2006).

Curricular governance also has two dimensions. First, it refers to those who are entitled to decide the contents and desired learning outcomes of secondary education, whether that is the central government, subnational units, schools, local communities, or private actors (Rizvi & Lingard, 2010). Second, the governance of the secondary school curriculum also refers to the orientation of its learning goals, which include comprehensive curricula, tracks with content and learning goals differentiated by student ability, or layers differentiated by various types of specialization (academic, vocational, scientific, artistic, etc.) (Benavot, 1983; Kamens, 1996; Kerckhoff, 2001).

Finally, evaluation governance refers to those who control the mechanisms by which students are examined, whether that is teachers, subnational units, or the central government. It also refers to who is accountable for assessment results. In secondary education, student evaluation can have consequences exclusively for students, such as granting a degree or university admission (Eckstein & Noah, 1993). Alternatively, evaluation may also be used to assess the implementation of the curriculum and reforms (Kamens & McNeely, 2010) or as a tool of test-based accountability by the use of government-led incentives, sanctions, or through parental school choice (Rizvi & Lingard, 2010; Verger et al., 2019).

Simultaneous changes in the areas of provision, curriculum, and evaluation produce complex transformations of the governance of secondary education. Scholarship on education policy suggests that educational systems are shifting away from a tight-loose bureaucratic arrangement toward a loose-tight post-bureaucratic form of governance (Baker & LeTendre, 2005; Maroy, 2009; H.-D. Meyer & Rowan, 2006b). The tight-loose bureaucratic arrangement includes, for the tight aspect, tracking or selective recruitment of students in public schools and a centralized curriculum that ensures the adequate training of human capital and future ruling elite (Astiz & Wiseman, 2005; Bruter et al., 2004; J. W. Meyer & Rowan, 1978). The loose part involves delegating student evaluation to teachers believing they would follow the established curriculum and the bureaucratic rules of the system (J. W. Meyer & Rowan, 1978; Scott et al., 1994). By contrast, the loose aspect of the loose-tight post-bureaucratic arrangement refers to the devolution of education delivery and curriculum decisions to subnational units, schools, communities, or private actors. It also includes the expansion of secondary education enrollment and provision of school choice for families (Astiz & Wiseman, 2005; Windzio et al., 2005). For the tight part, this arrangement involves centralizing student assessments through standardized tests and establishing incentives and sanctions for performance (Astiz & Wiseman, 2005; Rizvi & Lingard, 2010; Verger et al., 2019). Provision, curriculum, and evaluation are also empirically relevant, as their transformation in previous decades has modified the role of the different stakeholders in

Latin American education systems and has generated varied impacts on education quality and inequality.

The distribution of authority over provision, curriculum, and evaluation can be conceptualized as a continuum. On one end, we have a strong control of the state over schools; at the other end, authority is dispersed through smaller subnational units, communities, and private parties. This idea of continuum can be associated with the concept of decentralization or the distribution of authority between central government and subordinate, semiautonomous, or nongovernmental institutions (Jakobi et al., 2009; Pollitt, 2007; Rondinelli, 1981). Decentralization involves different degrees of transfer of authority and responsibility: (1) deconcentration is the shift of administrative functions and workload to subordinates at the local level without transferring authority; (2) delegation is the transfer of responsibility and some decision-making power to subnational units but within the boundaries established at the central level; (3) devolution involves the transfer of authority to autonomous local units or nongovernmental actors without the direct control of the central level; and (4) privatization implies responsibility and decision-making transferred to private actors, often regulated by a market rationale (Ball & Youdell, 2009; Rees, 2010; Robertson et al., 2012; Rondinelli & Nellis, 1986).

According to the continuum between centralization and decentralization, the areas of provision, curriculum, and evaluation adopt different arrangements that constitute distinctive governance models. To categorize these models, I build a classification based on the existing education governance literature. This classification identifies four typical combinations of governance arrangements that a country may adopt: bureaucratic model of governance or "teaching state" (Almond, 1991; J.W. Meyer & Rowan, 1978; Narodowski & Andrada, 2004; Newland, 1994), the semi-decentralized bureaucratic model or quasi-state monopoly[1] (Narodowski, 2008), the dualist model (Diaz-Rios, 2019; Narodowski & Nores, 2002), and the quasi-market model (Maroy, 2009; Walford, 1996; Whitty, 1997). Each of these combinations is associated with coordination problems addressed by distinctive institutionalized forms and capacities for collective action that define actors' interests and payoff schemes (Ostrom, 2015; Windzio et al., 2005). Yet, these combinations are ideal-types that in reality can be hybridized, as this book and many other studies show (Jakobi et al., 2009; Maroy, 2009, 2012; Windzio et al., 2005). Therefore, this classification presented in Table I.1 serves only heuristic purposes.

Table I.1. Policy Alternatives in Education Governance

Model / "Main Role of State"	Education Provision	Curriculum	Student Assessment
Teaching state / state monopoly	*Centralized* by selectively recruiting students for elite national schools.	*Centralized* through national curriculum.	*Delegated* to teachers.
Quasi-state monopoly / evaluator state	*Deconcentrated* to subnational levels with some school choice for families within the public system.	*Delegated* to local levels within the boundaries of centralized curricular standards.	*Partially delegated* to teachers but also *centralized* through standardized tests to define policy and programs.
Dualist system	*Privatized* for a segment of the demand. *Delegated* to local levels for those who attend public schools.	*Devolved* to the private sector. *Delegated* to local levels within a curricular framework.	*Centralized* to inform families in private schools and to define policy and programs in public schools.
Quasi-market of education	*Privatized* through full school choice.	*Devolved* to schools at least partially.	*Centralized* to inform parents and encourage competition.

Authors' elaboration based on Almond, 1991; Diaz-Rios, 2019; Maroy, 2009; J.W. Meyer & Rowan, 1978; Narodowski, 2008; Narodowski & Andrada, 2004; Narodowski & Nores, 2002; Newland, 1994; Walford, 1996; Whitty, 1997.

By the mid-twentieth century, secondary education in Latin America was highly selective. Since enrollment was low and secondary schools were not numerous, central coordination and management were not substantially problematic. Nevertheless, by the mid- to late twentieth century, secondary education enrollment rose significantly (Figure I.1), and therefore a centralized coordination of an increased number of schools, teachers, and staff became difficult. Problems of coordination run parallel to discussions about the negative effects of centralized curricula that neglected the needs and expectations of local communities and minorities.

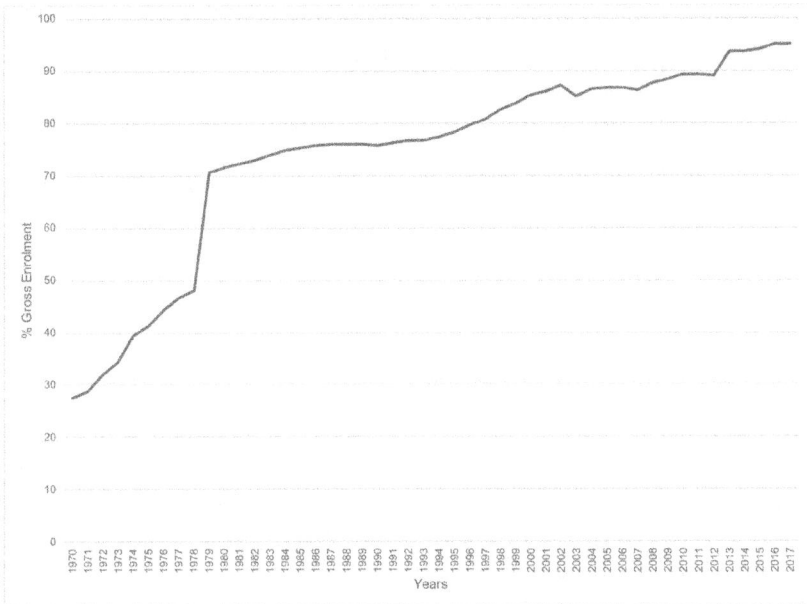

Figure I.1. Gross Enrollment Ratio in Latin America and the Caribbean, Secondary Education. Author's elaboration based on the World Bank, Education Statistics. Gross enrollment ratio, secondary, both sexes. Retrieved from https://databank.worldbank.org/source/education-statistics-^-all-indicators.

In this context, Latin American governments initiated a series of reforms. By the early twentieth century, only a handful of countries in the region had developed strong "teaching state" or bureaucratic governance models. Some of these countries (e.g., Argentina, Mexico) adopted characteristics of a quasi-state monopoly of education, including administrative deconcentration of education provision, delegation of some curriculum decisions, and increased although still limited room for school choice (e.g., between Catholic and public schools). A few others, and Chile in particular, embraced a quasi-market model of governance. Other countries that resembled a quasi-state monopoly of education increased the participation of nonstate and subnational actors, and some incorporated elements of a quasi-market model, such as school or community autonomy to hire and fire staff, competitive funding, test-based accountability, and so on (e.g., Peru, Brazil). Some remaining countries in the region that originally developed dualist models—in which public schooling grew in a slower pace and frequently targeted only poor students (e.g., Colombia,

El Salvador, Ecuador)—adopted characteristics of a quasi-market model by encouraging the expansion of the private sector, allowing more autonomy on curriculum, and implementing different forms of accountability.

The combinations and sequences of reforms undertaken by Latin American countries addressed certain coordination difficulties; however, they also created new policy problems and political struggles. The growth of private schools nurtured new constituents and sometimes exacerbated problems of educational segregation and inequality (Diaz-Rios, 2019). The oscillation between a centralized curriculum (centralized definition of curriculum contents), curricular autonomy (devolution of authority for teachers or communities to develop either parts of curriculum autonomously or the entire curriculum under very general national guidelines), and curriculum standardization (centralized definition of learning expectations) dispersed responsibility and prevented a consistent development of capacity for curriculum decisions in different governance levels (Gvirtz, 2002). Implementing standardized exams did not always translate into quality improvement but instead often increased teachers' political opposition, especially when used as an accountability mechanism. In chapters 2, 3, and 4, I analyze the consequences of these sequences of reforms.

Current Explanations of Changes in Education Governance

The mechanisms theorized and tested in this book build on a rich body of literature that explores the globalization of education policy. Some existing explanations have specified the mechanisms through which policy ideas are diffused, including world society theory and political economy approaches. Some others have described how these ideas change as they are adopted in different contexts, such as cultural political economy, policy-borrowing, and anthropological accounts. These descriptions provide detailed narratives of reinterpretation of global ideas in particular contexts but do not fully conceptualize the mechanisms that lead to diverse reinterpretations. Although this book acknowledges the uniqueness of each case, its comparative analysis of Chile, Argentina, and Colombia identifies patterns across cases that unpack these mechanisms and contribute to a better understanding of why and how the adoption of global ideas varies across different countries.

WORLD SOCIETY THEORY

As one of the leading approaches for the globalization of education policy, world society theory stems from the observation that education systems across societies present strikingly similar practices and arrangements due to external forces that push them to such isomorphism (H.-D. Meyer & Rowan, 2006b; J. W. Meyer & Rowan, 1977). This scholarship describes global ideas or global norms as part of a global culture that determine the appropriate behavior of actors, shape and legitimate identities, and constrain their practices (Drori et al., 2006; Finnemore, 1996; Kamens & McNeely, 2010; McNeely, 1995; J. W. Meyer, 2000). Put differently, these global ideas shape the ways in which decision-makers understand and solve education policy problems. This approach contests functionalist arguments by suggesting that global ideas are adopted not because they have been proved to work, but because of the perception of their legitimacy and appropriateness, thus transforming them into globalized myths that teach what has to be done (Kamens & McNeely, 2010; J. W. Meyer & Hannan, 1979; Ramírez, 2012). Such legitimacy is the driver of policy convergence.

Global norms travel through mimetic processes or through normative pressures. Mimesis describes a mechanism through which countries in uncertain circumstances imitate external models (e.g., mass schooling or national assessment systems) that international actors have framed and disseminated as the most appropriate solutions to specific policy problems (Beckert, 2010; DiMaggio & Powell, 1983; Finnemore, 1993, 1996; McNeely, 1995). My evidence suggests that international organizations such as the United Nations Educational Scientific and Cultural Organization (UNESCO), the United Nations' Economic Commission for Latin America (CEPAL), the World Bank (WB), the United States Agency for International Development (USAID), the Organization of American States (OAS), and some US universities were all engaged in diffusing educational policy ideas, including educational planning, decentralization, school choice, standardized assessments, test-based accountability, school autonomy, and so on. However, the interviews I conducted also demonstrate that elites do not take these recommendations for granted and instead transform them to avoid political costs of unpopular changes or to justify specific policy decisions that favor their interests (personal communications #1, #3, #50, and #58). Therefore, mimesis has not produced the theorized policy convergence. For instance, standardized exams are widely institutionalized in Chile and Colombia but not in Argentina, and curricular autonomy is adopted in Colombia but restrained in Chile and Argentina. The mechanism of mimesis only tells us part of the story, but it exaggerates the taken-for-granted nature attributed to global norms that depict domestic actors as unable to contest them or to think outside the template the norms provide (Campbell, 2004).

Normative pressures refer to processes of socialization through professional training, networks, and communities that favor the adoption of similar policies based on shared professional standards or norms (DiMaggio & Powell, 1983; Djelic, 2004; Owen-Smith & Powell, 2008; Ramírez, 2012). In fact, Chile developed robust and highly influential communities trained under educational planning ideas in the 1960s, as well as networks that argued for market-oriented education policies in the 1980s and 1990s. Actors of these networks often received foreign training and helped spread such socialization in domestic universities (Gauri, 1998; Picazo, 2013). Although smaller and less influential, similar networks emerged in Argentina and Colombia as well. Yet, evidence I collected posits that conflicting vested interests tied to existing domestic arrangements contest and transform foreign recommendations, alongside the size and position of these networks that account for different interpretations of global policy ideas. This factor is often neglected by world-society analyses.

World society theory suggests that education systems do not simply emulate global ideas but rather decouple the norm from the actual practice (Boxenbaum & Jonsson, 2008; J. W. Meyer, 2010; J. W. Meyer & Rowan, 1991). Put differently, education systems abide by global norms on a superficial level and adopt new structures without necessarily implementing the related practices. The acknowledgment of decoupling suggests that domestic actors can act pragmatically toward global ideas, identify the possibility of nonconformity, and act somewhat strategically. This notion contradicts—or at least relaxes—the original argument of a global culture that is taken for granted and calls for improved specification of the conditions and mechanisms through which domestic policymakers engage in conformity or decoupling (Silova, 2009; Steiner-Khamsi, 2012).

POLITICAL ECONOMY

Political economy approaches also acknowledge the existence of global policy ideas; however, rather than analyzing them as part of a global culture, the literature perceives and examines them as power-related dynamics. Traditional political economy scholarship emphasizes hard power, exercised through material means such as coercion, as a globalization force. Powerful international actors impose certain policies on other countries through incentives and sanctions, such as conditional loans, foreign aid, or technical assistance (Dobbin et al., 2007; Dolowitz & Marsh, 2000; Griffiths & Arnove, 2015; Samoff, 2007). During the 1980s and 1990s, Latin American countries struggled with harsh economic crises, which left them with little choice but to implement education reforms, such as privatization and decentralization, in exchange for loans and financial and technical assistance of the WB and the International Monetary Fund (IMF) (Arnove et al., 1996). Likewise, the WB, the Organization for Economic Cooperation and Development (OECD), and the Inter-American Development Bank (IADB) offer incentives for developing countries to implement standardized exams (Chmielewski et al., 2017, p. 19; Smith, 2014; Wiseman, 2010, p. 17). Nevertheless, governments often fail to implement the conditions required by external actors or ask for loans and conditions to further enforce their own agendas and interests (Dion, 2008). My findings show, for instance, that Argentina quickly dismantled the test-based accountability tools implemented in 1993 despite the financial and technical support of the WB (personal communications #58, #71, and #80). Likewise, in the 1990s, Chile requested a WB loan that the country did not need—only to guarantee the implementation of policy changes preferred by domestic policy elites (personal communications #50 and #52). Thus, the mere existence of loans or assistance is a weak test for coercion (Dion, 2008). Further evidence needs to verify that policymakers were actually forced to implement policies that they would not have adopted otherwise.

A more recent approach integrates an ideational perspective to the conventional, materially driven political economic analysis (Robertson & Dale, 2015; Verger et al, 2019). This strand conceives education policy as the product of the interaction between global and national civilizational projects (e.g., capitalism, national identity), the position of each society in global economic relations, and power struggles between different actors (Robertson & Dale, 2015). Beyond coercion, this scholarship shows how international agents build their power through the production and dissemination of meaning that establishes certain policy solutions as more adequate than others (Dale, 2000; Robertson, 2005; Verger, 2014). While this scholarship and world society theory coincide to some extent in the idea of globalized cultural projects, the cultural political economy approach further highlights the role of the local level by specifying mechanisms of domestic transformation of these projects; namely, variation, selection, and retention. Punctuated moments of crisis (e.g., economic, political, or humanitarian crises, social discontent with education, etc.) trigger a process of variation in which local actors look for alternative ways to govern education. This search makes room for international actors to disseminate policy solutions using hard (coercion) and soft (ideational legitimacy) power technologies (Verger et al., 2016). Nevertheless, local actors do not just emulate global policy ideas but also select solutions according to the domestic capacity and the evidence supporting policy recommendations. Yet, these scholars suggest that the process of selecting solutions is not rational or neutral but rather semiotic, as different governments select sources of evidence according to their ideological affinity (Verger et al., 2016; Verger, Fontdevila, et al., 2017). Finally, the retention of such solution is presented as a more contentious and materially oriented process depending on the conflict and negotiation with potential opponents of government proposals, such as teacher unions, political parties, and other interest groups. This conflict is shaped by formal institutions that define the influence of opponents, including government systems, electoral rules, veto players, president-assemblies distribution of power, and others (Takayama, 2012). Consequently, some solutions may be substantially transformed or may not be retained at all (Verger et al., 2016). Once chosen, the adopted solutions become resistant to change as they nurture new constituents invested in their continuity (Takayama, 2012, 2013). This cultural political economic approach has significantly advanced the explanation of variation amid convergence by integrating diffusion of global ideas with the specification of local reinterpretation mechanisms. However, my findings illuminate some aspects unexplained by the variation, selection, and retention mechanisms. Although cultural political economy aims at giving equal status to semiosis and social and material structures, it ultimately gives predominance to ideational processes while using material and extra-semiotic elements as constraining or mediating variables (Staricco, 2017). For instance, the role of material interests and how they interact with the selection of policy solutions is almost displaced by a semiotic analysis of how actors define and choose evidence. Although material-based conflict and institutional constraints are further acknowledged in the retention mechanism, their role seems to be an accessory to explain changes in the initial government's selection. Moreover, the retention mechanism does not fully explain how the material and semiotic strategies of supporters and opponents interact with institutions. Thus, we cannot know if actors' strategies can overcome unfavorable institutional arrangements or if institutional arrangements define the strategies and the result of the conflict. To complement these gaps, the mechanism specified in this book show how material interests can equally influence both the selection and retention of solutions in ways that are not always consistent or do not always give predominance to semiotic processes. The book also specifies the strategies supporters and opponents of educational reforms use to advocate for their preferences and the conditions under which they can be successful.

The Role of Local Context: Policy-Borrowing and Anthropological Accounts

Like cultural political economy, policy-borrowing and anthropological scholarship examine the role of domestic actors in the globalization of education policy. Yet, these approaches focus specifically on cultural processes. These scholars conceive globalization as a domestically induced process in which foreign references or global policy ideas are transformed and reinterpreted through local sense-making (Anderson-Levitt, 2003b; Schriewer, 2003; Steiner-Khamsi, 2014). Policy-borrowing literature identify different stages in which global ideas are reinterpreted. Although there is no consensus on the number and nature of these different stages, these scholars suggest that borrowing starts with selecting external references to follow (also called *cross-national attraction* by Phillips & Ochs, 2003; *externalization* by Schriewer, 2003; *reception* by Steiner-Khamsi, 2014; *lesson-drawing* by Dolowitz & Marsh, 2000, and Jules, 2012, among others). Three processes interact in the externalization stage. First, countries experience a crisis or protracted conflict that affects their education system; for instance, public discontent with education outcomes (quality, inequality, efficiency, etc.), poor results of management (distribution of responsibilities, salaries and labor conditions, etc.), or evidence that is interpreted as a country's educational deficit or decline (Steiner-Khamsi, 2012). Second, governments look for foreign references and strategically select those that are in line with their particular agenda (Silova, 2009; Steiner-Khamsi, 2004, 2012). Yet, third, these governments choose from a limited range of options that correspond to external sources of authority, including countries that have been portrayed as global education leaders, best practices disseminated by international organizations, and overall external references that confirm the fear of falling behind on a process of modernization or global-market competition (Steiner-Khamsi, 2014). Externalization then resembles the variation and selection mechanisms of cultural political economy. Both strands of literature accept diffusion and some of the characteristics of mimesis while simultaneously challenging the taken-for-granted nature attributed to global ideas by world society theory. Instead, policy-borrowing and cultural political economy indicate the agency of domestic agents in the process of selection.

A second stage of borrowing refers to the translation of global ideas.[2] During the translation stage, domestic actors make sense of imported models in a variety of ways that are shaped by contextual factors, such as cultural background, prevailing meanings attributed to education, economic conditions, vested interests, and political struggles (Anderson-Levitt, 2003b; Schriewer, 2003; Steiner-Khamsi, 2004). Both anthropological perspectives and policy-borrowing studies provide detailed descriptions of processes of translation, reinterpretation, and divergence (Bartlett, 2003; Jungck & Kajornsin, 2003; Rambla, 2014; Silova, 2009; Spreen, 2004; Steiner-Khamsi & Waldow, 2013). These descriptions challenge assumptions about global culture, isomorphism, and policy convergence by showing a complementary story of local variability and resistance (Anderson-Levitt, 2003b).

Nevertheless, these narratives—often based on single case studies—have not paid sufficient attention to commonalities and differences across cases (Schwinn, 2012), thus rendering the mechanisms behind translation as insufficiently theorized. Questions about the role context plays in the reinterpretation of global ideas are only addressed by descriptions that tell us what happened without fully shedding light on why things happened the way they did. Studies also approach these questions by identifying various intervening factors (prevailing interests, preexisting discourses, cultural legacies, etc.) without explaining how these factors trigger different processes across cases. Overall, studies describe *glocalization* processes (Anderson-Levitt, 2003b) and sometimes conceptualize particular types of *translation*, including *hybridization*, which refers to the mixture of domestic practices and global ideas in a single policy or program (Maroy, 2009); addition or *juxtaposition* of global ideas and domestic institutions, which may eventually produce a gradual change of both but not their displacement (Steiner-Khamsi, 2012); *reinforcement* of domestic institutions using global ideas to enhance the legitimacy of an existing policy (Silova, 2005; Steiner-Khamsi et al., 2006); and *inspiration*, which refers to the process of drawing lessons from knowledge organizations (international organizations, think tanks, etc.) or from other countries (Dolowitz & Marsh, 2000; Steiner-Khamsi & Waldow, 2013). Nevertheless, these studies do not explain the circumstances under which the translation of global ideas lead to any of these outcomes. While each case might be fairly unique, we can still identify patterns that drive us toward a more consistent conceptual understanding of the relationship between global dissemination of policy ideas and context-specific reinterpretations of them (Schriewer, 2012). This book's primary aim is to find these patterns and advance such conceptual understandings.

The Argument of the Book

World society scholarship on education reforms in Latin America has shown that global policy ideas have been disseminated through mimetic and normative pressures (Astiz, 2006; Astiz & Wiseman, 2005; Levy, 2006; Resnik, 2006). Political economic studies have demonstrated the role of coercion, globally structured policy agenda, and semiotic processes on both education policy convergence and variation (Arnove et al., 2012; Balarin, 2014; Robertson & Dale, 2015; Verger et al., 2016). Policy-borrowing and anthropological studies have uncovered significant policy variation across countries under global pressures (Bartlett, 2003; Beech, 2006, 2011; Jules, 2012; Verger, Moschetti, et al., 2017). Rather than competing, these theoretical approaches can complement each other and provide us with a better understanding of the global interdependence of the social world and the context-specific reinterpretation of global ideas (Anderson-Levitt, 2003a; Astiz, 2006; Edwards, 2012; Schriewer, 2012; Silova, 2013).

Nevertheless, the combination of these approaches still leaves us with gray boxes when it comes to mechanisms of translation. Demonstrating that cultural legacies or domestic prevailing interests reinterpret global policy ideas in education is not the same as explaining how these legacies and interests shape such translations, or why reinterpretations more closely resemble global ideas at times while, on other occasions, they deviate from global trends. Though cultural political economy proposes a more complete explanation of translation, their theorized mechanisms still do not fully account for cases in which globally inspired reforms succeed or fail to be passed despite (un)favorable institutional odds. Thus, this book builds on these bodies of literature and qualifies the conceptualization of the mechanisms that explain the domestic variation of education governance. I acknowledge the normative, mimetic, and coercive influence of global policy ideas on Latin American countries while also agreeing with political economic approaches that conceive domestic path dependence and semiotic processes as forces that differentially enact global ideas across countries (Maroy et al., 2017; Maurer, 2012; Takayama, 2012; Verger et al., 2016). Following the institutional literature of comparative politics, I use the concept of policy legacies described as path-dependent processes through which—once a particular policy has been chosen—it generates increasing returns for the actors who sustain it (Ellermann, 2015; Pierson, 2000a; Pribble, 2013). In turn, once institutionalized, chosen policies become norms that are perceived as morally appropriate and are there-fore used by actors to make sense of and negotiate the complexity of the world (Ellermann, 2015; Hall, 2010; Mahoney, 2000; Weir & Skocpol, 1985). In addition, policy legacies do not solely help the reproduction of previous arrangements but also generate negative consequences nur-turing coalitions of losers or opponents to existing policies (Falleti, 2010; Mahoney & Thelen, 2010; Pierson, 2004). These coalitions of losers have alternative perceptions of their existing arrangements that can potentially open opportunities for policy change favorable to global ideas. Thus, policy legacies create a material and semiotic context that can facilitate or constrain the selection and adoption of a global idea.

Furthermore, I explain how opponents and supporters engage in activ-ities that enhance their organizational capacity, influence decision-making, and mobilize power resources. The effectiveness of these activities defines the degree to which enacted policies resemble foreign prescriptions. The classification of different types of translation of global ideas developed in chapter 1 identify four degrees: conformity, compromise, avoidance, and defiance (Oliver, 1991; Pache & Santos, 2010). This classification organizes outcomes suggested by policy-borrowing scholarship (e.g., hybridization, reinforcement, juxtaposition) and explains the causal logics that link global governance ideas, domestic context, and different policy enactments.

Research Design, Methods, and Case Selection

To explain cross-national variation of education governance and uncover the mechanisms that produce it, my study combines two methodological approaches: comparative historical analysis and process-tracing. Compara-tive historical analysis is a method that permits a systematic comparison of long-term processes to explain large-scale outcomes, paying particular attention to the timing, sequence, and duration of events (Mahoney & Rueschemeyer, 2003). The constitution of mass state-sponsored educa-tional systems and posterior changes toward post-bureaucratic forms of managing the school system is a perfect example of this sort of process as it has unfolded over a long period, is a substantial part of the evolution of the modern world, signals the "crisis of the welfare state," and reflects dynamics of globalization (H.-D. Meyer & Rowan, 2006a; J. W. Meyer, 1977; Wiseman & Baker, 2006). My historical analysis uses three axes of comparison: longitudinal, cross-country, and across policy areas. My longitudinal comparison undertakes a careful assessment of the incidence of policy legacies and domestic coalitions as well as the institutionalization of global ideas across three periods of ideas on education governance: educational planning (1950s–1970s), state retrenchment (1970–1990s), and Education for All plus results-based accountability (2000s–2010s).

Along with comparing translation across time, this book also examines three countries: Chile, Argentina, and Colombia. These nations experienced the influence of similar global recommendations during the three periods analyzed in this study, along with convergent enrollment rates in secondary education (Figure I.2), and yet they developed different governance arrangements. On the one hand, Chile and Argentina had

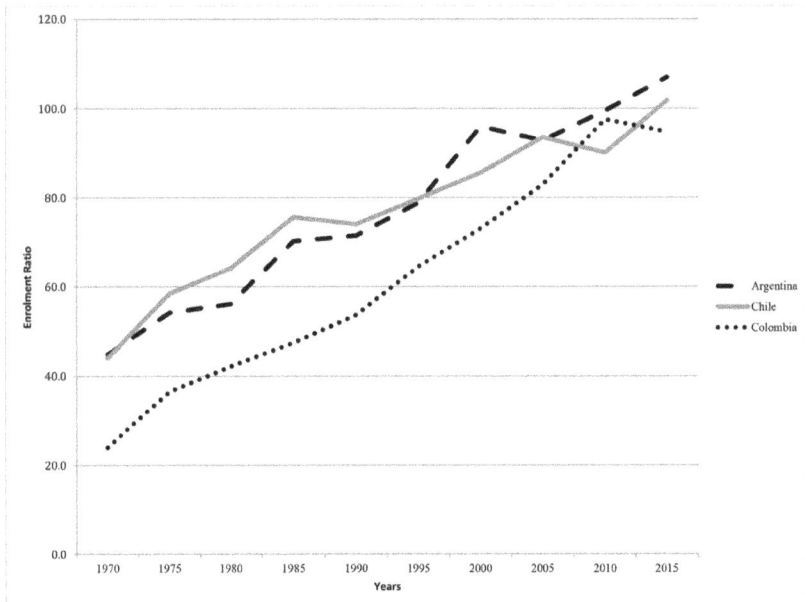

Figure I.2. Gross Enrollment Ratio in Secondary Education in Argentina, Chile, and Colombia. Author's elaboration based on Hanson, 1986; PIIE, 1984; Rivas, 2010; the World Bank, Education Statistics. https://databank.worldbank.org/source/education-statistics-^-all-indicators.

very similar starting points regarding education, including comparable state-managed secondary education models committed to train political and economic elites to sustain the nation-state project (Serrano et al., 2012; Tiramonti, 2003) and participation of the private sector (Figure I.3). Reforms in these two countries also occurred simultaneously with similar noneducation processes, such as authoritarian regimes prone to state-retrenchment ideas during the 1970s and 1980s, economic crises in the 1980s, and similar levels of development. Nevertheless, translation of global ideas in these countries went through very different pathways that led Chile to become a quasi-market of education (with a strong privatization of education provision and a clear centralization of curriculum and evaluation) and led Argentina to a quasi-state monopoly (with provision and some curriculum authority delegated to provinces while retaining the devolution of evaluation to teachers). Therefore, the comparison between these two countries facilitates the identification of causal processes through which cases with relatively similar contexts may end up with different outcomes (Locke & Thelen, 1995; Ragin, 1989).

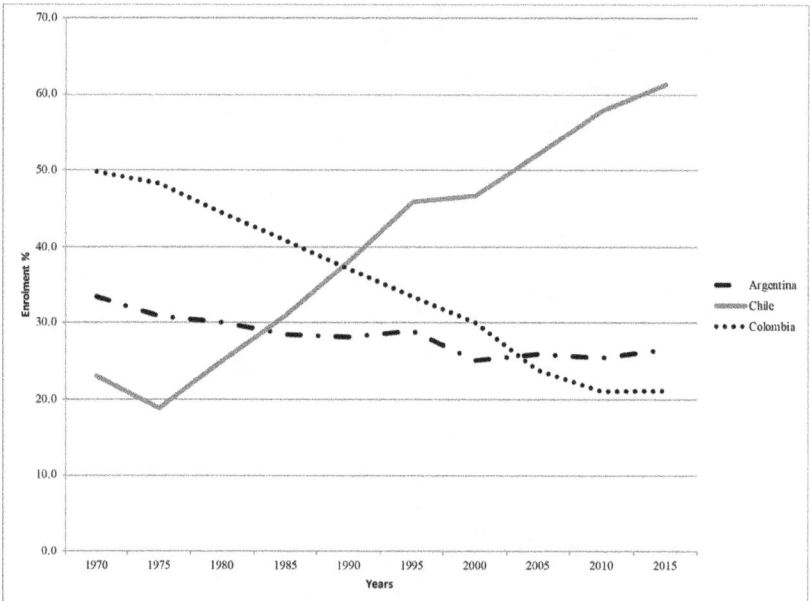

Figure I.3. Percentage of Enrollment in Private Schools out of Total Enrollment in Argentina, Chile, and Colombia, Secondary Education. Author's elaboration based on Hanson, 1986; PIIE, 1984; Rivas, 2010; the World Bank, Education Statistics. https://databank.worldbank.org/source/education-statistics-^-all-indicators.

On the other hand, Colombia's conditions of the educational system by the mid-twentieth century were significantly different from Chile and Argentina. Colombia did not consolidate a "teaching state" (Hanson, 1986; Helg, 1987) and therefore had a higher participation of the private sector (Figures I.3). Likewise, the country was more dependent on foreign technical and financial aid for education purposes (Arnove, 1980), and their reforms did not coincide with the type of military regimes that occurred in Chile and Argentina. Despite these different conditions, Colombia developed a governance system that holds some similarities with both the Argentinian and the Chilean governance models. This country devolved provision to the provincial and municipal levels, awarded some curriculum autonomy to schools, and partially centralized evaluation. Consequently, this contrasting case helps identify the mechanisms through which countries with different conditions may arrive at convergent governance models (Locke & Thelen, 1995; Ragin, 1989).

Table I.2. Changes in Secondary Education Governance in Chile, Argentina, and Colombia Between the 1960s and 2010s

Country	Time	Provision	Curriculum	Evaluation
Chile	1960s	Centralized	Centralized	Devolved to teachers
	2010s	Privatized, municipalized	Centralized	Centralized
Argentina	1960s	Centralized	Centralized	Devolved to teachers
	2010s	Decentralized to provinces	Centralized with some provincial autonomy	Devolved to teachers
Colombia	1960s	Privatized, municipal, provincial, and national	Uncoordinated	Devolved to teachers
	2010s	Decentralized to provinces and some municipalities	Central guidelines with provincial and school autonomy	Centralized

Author's elaboration.

Finally, my research also compares three different areas of governance: provision, curriculum, and evaluation. The assumption here is that even though foreign recommendations are packaged with ideas that affect multiple policy areas, the reinterpretation of an idea in a specific policy area is not necessarily the same that other ideas in the same package may achieve. For example, curricular autonomy may be achieved because of the support of grassroots education movements. Nevertheless, these same movements may block the implementation of standardized exams insofar as they undermine the authority that teachers, schools, or communities may have on curricular contents and desired learning outcomes. Yet, both curricular autonomy and standardized exams are part of the same global ideas in the 1990s.

My research pairs comparative historical analysis with process-tracing. Process-tracing is a method that uses "detailed, within-case empirical analysis of how a causal mechanism operated in real-world cases" (Beach & Pedersen, 2013, p. 1). I trace the processes that link global policy ideas with domestic education-governance decisions in each case by drawing on hundreds of causal observations collected through interviews and document analysis. Interviews were collected with international and national education policy experts as well as elected and appointed officials in government and in education interest groups such as teacher unions, organizations of private providers, and parent and student associations (31 in Chile, 24 in Argentina, and 26 in Colombia), who were asked about the context of the reforms, their interactions with other relevant actors, and their strategies to influence decisions. Document analysis included secondary sources, archival research in the Congress of each country, official documents from international organizations, and key national governmental and nongovernmental organizations and news outlets that further detailed the context for each reform, the ideas informing the position of different actors, and the conflict and negotiations between stakeholders.

Causal observations were used to identify empirical fingerprints or any observable manifestation of mechanisms behind the reinterpretation of global ideas, including the one theorized in this book as well as alternative explanations. For instance, three empirical fingerprints suggest that policy legacies facilitate the adoption of a global idea: (1) global ideas promise to solve domestic problems that emerged from previous policy decisions, (2) policy elites build on their inherited beliefs to select global ideas that are appropriate for their context, and (3) global ideas are favorable to constituents of existing domestic policies. Likewise, we can know that coercion is behind conformity with global ideas when we find four fingerprints: (1) the presence of financial assistance that stipulates a particular policy change as a condition for funding, (2) the perception of domestic policymakers that the policy solution was imposed upon, (3) the dismissal of other alternatives that otherwise would be considered, and (4) the adoption of the imposed policy decision under the conditions established by the financial agency. If we find independent evidence of each of these propositions, we will sum the small probative value of each, enabling a relatively strong confirmation of the presence of mechanisms leading to conformity to foreign recommendations (Beach & Pedersen, 2013, p. 248).

My research design and methods bring an innovative perspective to comparative education. By contrast to predominant small-N comparisons, my comparative historical analysis constitutes a medium-N research design with multiple cases (three periods X three countries X three policy areas). Therefore, process-tracing helps identify and test these mechanisms in each of these cases, enhancing the portability of my findings and the confidence that the theoretical framework established in this book can explain Latin American nations, and perhaps shed light on mechanisms of translation in other low- and middle-income countries.

Significance of the Book: Cross-Fertilization to Unpack the Global/Domestic Link

In addition to using approaches and methods from comparative politics to complement theories of education policy globalization in comparative education, this book contributes to the expansion of the still-emergent research on the influence of globalization on Latin American education governance. Such scholarship is based on single case studies (Astiz, 2006; Beech, 2011; Edwards, 2018; Parcerisa & Falabella, 2017; Rambla, 2014) and comparisons of a few countries in one time period (Astiz & Wiseman, 2005; Benveniste, 2002; Jules, 2012; Verger, Moschetti, et al., 2017). Single case studies leave us with the question of whether narratives that diverge from global ideas only reflect outliers or "black swans" (Beech & Barrenechea, 2011). Comparative studies of a limited time period—usually when global ideas are externalized and retained in domestic policy decisions—leave us with the notion that borrowed policies are implemented as intended and with little knowledge about what happens with previous domestic arrangements, their constituents, and the political impact of their changes. Without this knowledge, practitioners and scholars interested in Latin American education insufficiently understand the diversity of the translation of global ideas and their long-term consequences in future domestic policy decisions. My comparative historical analysis explores these consequences by taking difference and divergence as the starting point rather than a deviant situation. By acknowledging diversity, uncovering the mechanisms that produce it, and examining long-term consequences, this study also provides opportunities to reimagine education policies (Robertson & Dale, 2015).

The comparative politics tools used in this book also increase attention on the study of secondary education policy—an area that has often been neglected or conflated with basic education (Heyneman, 2003). This disregard is surprising, considering that the role attributed to secondary education differs from other educational levels. Secondary education has been considered crucial for future academic and professional choices, promoting job skills, fostering vocational training (Banco Mundial, 2005; Gropello, 2006; Pozo et al., 2002; Wolff & De Moura Castro, 2000), and shaping social stratification (Kerckhoff, 2001). Theoretical insights from comparative politics help us identify that these roles involve policy problems, actors, and interests that are different from those in basic and tertiary education. For example, the decision about curriculum goals in secondary education (e.g., prepare students for labor market, tracking student for different types of tertiary education) is an ongoing discussion between employers who want skilled workers, tertiary education institutions that want well-prepared students, and families that may want their kids to be more employable in the short term, or rather prefer them to continue their studies at a higher level.

Finally, the cross-fertilization presented in this book is also useful for comparative politics literature. Although scholars of comparative politics have conducted numerous studies on policy globalization and variation in many other policy areas such as pensions (e.g., Hennessy, 2014; M. Melo, 2004; Queisser, 2000; Weyland, 2005), healthcare (e.g., Cacace & Schmid, 2008; Clavier, 2010; Kaasch, 2013; Montanari, 2013), development policy (e.g., Sugiyama, 2011), or economic policy (e.g., Elkins et al., 2006; Jordana & Levi-Faur, 2005; Simmons et al., 2008), they have traditionally neglected the study of education policy (Busemeyer & Trampush, 2011; Jakobi et al., 2009). Only a handful of political-science scholars have researched education reforms in Latin America (Burton, 2011; Chambers-Ju, 2021; Corrales, 2004; Falleti, 2010; Grindle, 2004; Pribble, 2006; B. R. Schneider et al., 2019), but they have not addressed the role of global ideas in their studies. Nevertheless, the globalization of education policy deserves a place in comparative politics. International aid grew, in real terms, 360% between 1995 and 2010 (Riddell & Niño-Zarazúa, 2016), and increasingly more international organizations and other nongovernment actors engage in transnational education financial or technical assistance (Benavot et al., 2010). Likewise, education is frequently at the core of various human capital, wealth generation, and equity policy strategies and is often the largest among all government expenditures (Fan & Rao, 2003). These characteristics suggest that cutbacks in either international assistance or domestic expenditure could affect more constituents than retrenchment in other policy areas, and therefore relationships with international actors and the definition of the role of the state might be more contentious. Thus, the scholarship this book uses related to comparative education provides further insights to better understand the changing role of the state in social policy, the increasing participation of other nonstate (and nonnational) actors in the provision of social services, and the tension between policy convergence and variation.

Outline of the Book

This introduction is followed by five more chapters. Chapter 1 develops a theoretical framework that describes the two parts of the mechanism of translation of global education governance ideas in Latin America: (1) policy legacies that shape future problems, beliefs, and power distribution in ways that make the local political space (in)compatible with global ideas; (2) domestic conflict between advocates and opponents of global ideas, which outcome favors those who more effectively use their organizational capability, access to decision-making, and power resources. The combination between dynamics in policy legacies and domestic conflict can shift the translation toward conformity with global ideas, compromise, avoidance, or defiance.

Unlike other comparative studies, this book is not organized by countries but by historical periods (chapters 2 to 4). Each of these chapters follows the same logic of exposition. I start by introducing the global governance ideas that were dominant in the corresponding historical period, with special emphasis in the selected policy dimensions of analysis and the diffusion mechanisms through which these ideas traveled to the selected countries. Subsequently, I track the translation of these global ideas in each country, pointing at their interaction with domestic policy legacies and political coalitions. Finally, I develop a systematic comparison to identify similarities and differences in the translation mechanisms across policy areas and countries.

Chapter 2 explains the rise of manpower educational planning ideas and shows how they encouraged centralized provision and scientific planning of the curriculum, along with the expansion of secondary education with the purpose of generating adequate human capital for economic growth. In addition, the chapter demonstrates variation in policy legacies across countries regarding the previous consolidation and acceptance of the bureaucratic model in each country. Variation in legacies shaped the domestic conflict and, in particular, the role of a very influential actor—the Catholic Church—whose support helped Chile embrace manpower-planning ideas. By contrast, the Church's opposition led Argentina to keep its traditional bureaucratic system and drove Colombia to adopt a dualist model, shifting away from international recommendations.

Chapter 3 examines the translation of two different versions of state-retrenchment ideas that were predominant in Latin America during the 1980s and 1990s: (1) New Public Management or neoliberal prescriptions—namely market-based ideas—that recommended privatization of secondary education, curriculum autonomy but without vocational components, and standardized exams to inform parental school choices; and (2) active-state recommendations that argued for democratization and responsiveness to local participation demands through decentralization of provision and curriculum, along with standardized exams to guide the state's policy coordination and compensatory actions. I show how these recommendations were only compatible with Colombian policy legacies, as the country never consolidated the type of bureaucratic education model that Argentina and Chile held. Yet, this chapter shows how Pinochet's authoritarian regime was able to embrace market-oriented ideas, completely disrupting Chilean policy legacies. Conversely, the democratic context in which reforms were discussed in Argentina and Colombia encouraged greater opposition, especially from teacher unions, which led these countries to different outcomes. Colombia substantially compromised market-oriented reforms, while Argentina mostly dismissed them and compromised the adoption of active-state recommendations.

Chapter 4 focuses on the analysis of the modifications of the previous state-retrenchment versions toward a stronger role of the state. I show that negative consequences of previous reforms—such as inequality, segregation, poor teacher-labor conditions, and lack of education quality—moved advocates of both market-oriented and active-state recommendations to converge in their redefinition of the state's role in education governance. New ideas in the 2000s moderated privatization with public-private partnerships, called for a controlled decentralization, replaced curriculum autonomy with standards, and pushed forward government-led accountability. This chapter demonstrates that the adoption of these ideas was again shaped by policy legacies, in particular the effects of the 1990s reforms in each country. These effects structured the coalitions that supported and opposed reforms in the 2000s and onward. The relative success of 1990s Chilean reforms compared to the rest of the region helped this country reaffirm accountability, but the segregation produced by the very same policies also spurred strong student opposition that moderated the Chilean quasi-market of education. The failure of Argentinean reforms left state-retrenchment ideas without support and paved the way for a controlled decentralization. By contrast, the unsatisfactory outcomes in Colombia diminished the legitimacy of teacher unions and gave decentralization reforms a new push.

The conclusions synthesize the interplay between the two components of the proposed mechanism and the resulting translation pathways across countries: Chile exhibits a blend of conformity and compromise, Argentina leans toward avoidance and defiance, and Colombia navigates an oscillating trajectory between conformity and defiance. Moreover, this concluding section underscores the diversification of these translation paths across different policy areas, encompassing provision, curriculum, and evaluation, influenced by the unique coalitions within each sphere and the sequence of their reform initiatives. Furthermore, the conclusions discuss the theoretical implications suggesting a qualification of the mechanisms of globalization of education policy proposed by political economy and world society theories, while also stressing the importance for education reform policymakers, both internationally and domestically, to take into account the legacies of past policies and potential coalitions. Lastly, I discuss possibilities of future research, exploring how my theorized mechanisms can explain other cases and policy areas and shed light to studies on education inequality in the region.

Chapter 1

Policy Legacies and Domestic Conflict in the Translation of Global Ideas

Supported by the assumption that education is essential for the accumulation of human capital and economic growth, states around the world have faced the challenge to reform educational systems and increase enrollment across all educational levels (Ramírez & Boli, 1987; Wolf, 2002). This expansion of educational systems and the massification of secondary education in the 1950s and 1960s was often coupled with state-led educational planning, a model disseminated by UNESCO and other prominent international organizations (Williams & Cummings, 2005). This model proposed the centralization of education delivery and the definition of a national curriculum for primary education, complemented with diverse secondary tracks adapted to the manpower needs of the country (Coombs, 1970; ILO & UNESCO, 1963; The World Bank, 1974). Nevertheless, as educational systems grew, their state-led management became more expensive, complicated, and challenged by demands for the efficiency of the system and the recognition of cultural diversity (Blaug, 1967; Lewy, 1977; Psacharopoulos, 1986; Tedesco, 1989). This is especially true in Latin America, where fiscal constraints and weak government structures limited the capacity to fully implement state-led educational planning and expand educational systems to the extent supposedly required for economic growth (CEPAL & UNESCO, 1992; Tedesco, 1989). Consequently, since the 1980s, states have been struggling with the reorganization of their educational systems.

Two sets of ideas informed this reorganization: New Public Management (NPM), a public administration model that encourages the reduction of the role of the state and the implementation of businesslike approaches to manage public services (Pollitt & Bouckaert, 2011), and active-state approach, which recommended the democratization of decision-making through decentralization while the state was considered as a coordinator that should compensate for regional inequalities (CEPAL & UNESCO, 1992). Following these sets of ideas, international actors promoted reforms that delegated authority and responsibility over education to a variety of agents, including local units, schools, and nongovernment and private actors (Tolofari, 2005; Williams & Cummings, 2005). More recently, disparities derived from privatization and decentralization processes spurred recommendations that attributed a stronger role to the state through result-based accountability mechanisms and as a guarantor of the right to quality education (The World Bank, 2011; UNESCO, 2000).

If Latin American governments were influenced by similar globally disseminated ideas, what explains the variation in the organization of their educational systems? For the countries that more closely followed diffused educational solutions, how did they proceed and how did other countries avoid a full implementation of these models? In this chapter, I present a set of propositions that describe the mechanism of the translation of global ideas and that will be empirically tested in the subsequent chapters.

While scholars have used various terms for the reinterpretation of global ideas, I employ the term translation to describe the process through which foreign ideas are reinterpreted through existing institutionalized educational practices at the domestic level in ways that involve a process of recombination of local and global elements (Campbell, 2004; Cowen, 2009; Czarniawska-Joerges et al., 1996; Sahlin, 2008; Steiner-Khamsi, 2014). This definition of translation puts an emphasis on the recombination of institutions—or formal and informal rules, procedures, and cognitive and cultural frameworks—to signal the rule-like character of both local arrangements and global ideas, as well as the ideational and interest-based struggles between local and global institutions in the process of reinterpretation of foreign recommendations (Campbell, 2004; Djelic & Quack, 2008; Mahoney & Thelen, 2010; Oliver, 1991; Pache & Santos, 2010; Sahlin, 2008; Thelen, 2014).

The translation mechanism involves two parts, each one involving particular entities and activities. The main entities of the first part are policy legacies. These legacies shape the extension to which global ideas are compatible with domestic arrangements. The more incompatible are global ideas and domestic arrangements, the greater the chances for foreign recommendations to be significantly modified or rejected.

The second part of the mechanism involves different domestic actors, including political parties, education interest groups, social movements, and civil society organizations, among others. These actors engage in forming coalitions to support or oppose global ideas depending on whether these recommendations favor their interests. The more opponent coalitions are able to mobilize their influence, the greater the chances for the modification or rejection of foreign recommendations. Table 1.1

Table 1.1. Outline of Translation Mechanism

Triggering Condition	Mechanism Part 1 "Shaping Context"	Mechanism Part 2 "Conflict Between Coalitions"	Translation Outcomes
International actors diffuse global ideas through hard and soft power.	Policy legacies *shape* the compatibility between domestic context and global ideas through: — *Creating problems* that global ideas can solve — *Nurturing domestic dominant beliefs* consistent with global ideas — *Generating interests* that global ideas may perpetuate	When global ideas and policy legacies are compatible, coalitions of winners of domestic arrangements become supporters of foreign recommendations while losers become opponents. When global ideas and policy legacies are incompatible, losers become supporters while winners become opponents. To influence translation, winners and losers engage in: — *Enhancing organizational capacity* — *Accessing decision-making* — *Mobilizing power resources*	Conformity Compromise Avoidance Defiance

Author's elaboration. Entities are underlined and activities are in italics following Beach, 2016.

summarizes the mechanism while the next sections explain in detail the entities and activities enunciated in the figure and the way they lead to different translation outcomes.

Compatibility with Domestic Arrangements: The Role of Policy Legacies

Scholars examining the globalization of education have shown that global ideas act as international norms that constrain domestic decisions to solve policy problems (Finnemore, 1998; McNeely, 1995; J. W. Meyer, 1977; Ramírez, 2012; Ramírez & Boli, 1987). Likewise, political scientists have demonstrated that previous domestic policy decisions also generate institutional routines constraining future policy choices (Béland, 2005; Pierson, 2000b, 2004; Pribble, 2013; Weir & Skocpol, 1985). If we accept that both global norms and domestic legacies can operate as institutions that shape policy decisions, then we must analyze the similarities and differences between them and study the reactions their encounter is likely to spark to understand the context in which the translation of foreign recommendations takes place.

I build on existing explanations about the role of policy legacies in policymaking (Béland, 2010; Béland & Schlager, 2019; Mahoney, 2000; Pierson, 2000a; Pribble, 2013; Weir & Skocpol, 1985) to clarify how these legacies shape translations of global ideas. These legacies influence decisions through three activities. Two activities (activities one and three) are related to material interests and have been extensively explored by Pribble (2013) to analyze the education sector. I also proposed another activity (activity two) building on another branch of institutional scholarship that stresses the ideational components of policy legacies and their potential impact on future decisions (Béland, 2010; Béland & Schlager, 2019; Campbell, 1998; Mahoney, 2000).

First, policy legacies shape future reforms by structuring the type of problems and conflicts that require attention (Pribble, 2013). Thus, when global ideas promise to solve these perceived problems or the conflicts generated by them, they are likely to be adopted (Steiner-Khamsi, 2014). For instance, Latin American countries embraced state-led planning to expand a previously elitist secondary education that was not considered able to provide the human capital required for development. Yet, along with the problems of centrally managing massive education systems, centralized curriculum spurred demands of new communities in the education system for recognition of diverse identities and needs, which made attractive foreign prescriptions around curricular autonomy.

Second, policy legacies also structure the attitudes, beliefs, perceptions, and behaviors of policy elites and public opinion (Béland & Schlager, 2019; Campbell, 2004; Diaz-Rios, 2020). On one hand, policy legacies influence what public opinion perceives as appropriate to solve policy problems fueling a positive feedback cycle that reproduces existing decisions (Béland, 2010; Mahoney, 2000; Pacheco, 2013). For example, in educational systems that have historically developed a significant participation of private provision, public opinion tends to highly value parental school choice. On the other hand, previous policies also shape the beliefs and expertise of policymakers and the distribution of state capacity, which in turn affects future policymaking (Béland & Schlager, 2019; Orloff, 1993; Skocpol, 1995). The cases of Argentina and Chile show that a tradition of national curriculum concentrated curriculum expertise at the central level, making decentralization of learning contents unattractive. Without such central capacity in Colombia, policymakers were more open to transfer this responsibility to subnational governments and schools. This role of policy legacies acknowledges the importance of the production of meaning in the translation of global ideas as cultural political economy does, but rather than focusing only on global ideas and associated strategies to "sell" reforms, it identifies how local meanings can help or prevent globally inspired changes. Thus, even though global ideas may promise to solve existing problems, when such solutions radically challenge existing domestic beliefs and capacities, I expect them to be more prone to modification and even rejection.

Third, in addition to shaping views of policymakers and public opinion, previous policy designs generate increasing returns that nurture a set of constituents or supporters (Dale, 2012; Mahoney, 2000; Pierson, 2000a). Thus, policy legacies structure the distribution of power by empowering some groups and transforming them into coalitions of winners with the incentives to maintain existing policies or favor only minor changes (Béland, 2010; Pribble, 2013). Policy legacies can fuel different interest groups inside and outside the government. Some examples of increasing returns and distribution of power outside the government are the expansion of private education that nurtures organizations of private providers advocating for additional mechanisms of privatization (subsidies, charter schools, vouchers, etc.), or the expansion of public education that often enhances the membership and influence of teacher unions in future education policy. Inside the government, previous policies create bureaucracies that can be very influential in the reproduction and expansion of programs under their management (Béland & Schlager, 2019), such as bureaucrats in agencies managing standardized assessments who may see the benefits in expanding the number and importance of testing. Although which groups gain and maintain prominence varies across countries (as a result of previous decisions), I expect powerful organized interests to support global ideas when they expand or bring further legitimation to existing, beneficial arrangements. Alternatively, these groups will oppose global ideas when they threaten to change their status quo.

Shortly put, these three activities—creation of future problems, shaping of local beliefs, and structuring of power distribution—create the context for the translation of foreign recommendations. When global ideas promise to solve perceived problems, are consistent with domestic capacities and beliefs on how education should be managed, and do not threaten the interests of prominent groups, policymakers are more likely to accept and emulate foreign recommendations because they reinforce the domestic arrangement. Such reinforcement fuels a path-dependent pattern of the domestic policy and enhances the legitimacy of the global idea. By contrast, when global ideas and policy legacies are incompatible—that is, when foreign recommendations do not seem able to solve domestic problems, are contradictory to domestic beliefs, and/or threaten powerful interests—I expect that these inconsistencies will challenge the legitimacy of both global ideas and policy legacies, triggering the activation of coalitions of support and opposition to foreign recommendations. The conflict between these coalitions increases the chances of modifying or even rejecting the global idea. I explain this conflict in the following section.

Domestic Coalitions: Organizational Capability, Access to Decision-Making, and Power Resources

The concept of policy legacies is consistent with path-dependent dynamics that scholars studying education policy have used to explain how past decisions become resistant to change in the long term (Dale, 2012; Maroy et al., 2017; Pribble, 2013; Verger et al., 2016). Nevertheless, past policy decisions not only produce increasing returns for some, but also generate downstream negative consequences for others that may gradually diminish policy benefits, erode the policy's rule-like character, promote reactions that create coalitions of opponents or losers, and stimulate their mobilizations for change (Falleti, 2010; Mahoney & Thelen, 2010; Pierson, 2004). Hence, I argue that coalitions of losers of existing domestic policies can use global ideas to push for a more favorable arrangement or oppose foreign recommendations if they threaten to increase their losses. The recognition of negative consequences and the potential of coalitions of losers has two implications for my understanding of the translation of global ideas. First, translation does not always favor the most powerful domestic groups. Second, since the accumulation of negative consequences of domestic arrangements and the constitution of losers' coalitions is gradual, acknowledging them assumes that educational policy transformations are not only rapid and revolutionary as the traditional understanding of path dependence suggests, but they can also be slow and still significant in the long run. The book provides examples of these different types of change. For instance, the Chilean implementation of a voucher system during Pinochet's regime illustrates radical and rapid transformations due to the action of powerful actors who took advantage of the crisis caused by the dictatorship to emulate market-oriented education ideas. By contrast, similar powerful actors in Colombia were not able to implement the same type of reform due to the opposition of teacher unions, who bargained changes that, in the long run, limited the growth of publicly subsidized private education.

The literature on groups and coalitions engaged in education politics can be divided into two groups. On the one hand, we find scholars who have focused on analyzing the particular role of specific actors, individual or collective, in policy change. A focus within this group has been set on political parties, or more specifically, how party ideology, internal organization, and/or relationships with their core constituents influence education policy outcomes (Burton, 2011; Pribble, 2013). A second emphasis rather examines how the organizational capacity and power resources of teacher unions give them more or less leverage to influence policy outcomes (Chambers-Ju, 2017; Moe & Wiborg, 2017; B.R. Schneider, 2022). Finally, others have focused on showing how social movements have been able to organize and push for structural reforms that produce significant shifts in educational arrangements (Anyon, 2009; Bellei, 2014; Bellei & Cabalín, 2013).

On the other hand, a second group has studied coalitions between these different actors. Some of them focus on explaining how interests shaped by past institutional designs facilitate the formation of cross-class coalitions (e.g., coalitions between unions, business, and parties shaping skill regimes; see Busemeyer, 2009; Dobbins & Busemeyer, 2015; Thelen, 2004, 2014) or coalitions between territorial interests (national and subnational) and civil society groups (Falleti, 2010). Others have explored how ideas are mobilized to attract specific actors, such as advocacy groups, research organizations, policy experts, and policy entrepreneurs (Ansell et al., 2009; Béland & Cox, 2016; Betancur, 2016; DeBray et al., 2014; Mintrom & Vergari, 1996). Finally, some others explore the internal operation of coalition by analyzing how different government and policy elite actors network and strategize to beat their opponents (Corrales, 2004; Grindle, 2004).

My approach to coalitions is closer to this second group, as my goal is to identify alliances due to both interest and ideological alignment. Thus, I do not focus on a particular group but rather observe the strategies and interactions of parties, teacher unions, territorial interests, social movements, civil society organizations, and their individual members. Yet, the first group of literature has been helpful to pinpoint the three activities in which coalitions engage to push for or against global ideas. First, supporters and opponents *enhance their organizational capability through increasing their membership and coordinate mobilization around consistent policy preferences* (Chambers-Ju, 2017; Pribble, 2013; B.R. Schneider, 2022). Actors with a formal structure, such as political parties, teacher unions, and organizations of private providers, have more opportunities to rally a larger set of members around the defense of uniform preferences and interests (B.R. Schneider, 2022). By contrast, students and parents—although large in numbers—find it harder to coordinate and are more likely to be co-opted by other groups or simply dismissed in the decision-making process. Although some groups can be more cohesive, coalitions are hardly homogeneous and may contain different segments with sometimes conflicting interests or beliefs, which diminishes their organizational capability and their ability to influence the translation of global ideas. For example, the expansion of school choice in Chile convinced large constituents of middle-class parents of the advantages of private education. At the same time, low-income parents and public-school teachers wanted education policy to favor public schools. In this way, left and center-left parties, such as Christian-Democrats and Socialists, struggled to reconcile the different interests of these segments that had traditionally been part of their constituents.

Second, coalitions also influence the translation of global ideas by *accessing the decision-making process* (Grindle, 2004; Ross Schneider, 2022).

For such activity, coalitions can use formal channels, such as participation in law reform commissions or legislative debate, or informal means, such as personal or business ties with members of the legislative or political parties. To understand this access, we need to identify the key actors in the coalitions, as well as their political calculations, ideas, and strategies to influence decision-making (Teichman, 2001). While accessing decision-making might be easier for powerful groups (e.g., dominant political parties, the military during authoritarian regimes), less powerful groups sometimes take advantage of opportunities like mandatory collective bargaining of education policies, as was the case of the constitutional request for teacher unions' participation in the Colombian 1990s reform. These groups can also strategize to reach influential positions directly or through alliances, as in the case of the Chilean student movement that used their popularity to position leaders in the National Congress.

The third activity coalitions engage with is *mobilizing their power resources*, which includes strikes, protests, votes, oppression, research dissemination, and mobilization of public opinion, among others (Chambers-Ju, 2017; Grindle, 2004; B.R. Schneider, 2022). While some of these resources are more accessible to dominant groups (votes, oppression, media influence, etc.), coalitions of losers often have other important sources of influence. Most notably, these coalitions achieve a heightened degree of legitimacy when they frame their demands as problems that have emerged from their social position of disadvantage. Therefore, they present themselves convincingly as bearers of unfair decisions with the right to make claims for change (Anyon, 2009; Bellei & Cabalín, 2013; Trumbull, 2012). Using this legitimacy, coalitions of losers can either frame global ideas as changes required to modify unfair domestic policies, or oppose the adoption of global ideas, arguing that they would increase injustice. Examples of the latter are more common in the literature that show teacher unions as opponents of privatization and accountability measures (Chambers-Ju, 2017; Moe & Wiborg, 2017). However, I also find examples of the former in Colombian teachers arguing for curriculum autonomy in the 1980s, as well as in the Chilean student movement using ideas rooted in the right to education to criticize the domestic market-oriented system.

These three activities—enhancing of organizational capability, accessing decision-making, and mobilization of power resources—vary independently of one another, thus producing different degrees of influence of the supporters and opponents of global ideas. If a coalition has consolidated a highly cohesive group, has members influencing decision-making, and mobilizes high-impact resources, it will have a strong influence in the translation. When coalitions do not engage in one of these activities, they will have a moderate or limited influence. Finally, their influence will be weak when they have dispersed members with scarce ties with the decision sphere, and few significant resources. Along with policy legacies, the asymmetry of influence between the two coalitions defines the outcome of the translation, as the next section explains.

Outcomes of Translation: From Conformity to Defiance

If we combine the propositions derived from the two parts of the mechanism—the (in)compatibility between global ideas and domestic policy legacies, and asymmetries in the influence of coalitions—we obtain several hypothetical translation outcomes. I build on typologies established by organizational studies to classify these outcomes in four categories that make a continuum, ranging from conformity to defiance of global ideas (Oliver, 1991; Pache & Santos, 2010). These categories are also similar to some of the concepts used in the literature about globalization of education policy. *Conformity* refers to emulation or full compliance with foreign recommendations. The notion of conformity can be associated with policy convergence or isomorphism (Beckert, 2010). *Compromise* involves a moderate modification of the global idea to accommodate domestic conflicting pressures. This accommodation can be considered similar to hybridization (Maroy et al., 2017) and juxtaposition (Steiner-Khamsi, 2012). *Avoidance* refers to a disguised nonconformity or a ritual adoption of the global idea by manipulating its content to accommodate domestic interest or to avoid changing domestic practices. Avoidance is close to the notion of decoupling in sociological institutionalism (Boxenbaum & Jonsson, 2008). Finally, *defiance* involves a more active form of resistance that leads to the contestation and rejection of the global idea.

As Table 1.2 indicates, compatibility between policy legacies and global ideas tips translation toward conformity because beliefs of domestic policymakers are consistent with the foreign recommendations, and global ideas attract the support of existing winners. Nevertheless, compatibility does not preclude conflict between domestic coalitions, as losers of existing domestic arrangements may oppose global ideas when their implementation worsens their situation. Thus, the translation outcome will be conformity only when current winners actively support global

Table 1.2. Translation Outcomes According to the Interaction
Between Global Ideas, Policy Legacies, and Domestic Coalitions

Interaction Between Global Ideas and Policy Legacies	Influence of Global Ideas' Supporters	Influence of Global Ideas' Opponents	Translation Outcomes
Compatible	Strong	Weak	Conformity
		Moderate	Conformity
		Strong	Compromise
	Moderate	Weak	Conformity
		Moderate	Compromise
		Strong	Compromise
	Weak	Weak	Avoidance
		Moderate	Avoidance
		Strong	Avoidance
Incompatible	Strong	Weak	Conformity
		Moderate	Compromise
		Strong	Compromise
	Moderate	Weak	Avoidance
		Moderate	Avoidance
		Strong	Avoidance
	Weak	Weak	Avoidance
		Moderate	Defiance
		Strong	Defiance

Author's elaboration.

ideas and possess stronger organization and effectiveness in accessing decision-making and mobilizing power resources compared to their opponents. Yet, when supporters and opponents are equally engaged in activities that influence translation, I expect the outcome to move away from conformity toward a compromise that accommodates the demands of the opponent coalition. Finally, when the influence of the opponent coalition is more effective, avoidance is the expected outcome, as supporters will not have the strength to fully adopt foreign recommendations but will act as if they were embraced without the need to substantially change the status quo.

By contrast, incompatibility between policy legacies and global ideas shifts the translation toward defiance because winners of the current domestic arrangement will oppose transformations that threaten their dominance. Yet, opposition of powerful domestic actors does not guarantee rejection of the global idea. Only when this coalition of opponents outpace the influence of supporters (current losers of the domestic arrangements) are global ideas effectively defied. However, when opponents and supporters are equally influential, the most likely result will be avoidance, as opponents will behave as if they were implementing foreign changes that promise to solve problems of the group of losers but deflecting real transformations. Lastly, when these losers as supporters of a global idea have far more influence than opponents do, they may shift translation outcome to a compromise, and eventually conformity, that provides them with a more favorable arrangement.

Conclusion

In the remainder of this book, I will test these propositions by focusing on the role of policy legacies and political contestation between domestic coalitions in shaping the translation of global ideas. I identify patterns in all three historical periods analyzed in this book. Chile mostly shifts toward the conformity and compromise end of the continuum. In the 1960s, the compatibility between a state-run model of governance and global recommendations on state-led educational planning attracted the support of the party in power and technocratic elites. Yet, the connections of the Catholic Church with parties and decision-making spheres forced these supporters to compromise on global ideas and accommodate the Church's participation in education delivery and curriculum planning. In the 1980s, the Chilean version of state-led planning was disrupted by a market-oriented model based on vouchers, curricular autonomy, and standardized tests to inform school choice. The conformity to such an incompatible global idea was achieved due to the support of an authoritarian regime and market-oriented technocratic elites that repressed the opposition of teachers and the Church. This conformity continued through the transition to democracy, as policy legacies nurtured strong supporters of the market-oriented model and shaped the orientations of policymakers. In the 2010s, the accumulated levels of educational inequality motivated students to realign and oppose market-oriented ideas. Students supported global ideas on the right to education through massive mobilization and alliances with other actors (e.g., teacher unions and parent organizations). With these strategies, students achieved the reversal of some education policies implemented during the 1980s and 1990s and conformed to their own interpretation of a stronger state, which slightly compromised the Chilean market-oriented model.

Argentina mostly shifts toward avoidance and defiance. Although 1960s state-led planning ideas were compatible with the teaching state model of the country, the opposition of the Church in Argentina and the lack of organizational capacity of supporters of educational planning led the country to avoid foreign recommendations. The 1990s NPM recommendations instead found incompatible policy legacies, and although a popular government supported the adoption of state-retrenchment ideas, the opposition of teachers and public opinion compromised decentralization and avoided standardized tests. By the 2000s, the influence of the coalition supporting NPM policies was so diminished that the previously adopted decentralization was downplayed and test-based accountability was defied.

Colombia shows evidence of all translation outcomes. Despite a very active dissemination of state-led educational planning ideas in the 1960s, Colombia avoided and even defied their implementation, as such recommendations were at odds with the elitist character of secondary education. Indeed, state-led educational planning attracted moderate to little support from policymakers and teachers. By the 1990s, however, NPM ideas were compatible with the domestic arrangement, but a strong teachers' opposition avoided the implementation of some of the proposed measures (e.g., vouchers and accountability) and compromised on others (e.g., decentralization and curriculum autonomy). In the 2000s, this compromise increased as teachers' influence weakened, and supporters of NPM seized the opportunity to further decentralize the responsibility for delivery and increase curriculum standardization.

Despite these patterns, countries' responses still vary across time and, more importantly, policy areas. This variation does not invalidate the mechanism proposed in this chapter. On the contrary, variation across time and policy areas shows that we cannot assume uniformity of policy legacies and/or coalitions in each country, and therefore the examination of translation processes needs to consider longer historical processes and the identification of diverse and changing interests in local educational arenas. I examine these processes in each of the next three chapters of this book.

Chapter 2

Translation of Manpower Education Planning Ideas

Until the 1940s, secondary education in several Latin American countries was closely related to the education of the future ruling class (Helg, 1987; Ruiz & Schoo, 2014, p. 75; Serrano et al., 2012; Tenti, 2003, p. 15). The governance of this educational level was usually state-centered, with national schools or schools that were part of universities (Serrano et al., 2012; Tenti, 2003). These schools often taught a national "encyclopedic" curriculum that encompassed a comprehensive knowledge, including multiple humanistic disciplines and excluding practice-oriented learning (White, 2011). Secondary education was not necessarily tuition free, and admissions were sometimes regulated through exams (Acosta, 2011; Aedo-Richmond, 2000; Helg, 1987; Ruiz Berrio, 2006). Although students occasionally needed to write exams for university admission, assessment of student learning at secondary schools was mainly teachers' responsibility (Eckstein & Noah, 1993). Instructional inspectors were supposed to monitor the teaching process, but they often just checked compliance with administrative and bureaucratic rules (Gvirtz, 2002).

Nevertheless, by the 1950s, the rise of human-capital theories challenged this governance model by depicting education as the engine for economic development and modernization (Ramírez & Boli, 1987; Wolf, 2002). A new governance model, denominated Manpower Educational Planning (MEP), suggested that secondary education should respond to systematically identified workforce needs (Coombs, 1970; ILO & UNESCO, 1963; The World Bank, 1974). Although this new model still followed a teaching-state template, it had implications for the policy dimensions analyzed in this study. Regarding provision, MEP recommended a shift from elitist secondary education toward massive schooling to train future workers (Tenti, 2003). The massification of secondary schooling was framed as a responsibility of the state through public schools (OEA, 1963, p. 51). Although global recommendations acknowledged "the right of parents to educate their children in their preferred institutions" (OEA, 1963, p. 52), decisions about secondary education provisions were implicitly submitted to manpower requirements with the purpose of diverting students from the typical humanistic secondary education and traditional university studies and directing them to vocational secondary school (VOCSED) (Coombs, 1968; The World Bank, 1971). This tracking also challenged ideas regarding curriculum. International recommendations suggested the replacement of the encyclopedic curriculum with measurable skills relevant to countries' development needs and identified through scientific procedures (Benavot, 1983; Haddad, 1987). Although the curricular orientation for secondary education changed, decisions remained highly centralized, as central specialized agencies were expected to design and test the curriculum while teachers were considered technicians in charge of applying these scientifically designed procedures (H. González, 1976). Finally, regarding evaluation, MEP did not challenge the authority of teachers on student assessment, and neither did it question the role of inspectors in monitoring teachers' practices. Yet, MEP promoted the employment of occasional standardized tests as a tool to monitor reforms and measure the fit between curriculum and socioeconomic needs (Schiefelbein, 2003). Table 2.1 summarizes changes between the predominant model until the 1940s and MEP recommendations in the three policy areas of this study.

MEP ideas were disseminated in Latin America through channels that suggest the presence of coercion, mimesis, and normative pressures. Within the context of the "Alliance for Progress"—a US foreign-assistance program established in 1961 to promote economic development and avoid the expansion of communism in Latin America (Agency for Aid Development, 1966)—international organizations such as the WB and USAID sought to exercise coercion through conditional aid (Taffet, 2012). UNESCO, CEPAL, and OAS also employed mimetic pressures in their technical assistance and their regional conferences that sought to persuade Latin American countries of the benefits of MEP and the implementation of education planning offices (Blat Gimeno, 1983; e.g., ILO & UNESCO, 1963). Finally, these international organizations also

Table 2.1. Changes in Global Education Ideas in the 1950s

Policy Dimensions	State-Centered, Elitist Model of Secondary Education	Manpower Educational Planning Approach (MEP)
Provision	State-run, elitist education to train future elite.	State-run, massive education to train future workers.
Curriculum	Encyclopedic humanistic national curriculum.	Scientifically planned national curriculum promoting VOCSED.
Evaluation	Delegated to teachers.	Delegated to teachers with occasional tests used to inform reforms.

Author's elaboration.

used normative diffusion by training and promoting networks of education-planning specialists who often became government officials and policymakers.

While mimetic pressures were similar across the countries analyzed in this study, coercive and normative diffusion varied slightly. Argentina received about a third of the financial aid that the Alliance for Progress provided to Chile and Colombia, suggesting that coercion was likely stronger in these two countries (Sigafoos, 1962, p. 51; Taffet, 2012). Moreover, foreign aid in Colombia accounted for half of the education investment in the country, which transformed it into a laboratory for designing and testing educational innovations of several international organizations, including UNESCO, the United Nations Development Program (UNDP), the USAID, and the WB (Arnove, 1980; Martinez et al., 2011). Normative diffusion was stronger in Chile through two channels. First, international grants facilitated the training of a cohort of educational planning and assessment experts who returned to the country to actively participate in educational reforms (Schiefelbein, 1976). Second, UNESCO and CEPAL[1] advised the implementation of local graduate educational planning programs, such as Latin American Faculty of Social Sciences (Facultad Latinoamericana de Ciencias Sociales - FLACSO) and professional training at the University of Chile (Biglaiser, 2002; Gill, 1966). Although similar local training programs were established in Argentina in 1958 (Rein, 1998), the military governments of 1962 and 1966 continuously intervened, thus preventing the development of a sufficient number of educational planning experts (Biglaiser, 2002). Moreover, in the area of evaluation, Argentina did not receive any training for the development of standardized assessments (Diaz-Rios, 2020). While Colombia did receive some support to establish the first standardized assessments, the country developed only some planning programs, and the most important ones, such as those administered by the National University of Colombia, were interrupted by the rejection of financial support from UNESCO and the Rockefeller Foundation, arguing that this funding was an action of "American imperialism" (Tarazona, 2015; Uribe, 2014). In sum, while coercive pressures were stronger in Colombia, normative diffusion was more evident in Chile.

One would expect that Chile and Colombia were more likely to conform to or closely emulate MEP recommendations compared to Argentina where diffusion pressures were relatively weaker. However, the translation of foreign recommendations in the 1960s and 1970s did not reflect this expectation. While Chile indeed conformed to MEP ideas, Colombia mostly avoided and defied them. Meanwhile, Argentina went through a middle-ground path of compromise and avoidance. In this chapter, I examine the role that policy legacies and domestic coalitions played in the translation pathways. While actors involved in this translation are similar across countries, including the Church, teacher unions, and political parties, the ways in which they perceived problems and solutions—as well as the coalitions they formed—varied according to the policy legacies in each nation.

Chilean Conformity to MEP Ideas (1964–1973)

In terms of diffusion, one could argue that strong coercive, mimetic, and normative pressures drove Chile to mostly conform to MEP global ideas. Yet, a closer look at domestic politics shows that such conformity was also motivated by the perception that MEP could fix inherited problems in a way that was appropriate for the dominant beliefs and power distribution in the existing domestic governance arrangement. Frei-Montalva's government (1964–1970) managed to follow MEP recommendations by establishing an alliance with the Church and allowing this organization to participate in provision and curriculum decisions. By contrast, Allende's administration (1970–1973) faced a powerful coalition composed by the most influential political parties and the Church, which mobilized important power resources to defeat Allende's attempts to exclude private actors from provision and to further strengthen vocational curriculum.

Policy Legacies: The Influence of the Church and the Need to Expand Secondary Education

The inherited problems that influenced the 1960s education reforms in Chile resulted from the expansion of primary education initiated in the 1920s, which reached 74% enrollment by the 1950s. This expansion generated a bottleneck at the end of primary schooling, reflected in an enrollment rate of only 10% for secondary education. This bottleneck signaled a pressure to expand secondary schooling (Schiefelbein, 1974, p. 17). This pressure also challenged the elitist character of the secondary school curriculum, its emphasis on university preparation, and its exclusionary admission procedures (Bellei & Pérez, 2016). Working-class children had limited secondary education opportunities; at best, they were trained for specific occupations at technical schools (Cox, 1988; Leyton, 2010). A former official of the education ministry noticed that inherited beliefs regarded technical schools as second-rate organizations and, by contrast to traditional secondary schools, vocational education was highly uncoordinated, as illustrated by the varied duration of their specialties (four to seven years), the proliferation of different curricular plans, and their terminal character (personal communication #36). Thus, while MEP ideas were appealing to policymakers facing pressures to expand educational opportunities (Cox, 1988), prevailing beliefs were somewhat at odds with the expansion of technical education.

Additionally, the 1960s reforms inherited a highly legitimate participation of the Catholic Church in education policymaking. Private schools constituted 25% of total enrollment in secondary school, and most of them were Catholic. Although the state strictly regulated these schools, the Catholic Church had a significant influence in shaping these regulations through the Federation of Secondary Schools (Federación de Institutos de Educación Secundaria—FIDE), an organization created in 1948 to coordinate the relationship between Catholic private schools and the education ministry (Brahm et al., 1971). Through the lobby of FIDE, Catholic schools received regular state subsidies, had influence on curricular decisions (Aedo-Richmond, 2000), and promoted a "social Christian" ideology in education that focused on the alleviation of inequalities and social justice (Caiceo Escudero, 2012; Fischer, 1979). The legitimacy of the Church in education policy decisions was also a powerful legacy that empowered Catholic organizations and gave them incentives to reproduce arrangements that favored the continuation of their participation in the governance of secondary school.

MEP ideas were arguably promising to solve Chile's education problems, and the capacity that the state had consolidated in the governance of primary education and the development of a national curriculum were also favorable for centralized educational planning (Celis Muñoz, 2004). Nevertheless, foreign recommendations were not entirely compatible with policy feedback and power distribution of previous governance institutions. In both education provision and curriculum, the centralization of secondary education could facilitate an expansion of state schooling with a centrally defined curriculum, but the legitimacy and power of the Church also anticipated a limitation for full development of an exclusive state-run governance of secondary schools (Aedo-Richmond, 2000). Likewise, expansion and changes in the hierarchical status of technical schools attracted little support within political elites who considered humanistic education as superior knowledge compared to practical education (Serrano et al., 2018). Thus, despite the compatibility of MEP ideas with inherited problems and the relative centrality of the Chilean state in education governance, supporters of global recommendations still required some modifications to prevent the opposition of the Church, which could potentially lose from a stronger presence of the state in education.

Although the area of evaluation was not a central part of MEP recommendations, a brief mention of the policy legacies in the country also shows a favorable environment for occasional standardized tests. Chile developed a national school inspection system in the nineteenth century. Inspectors were responsible for guaranteeing that teachers followed the national curriculum and for collecting data about the school system (Falabella & Ramos, 2019; Leal Vásquez, 2014). Yet, while inspectors were considered hierarchical superiors to public-school directors, they just monitored private schools, a situation emerged from the Church's historical contestation and search for freedom of education (Leal Vásquez, 2014). In such context, occasional standardized tests to monitor reforms seemed like a convenient compromise to assist the inspection of a growing number of schools without disrupting the autonomy of private organizations. Table 2.2 summarizes the compatibility of policy legacies and MEP ideas in provision, curriculum, and evaluation.

Table 2.2. Compatibility Between Chilean Policy Legacies and MEP Ideas

Policy Area	Inherited Problems	Inherited Beliefs	Inherited Power Distribution	Compatibility Outcome
Provision	Expansion of primary education pushed for massification of secondary schooling.	State as main education provider but with the support of the Church.	Church's influence in education provision regulations	Relatively compatible with public school expansion.
Curriculum	Predominance of a national humanistic curriculum oriented toward university.	Technical schools as second-rate education.	Church's influence in curriculum decisions. Technical secondary schools without powerful constituents.	Relatively compatible with a national curriculum but not with VOCSED.
Evaluation	Difficulties to oversight a growing number of schools.	State as main responsible party for school supervision.	Inspection authority concentrated in the government but with autonomy for private schools.	Relatively compatible with a minor use of tests.

Author's elaboration.

COALITIONS AND ACTIVITIES: PERSUADING AND ACCOMMODATING THE CHURCH

With policy legacies in their favor, advocates of MEP ideas only needed to persuade the Church of the benefits of educational planning and grant their representatives participation in education policy decisions to secure the support of the winners of the current Chilean arrangement. During the presidencies of Jorge Alessandri (1958–1964) and Eduardo Frei-Montalva (1964–1970), foreign- and domestic-trained experts on educational planning became leaders of educational reforms, signaling the presence of normative dissemination of global ideas. Alessandri appointed a commission of these experts to examine the conditions of the Chilean education system that established the foundations for educational planning (Fischer, 1979; Picazo, 2013). Likewise, Mario Leyton, a graduate in educational planning from the University of Chicago, later became Frei-Montalva's education secretary, and Juan Gomez Milla, a former dean of the University of Chile and the founder of the first center for educational research, was appointed as education minister (Leyton, 1970; Ruiz Schneider, 1994). Although trained in ideas of state-based educational planning, following domestic beliefs, these specialists did not consider that a stronger role of the state would mean a diminished influence of the Church. Therefore, they promoted the creation of the Catholic Centre for Educational Research and Development (Centro de Investigación y Desarrollo de la Educación - CIDE) as a way to train Catholic experts and improve FIDE's capacity in educational planning (Picazo, 2013). Indeed, CIDE became a peer agency for the Center for Improvement, Experimentation and Pedagogical Research (Centro de Perfeccionamiento, Experimentación e Investigación Pedagógica—CPEIP), a division responsible for curricular planning within the national education ministry also created by Frei-Montalva's government (Leyton, 2010).

This alliance between educational planning specialists and the Church was further supported by a plural coalition of different center-right parties, including the Christian Democratic Party (CDP) and the Conservatives (Fischer, 1979). This coalition had significant organizational capability as they were cohesive in their goals of expanding secondary education without diminishing the influence of the Church. They also had direct access to decision-making and important power resources, including well-reputed research, educational planning centers, and the potential mobilization of constituents of private (Catholic) education. The mobilization of the government to create an alliance with the Church that did not challenge previous beliefs or the Church's authority in education shaped the support for reforms inspired by MEP ideas, including the rapid expansion of education (especially for the poorest sectors), scientific-based curriculum reform, adaptation of education to socioeconomic development, subsequent integration of technical schools to the formal education system, and testing for monitoring the implementation of reforms (PIIE, 1984; Schiefelbein & Davis, 1974).

With the accommodation of the Church's interests, the goals of Frei-Montalva's education reforms appealed to most sectors of society, with only a mild opposition coming from teacher unions. Regarding provision, these unions disagreed with the existence of elite private schools and public subsidies to private institutions that, according to them, reproduced the antidemocratic character of the Chilean education system (Farrell, 1986). In the area of curriculum, the unions criticized the top-down character of educational planning that limited teachers and community participation in education policy and curriculum decisions (Nuñez, 1989; Ruiz Schneider, 1994). Moreover, the employment of North American theories in the curricular planning was deemed as an exaggerated influence of foreign ideas not fully appropriate for the Chilean context (Aedo-Richmond, 2000; Nuñez, 1990). This opposition, however, was not effective to mobilize for changes. While unions had access to decision-making through their participation in the National Education Council—an independent agency that had to be consulted about educational, and particularly curricular, policy—they did not use their influence, as sometimes they abstained to vote and other times they approved government proposals with some observations (Nuñez, 1990). Moreover, teacher unions' priorities were much more focused on bargaining new salary rates and linking them to increases of public servants' salary scales as a way to address historically low remunerations for teachers (*Ley 16.617*, 1967, art. 25). This bargain probably prevented the scalation of opposition—at least until 1968, when an economic crisis forced the government to set public salary increase to 12.5%, 9 percentage points under the growth of the cost-of-living index (Nuñez, 1990). Teacher unions responded with a fifty-nine-day strike that drove the government to offer a mid-ground agreement in salaries, but secondary education reforms were not consistently advocated, thus showing a lack of cohesiveness around these goals. Nevertheless, the opposition of the teacher unions persisted and were consolidated with the new government of Salvador Allende (1970–1973). Table 2.3 summarizes the coalitions supporting and opposing Frei-Montalva's reforms.

A comparison between Allende's attempts to change education policy and Frei-Montalva's reforms confirms the need to accommodate the Church in order to conform to MEP ideas. The most important education proposal of Allende's administration was the Unified National School (Escuela Nacional Unificada—ENU). According to a former education ministry of Allende's government, the ENU was expected to move MEP

Table 2.3. Coalitions' Actors and Activities During MEP-Inspired Frei-Montalva's Reform by Policy Area (1964–1970)

Policy Area	MEP Supporters (Fre-Montalva's Reform)	Opponents to Reforms
Provision and Curriculum	<u>Actors</u>: CDP, Conservatives, Radicals, the Church, education planning experts. <u>Activities</u>: Enhanced organizational capacity: strong. Access to decision-making: strong. Mobilization of power resources: strong.	<u>Actors</u>: Socialists, Communists, teacher union. <u>Activities</u>: Enhancement of organizational capacity: weak. Access to decision-making: limited. Mobilization of power resources: weak.
Evaluation	<u>Actors</u>: Educational planners. <u>Activities</u>: Enhancement of organizational capacity: limited. Access to decision-making: limited. Mobilization of power resources: limited.	No opponents to assessments.

Author's elaboration.

ideas forward through the merger of vocational and general secondary education into a single track, the constitution of a lifelong education system with a diversified postsecondary education, and the subsequent reduction of the demand for humanistic higher education while promoting diversified skills (personal communication #43). Allende also sought to further strengthen the role of the state by nationalizing private schools to change the elitist character of education and by consolidating the national inspection system (Unidad Popular, 1969). Yet, the organizational capacity to support ENU was weak. The Popular Unity (Unidad Popular—UP), Allende's left party coalition, was not entirely cohesive, as reflected by its division into two different factions. On one hand, the Socialist party and the Popular Unitary Action Movement (Movimiento de Acción Popular Unitaria—MAPU) advocated for education as a tool to make the transition to socialism under teachers' authority (Cox, 1988; Farrell, 1986; Fischer, 1979). On the other hand, Communists and Radicals acknowledged some of the achievements of Frei-Montalva's reforms, regarded educational planning as necessary, and preferred to ground this planning in a broader and pluralist participation of teachers, parents, students, and other education stakeholders (Farrell, 1986; Nuñez, 1990, 2003). This division, the threats to displace the Church's influence on the education system, and ENU's narrative about "build[ing] a socialist society" (Informe ENU-1973, 2014, pp. 158, 164, 166) spurred a fierce opposition of the CDP, Conservatives, and the Church that contrasted with the support received by Frei-Montalva's reforms.

ENU's opponents gained access to decision-making that gave them strong influence to block Allende's policies. First, to get ratified as president without a majority of votes, Allende was forced to bargain a Statute of Constitutional Guarantees with the CDP (Farrell, 1986). This statute prevented the nationalization of private education proposed by ENU through the protection of private schools' autonomy and the responsibility of the state to provide subsidies to tuition-free and nonprofit private organizations (Estatuto de Garantías Constitutionales, 1970, art. 10). Second, ENU's opponents mobilized their resources through the dissemination of CIDE's research showing the contribution of private schools to Chilean education and the limited financial ability of the government to assume the expenditures of all private providers (Brahm et al., 1971). The opposition also engaged in active media campaigns and promoted massive protests against ENU, portraying it as a "system of ideological infiltration into all sectors and ages of the population" (Editorial, 1973). The education ministry and the state minister of Allende explained that this media campaign undermined ENU's legitimacy, and the proposal never reached legislative debate (personal communications #33 and #43). Moreover, the military coup of 1973 delivered the final blow to Allende's educational reform. Table 2.4 summarizes the actors and their activities in the Chilean education coalitions during Allende's administration.

Table 2.4. Coalitions' Actors and Activities During MEP-Inspired Allende's Reform by Policy Area (1970–1973)

Policy Area	MEP Supporters (Allende's Reform)	Opponents
Provision and Curriculum*	Actors: Socialists, Communists, teacher union, MAPU, Radicals.	Actors: CDP, Conservatives, the Church.
	Activities: Enhanced organizational capacity: limited.	Activities: Enhancement of organizational capacity: limited.
	Access to decision-making: strong.	Access to decision-making: limited.
	Mobilization of power resources: weak.	Mobilization of power resources: strong.

Author's elaboration.

*Allende's discontinued tests but did not have strong preferences in evaluation.

OUTCOMES: SELECTIVE CONFORMITY TO MEP IDEAS

Due to the strong support of domestic winners and the weak opposition to Frei-Montalva's educational reforms, educational policies in Chile during the 1960s conformed to global recommendations. Yet, the accommodation of the Church and domestic beliefs made this conformity selective in the areas of provision and curriculum. In general, the Frei-Montalva administration established influential planning offices[2] with a strong cadre of planning experts (Hira, 1998; Leyton, 2010). More specifically, regarding education provision, Frei-Montalva's government significantly expanded public secondary schooling, shifting away from the former elitist character of secondary education, as MEP ideas suggested (Table 2.5). Public expenditure on education grew from 2.7% to 4.5% of the GDP, and enrollment in secondary education rose from 17.5% to 32.8% between 1965 and 1969 (PIIE, 1984). Admission exams for secondary education were gradually eliminated (Cox, 1988), and around 3,000 new public schools were constructed, including specialized infrastructure for secondary education, such as workshops and laboratories (UNESCO,

Table 2.5. Translation of MEP Ideas in Chile

Policy Area	Compatibility with Policy Legacies	Support	Opposition	Translation
Provision	Relatively compatible	Strong	Weak	Conformity: Expansion of state-led public-private provision.
Curriculum	Relatively compatible	Strong	Weak	Conformity: National scientific curriculum and adoption of VOCSED.
Evaluation	Relatively compatible	Moderate	Weak	Conformity: Emergence of testing to inform reforms.

Author's elaboration.

1971, p. 516). Nevertheless, state subsidies and access to foreign funds also promoted growth in the private sector (Aedo-Richmond, 2000). Although the participation of public schools in the total enrollment of secondary education increased from 66.9% to 76.3% between 1965 and 1969, and private enrollment share decreased from 33.1% to 23.7%, in absolute numbers, both sectors grew constantly during Frei-Montalva's administration (PIIE, 1984). Moreover, the influence of supporters of this model of public-private provision blocked Allende's proposal to nationalize private schools even when the CDP was no longer in office.

Regarding curriculum, Chile also conformed to centralized planning processes but retained the secondary role of VOCSED. Frei-Montalva's reforms promoted scientific, centralized curricular planning through CPEIP (Superintendencia de Educación, 1966), although in collaboration with the Catholic agency, CIDE, thus signaling the accommodation of the

Church once more in this policy area. By contrast, the consolidation of VOCSED received less attention. On the one hand, the government declared "workers training" as one of the goals of educational reforms (Superintendencia de Educación, 1966), technical education specialties were unified and formally acknowledged as part of secondary education, and the share of the enrollment in VOCSED rose from 25.2% to 32.1% between 1965 and 1969 (PIIE, 1984). On the other hand, VOCSED schools continued to be a second-rate option, and lower achievers were often tracked into vocational education through pre-secondary tests (Aedo-Richmond, 2000). This compromise in the translation of VOCSED reflected the lack of constituents of technical education in the country and the inherited bias toward a liberal and humanistic curriculum (Fischer, 1979). As a result of this unequal recognition, the reformed structure of secondary education did not provide manpower resources or divert graduates from university studies, as students preferred attending humanistic schools with greater prestige (Nuñez, 2003). Later, when Allende tried to dismantle these tracks and diversify secondary education, his proposal did not attract enough support and was easily defeated—not because of its content, but because of its socialist framing, as Allende's former education ministry asserted (personal communication #43).

Finally, while student evaluation was not a substantial part of MEP ideas or Frei-Montalva's reforms, the scientific character of educational planning recommended by MEP drove the government to introduce a standardized assessment for students completing primary education that was applied annually between 1968 and 1971 to monitor the reform (Ortiz Cáceres, 2012). This assessment did not trigger substantial opposition because it did not constrain the autonomy of the Church. While discontinued during Allende's administration—likely because of the lack of interest in evaluation—this assessment initiated an evaluation tradition in the country that would later facilitate the expansion of testing. Ultimately, selective conformity of MEP ideas in Chile shows how domestic policymakers translate global recommendations in line with policy legacies and through the accommodation of powerful interests.

Argentina's Shift Away from MEP Ideas (1958–1971)

Compared to Chile, Argentina experienced weaker coercive and normative pressures that could partially explain ritual implementation or avoidance of MEP ideas in the country. A smaller aid through the Alliance for Progress and fewer foreign-trained specialists in educational planning may have driven Argentina to use only MEP rhetoric without implementing significant changes in the governance of secondary education. Yet, in addition to these weaker global pressures, policy legacies in Argentina diminished incentives for domestic actors to advocate for educational planning and drove the Church to block attempts to strengthen the role of the state in education. Unlike Chile, where the Church established an alliance with a right-center coalition to embrace MEP educational planning, the Argentinean Church, right-wing parties, and the military fiercely opposed and avoided an expansion of the state that could have threatened a rising and hardly earned control over education. The ambiguous compatibility of policy legacies in Argentina only helped the compromise over VOCSED as education planning experts found a middle-ground solution that appealed to both statist and anti-statist advocates.

POLICY LEGACIES: EARLY EXPANSION OF PUBLIC SECONDARY EDUCATION AND CONFLICTS FOR ITS CONTROL

Although Argentina developed early a "teaching state" governance model that seemed favorable for MEP recommendations, policy legacies in this country were structured in a different way compared to Chile. First, although policy feedback encouraged the centrality of the state in education provision and curriculum, the Church contested this centrality that kept private schooling as marginal (Vior & Rodríguez, 2012). By the time of the arrival of MEP ideas, national schools delivered secondary education, and the growth of the private sector was restricted by private providers' inability to grant certificates to students, their obligation to follow the national curriculum, and the imposition for students to write a final examination in public schools (Narodowski & Andrada, 2001). Catholic representatives advocated for the "freedom of education" or the need for the state to give parents the right to choose their children's school according to their beliefs (Llerena, 1998). A similar though less heated tension was present in the area of evaluation. Student evaluation was delegated to teachers in Argentina, but the country developed a strong tradition of inspectors through which the state guaranteed that schools followed national curriculum. While teachers praised the pedagogical assistance of inspectors, they also criticized the state's intervention and desire to control teachers' work (Southwell & Manzione, 2011). Thus, inherited beliefs might have been consistent with MEP ideas, but ideological challenges of losers of the existing arrangement in Argentina anticipated a difficult environment for recommendations that further strengthen the role of the state.

By contrast, vocational education was a less contested area and had a higher status in Argentina compared to Chile. Before the arrival of MEP recommendations, the first administration of Juan Domingo Perón[3] (1946–1952) created the "Factory Schools," an alternative type of secondary education for working-class children (Pineau, 2004). Although some scholars have argued that Factory Schools reproduced education inequality through hierarchical tracks (Tedesco, 1980; D. Weinberg, 1967; G. Weinberg, 1982), these schools also elevated the status of education and knowledge of workers (Balduzzi, 1988; Cucuzza, 1997; Dussel & Pineau, 1995; Pineau, 2004). In addition, two vocational education experts explained that through Factory Schools, Argentinean bureaucracy developed capacity to centrally coordinate the education decisions of employers, workers, and the state, making these schools important for the country's industrialization (personal communications # 69 and #70). Moreover, education at Factory Schools was not terminal, as students were able to continue postsecondary education in the National Workers University (Pineau, 2004). Thus, enrollment in vocational schools had already reached 36% of total enrollment in secondary education by 1955, nurturing constituents such as working-class families, unions, and business sectors (Tedesco, 1986, p. 257).

Second, although power distribution favored advocates of a state-centered education system until the early 1950s, the secondary role of the Church fed its motivation to reject the expansion of the state in education governance (G. Torres, 2014). Moreover, this secondary role did not mean that the Church was powerless. On the contrary, through its alliances with the military and Conservatives, the Church was able to retain significant influence, especially during the authoritarian regimes of 1930 and 1943 (L. Rodríguez, 2015). Tensions between secular and anti-secular forces in education became critical during Perón's first administration. Initially, Perón's administration showed an anti-secular trend by reinstating religious education and regularizing subsidies to private schools (Narodowski & Andrada, 2001). These subsidies attracted substantial support of the Church (Vior & Rodríguez, 2012). However, they were also meant to increase the support for Peronism among private-school teachers and the intervention of the state in private schooling (G. Torres, 2014). Moreover, Perón also promoted a pervasive exaltation of his own figure in the national school curriculum (Rein, 1998; G. Torres, 2014). This exaltation was not only at odds with MEP's scientific curriculum planning recommendation, but it also displaced the Catholic discourse from schools and fueled opposition from the Church to Peronist education initiatives (Bianchi, 1992; Rein, 1998; G. Torres, 2014). Similarly, although Perón's administration initially created the Direction of Religious Education that gave more participation to the Church in inspection, his government also later eliminated this direction, fueling the conflict with the Catholic representatives (Petitti, 2013). By contrast to Chile, power distribution did not clearly favor advocates of state-led education, and tensions between secular and anti-secular forces made it harder to establish a partnership between them and the Church to implement MEP ideas.

Ultimately, policy legacies created problems that MEP did not necessarily promise to solve. The early expansion of secondary education in Argentina, which reached almost 30% gross enrollment by the late 1950s, and the early implementation of Factory Schools made MEP recommendations less attractive to solve problems with which Argentina seemed to be dealing adequately through their own policies. Moreover, fluctuating tension between advocates of a secular education system, Peronists, and the Church created a persistent struggle over the control of secondary education that the state-centered nature of MEP recommendations did not promise to settle—at least in favor of opponents to the expansion of the state's role in education. Problems created by previous decisions therefore anticipated a more contested translation of MEP ideas. Table 2.6 summarizes the ambiguous compatibility of policy legacies in Argentina with MEP recommendations, including the challenges these global ideas would face in their translation.

COALITIONS AND ACTIVITIES: EDUCATIONAL PLANNERS BETWEEN PERONISTS AND THE CHURCH

The influence of MEP ideas in Argentina started with the administration of Arturo Frondizi (1958–1962). The apparent consistency between Peronists and Argentinean education planning experts in their advocacy for a strong state (Minteguiaga, 2009) suggests a potential coalition between these groups. Nevertheless, Perón was overthrown in a civilian-military coup in 1955, and Peronism was banned from the electoral competition

Table 2.6. Ambiguous Compatibility Between Argentinean Policy Legacies and MEP Ideas

Policy Area	Inherited Problems	Inherited Beliefs	Inherited Power Distribution	Compatibility Outcome
Provision	Conflict over the autonomy of private (Catholic) schools.	High legitimacy of state-centered education system but challenged by Church's advocacy for parental freedom to choose education.	Peronist control of education provision but significant influence of the Church.	Relatively compatible with state-led schooling but with important opposition.
Curriculum	Church's inconformity with exclusion of religious education.	Predominance of a national curriculum. High legitimacy of vocational education.	Peronist control of curriculum contested by the Church. Business, working-class families, and unions as constituents of vocational education.	Relatively compatible with national curriculum and vocational education but unfavorable for scientific design.
Evaluation	No significant evaluation problems.	State as main responsible party for school supervision without testing experience.	Strong constituents of inspection but with some contestation from teachers.	Relatively incompatible with the use of tests.

Author's elaboration.

until 1970, which weakened Peronists' access to decision-making. This access was also weakened for education planning experts. Although Frondizi—assisted by CEPAL—attempted to modernize higher education and implement MEP ideas in university programs, three military coups between 1962 and 1976[4] continuously intervened in higher education, thus preventing the expansion of training for educational planning (Biglaiser, 2002; Rein, 1998). A former senior researcher of the Latin American Institute for International Relations (Instituto Latinoamericano de Relaciones Internacionales—ILARI)—an organization created in the 1960s, funded by the Ford and Rockefeller Foundations, to promote development and planning studies—explained that although Argentinean planning experts were not completely excluded from the subsequent democratic and nondemocratic governments of Jose María Guido (1962–1963), Arturo Illia (1963–1966), and Juan Carlos Onganía (1966–1970), their scarce numbers and high turnover rates prevented their ideas from being transformed into concrete policies (personal communication #81). Moreover, these experts often went to private research centers to preserve their autonomy from political instability (Suasnábar & Merodo, 2007). In sum, and in contrast to Chile, education planning experts had very limited access to decision-making.

Additionally, the support for a stronger role of the state in education lacked organizational capacity and only mobilized moderate power resources. The pressure to "stamping out" Peronism from Argentinean education made education planning experts distance themselves from Peronists' alliances (Rein, 1998, p. 136). While both supported the expansion of public secondary education and VOCSED (CONADE, 1968; Pineau, 2004; Puiggrós & Gagliano, 2004), educational experts attempted to introduce technical and scientific criteria in education governance (Palamidessi & Feldman, 1994), which was at odds with Peronist employment of education as a political tool. These situations prevented the development of a stronger coalition between Peronists, the winners of the existing arrangement, and education planning advocates. Nevertheless, statist supporters retained some influence through the secret endorsement Frondizi received from Perón to win the presidency (Rein, 1998) and through the support of teacher unions of public schools, which were traditional constituents of a state-run education system (Puiggrós, 2003).

While the influence of advocates of MEP ideas was weakened, opponents gained terrain. Despite its secret alliance with Peronism, Frondizi's administration was also influenced by the Catholic Church (Vior & Rodríguez, 2012). His government created the National Office for Private Education (Superintendencia Nacional de la Enseñanza Privada—SNEP) in 1959, which gave the Church direct access to education decision-making (L. Rodríguez, 2015). SNEP was an organization within the education ministry responsible for coordinating private schools. Although Catholic education staff from Frondizi's administration and subsequent governments participated in UNESCO planning networks, they persisted in their rejection of statist ideas and rather engaged in enhancing the influence of private schools (see, e.g., Van Gelderen, 1963). The Church did not challenge the centralized control of secondary school curriculum (Southwell, 1997), but its alliances with the military aimed at abolishing "Peronist" learning content from schools and reestablishing Catholic discourse rather than implementing scientific curricular planning (Rein, 1998). Moreover, while this opponent coalition agreed on the importance of technical education, they considered this type of schooling a terminal level for poor students and deemed it not conducive to postsecondary studies—a preference that mirrored the elitist character of secondary education (Tedesco, 1986). The influence of this coalition of opponents to MEP ideas increased with the military governments that followed Frondizi's administration (1962–1963 and 1966–1970), which appointed Catholic staff in important positions in the education ministry, thus expanding their access to decision-making beyond the governance of private schools (L. Rodríguez, 2013). This coalition also gained considerable power resources as the Church was able to mobilize private-school teachers and families, and authoritarian regimes eliminated the teacher unions established during Perón's administration (Puiggrós, 2003; L. Rodríguez, 2015).

While the conflict around provision and curriculum was intense, the area of evaluation was less contested. First, Argentinean education planners were not sufficiently socialized in assessments (personal communication #81). Second, neither Peronists nor Catholic representatives engaged in centralizing evaluation through testing; instead, both used inspectors to control how and what to teach (Southwell & Manzione, 2011). Table 2.7 summarizes the coalitions in Argentina during the predominance of MEP ideas.

OUTCOMES: AVOIDANCE AND COMPROMISE OF MEP IDEAS

By contrast to Chile, the ambiguous compatibility of MEP ideas with Argentinean policy legacies was not enough to produce conformity with

Table 2.7. Coalitions' Actors and Activities During MEP Ideas in Argentina by Policy Area

Policy Area*	State-Led Planning for Secondary Education	Private Secondary Education Coalition
Provision and Curriculum	Actors: Education planners, Peronists, teacher unions of public schools. Activities: Enhanced organizational capacity: weak. Access to decision-making: weak. Mobilization of power resources: limited.	Actors: Church, military governments, Conservatives, some (anti-Peronist) liberals. Activities: Enhanced organizational capacity: strong. Access to decision-making: limited. Mobilization of power resources: limited.
VOCSED**	Actors: Education planners, Peronists, VOCSED teachers, business associations. Activities: Enhanced organizational capacity: strong. Access to decision-making: weak. Mobilization of power resources: strong.	Actors: Church, military governments, Conservatives, some (anti-Peronist) liberals. Activities: Enhanced organizational capacity: strong. Access to decision-making: strong. Mobilization of power resources: weak.

Author's elaboration.

*Changes in evaluation were not part of MEP reforms in Argentina.

**Although VOCSED is a part of curriculum policy, this policy dimension is highlighted here as a separate one due to differences in coalitions.

global recommendations. A stronger opposition from the Church and its allies to the expansion of the state's role in education, as well as weak support for scientific educational planning, prevented conformity to MEP. Although Frondizi established different planning agencies following the lead of other Latin American countries, such as the National Development Council (Consejo Nacional de Desarrollo—CONADE) and education planning offices within CONADE and the education ministry (Salonia, 1981; Southwell, 1997), a former coordinator of CONADE's education department and a former ILARI researcher explained that due to their short tenure and lack of influence in the government, education planners were only able to conduct some studies, like the Mediterranean Regional Project—a pioneering manpower planning initiative—and "Education, Development, and Human Resources," but did not develop significant education reforms (personal communications #65 and #81).

In the area of provision, advocates of private education used their position of power within the education ministry to expand private schooling and restrict the expansion of secondary education. Catholic officials used their influence on Frondizi's administration and subsequent governments to issue laws that deregulated private education, thus increasing subsidies for private schools and devolving them the authority to grant secondary education certificates to students (Narodowski & Andrada, 2001; Vior & Rodríguez, 2012). Later, these officials pushed to break the legacies of a strong state through a reform called "Escuela Intermedia" (Middle School). This reform sought to reduce mandatory secondary education by two years and replace it with a new, nonmandatory, privately paid, and mostly privately provided lower secondary school (Ministerio de Educación y Cultura, 1969, p. 13). These changes in secondary education eroded the authority of the state and substantially affected constituents of public education who rapidly became opponents of this proposal (L. Rodríguez, 2008). Although support for MEP recommendations was not strong in the country, teacher unions, Peronists, and education planning experts came together and used MEP rhetoric to delegitimize the Escuela Intermedia proposal by denouncing the reform as elitist, regressive, and against global recommendations and CONADE's call for public secondary education expansion (ATEP, 1971; L. Rodríguez, 2013). Opponents mobilized their power resources through massive strikes organized by public-school teachers (J. González, 1971) and provincial influence that forced the refusal of 13 out of 22 provinces to implement the reform (Villaverde, 1971). Ultimately, Catholic officials were unable to break the strong legacies of a state-run education system and they gave up the Escuela Intermedia project by 1971. Despite this defeat, the private sector gained ground in education governance, as reflected not only by the deregulation measures in place since the 1950s but also by the increase in the percentage of students enrolled in private secondary schools from 23% to 33% between 1960 and 1970 (Tiramonti, 2003). This increase contributed to a rise in secondary education enrollment from 34% to 44%, disguising the Church's lack of interest in the expansion of secondary education.

While in the area of provision avoidance was the result of conflict between statist and anti-statist forces, in the area of curriculum, ritual implementation was produced by the lack of interest of both sides in scientific planning. While using MEP rhetoric, Frondizi preserved the traditional encyclopedic curriculum by linking the appointment of teachers to existing subjects instead of to specific schools (Salonia, 1981). Consequently, teachers became constituents of the encyclopedic curriculum that defined their job positions and mainly retained the characteristics of the nineteenth century (Acosta, 2012; Dussel, 2006). Briefly put, despite compatible policy legacies with global ideas, avoidance was the outcome of supporters' lack of engagement with scientific planning.

Although scientific planning of curriculum was avoided, MEP recommendations on technical education were compromised through a middle-ground reform that pleased both anti-Peronists and advocates of technical education. On the one hand, Frondizi removed Factory Schools from the ministry of labor to erase Peronism legacies from technical education (Pineau, 2003). On the other hand, two former education officials of the International Labor Organization (ILO) and OAS explained that despite the dismantling of Factory Schools, Frondizi replicated their structure by creating the National Council for Technical Education (Consejo Nacional de Educación Técnica—CONET), a semiautonomous agency within the education ministry with a board composed of CONET's officials, business, and union representatives (personal communications #69 and #70). In this way, Frondizi's administration compromised or mixed new global ideas with existing domestic legacies by pleasing opponents of Peronism, while also satisfying the strong constituents of technical education in the country.

Regarding evaluation, none of the coalitions actually engaged with changing the existing model. Incompatible policy legacies, poor domestic engagement with scientific planning, and the functional role of inspectors to make schools aligned with centralized decisions, regardless of the ideology in power, made assessments completely unattractive. Therefore, both coalitions avoided their implementation. Table 2.8 summarizes the operation of the translation mechanism in each policy area during MEP predominance in Argentina.

Table 2.8. Translation of MEP Ideas in Argentina

Policy Area*	Compatibility with Policy Legacies	Support	Opposition	Translation
Provision	Relatively compatible	Weak	Moderate	Avoidance: expansion of secondary education, more autonomy of private sector.
Curriculum	Relatively compatible	Weak	Moderate	Avoidance: national encyclopedic curriculum disguised by MEP rhetoric.
VOCSED**	Relatively compatible	Strong	Strong	Compromise: cancelation of factory schools but continuation of technical education.

Author's elaboration.

*Changes in evaluation were not part of MEP reforms in Argentina.

**Although VOCSED is a part of curriculum policy, this policy dimension is highlighted here as a separate one due to differences in coalitions.

Colombia's Rift Between MEP Ideas and Domestic Policy (1958–1985)

In terms of the strength of diffusion pressures, Colombia can be described as an intermediate case. The country received stronger pressures compared to Argentina, but smaller normative influence compared to Chile. Nevertheless, Colombia did not conform to MEP ideas and instead avoided and defied most foreign recommendations. The explanation of these outcomes lies in the incompatibility of the country's policy legacies that did not nurture strong constituents for a state-run secondary education. On the contrary, the benefits produced by a semi-anarchic organization and extensive privatization of the education system for the Church, policy elites, and local leaders gave them little incentives to support centralization of the authority over education. These actors used their veto-power position within the government to block the timid attempts that some educational planning advocates did to implement provision recommendations. Similarly, teacher unions only needed to employ their alliances with domestic intellectuals to effectively oppose a proposal that was not a priority for the government: the centralization and scientific development of the curriculum.

The only area in which Colombia followed MEP ideas more closely was the implementation of VOCSED. Policy elites compromised on this implementation because VOCSED gave them access to important international funding without changing their beliefs of a minimal role of the state in education. VOCSED expansion did not disturb the authority of the Church on education, the elitist character of secondary education, or the authority of teachers on curriculum matters. Therefore, the implementation of a few VOCSED schools pleased the requirements of international organizations without triggering any significant domestic opposition.

POLICY LEGACIES: WEAK STATE IN THE GOVERNANCE OF SECONDARY EDUCATION

Unlike Chile and Argentina, policy legacies in Colombia were incompatible with MEP ideas. First, inherited problems in the country by the 1950s did not make global recommendations attractive for the Colombian education system. By contrast to the highly centralized educational systems of Chile and Argentina, in Colombia local authorities designated most education staff, and appointments throughout the entire education system (teachers, supervisors, education secretaries, and education ministers) served clientelist purposes (Duarte & Restrepo, 2003; Hanson, 1986). The secondary school curriculum was also highly uncoordinated, as evidenced by the 21 curriculum reforms formulated during the first half of the twentieth century as the government changed or the education minister was replaced (Henao, 1956). By 1948, the education ministry also stopped the creation of new national secondary schools and delegated this task to subnational and private actors, which increased the local contribution to funding for secondary education to 59% (Helg, 1987; Lebot, 1971). Thus, the national government did not have fiscal control over secondary schools. Subnational governments typically ignored national education policy and guidelines, and appointed education staff were often unprepared for their positions (Duarte & Restrepo, 2003; Hanson, 1986; Lebot, 1971). Likewise, the country did not develop the centralized inspection system that Chile and Argentina achieved. Originally, the school inspection was in charge of municipalities. Later attempts to centralize inspection for secondary schools were resisted by local authorities and diminished by the limited capacity at the central level (Helg, 1987). Although MEP ideas could have been promising to solve this lack of coordination, expanding and reforming secondary education was not yet a priority for the country. Efforts were concentrated in expanding primary education, which had only reached 44% by the early 1950s (Helg, 1987; Lebot, 1971).

Second, the legacies of an uncoordinated and highly privatized secondary education structured beliefs of policymakers that supported a small role of state in this educational level. By the 1950s, more than 60% of the total students in secondary education attended private—mostly Catholic—schools, which were permitted to run parallel to public schools with almost no regulation by the state (Helg, 1987). Indeed, policy elites and their children had been educated in private schools, which drove them to support the significant share and autonomy of the private education sector. Moreover, these elites believed that since public capacity to expand education was insufficient, the state should concentrate on the population not served by the private sector (Helg, 1998). While this belief officially transformed technical education into a priority of Colombian governments starting in the 1940s, technical schools were regarded as second-rate, and parents preferred to send their children to academic schools if they were able to afford them (Saldarriaga, 2003). Like in Chile, technical education was highly heterogeneous with substantive program variation in length, quality, and relevance, as well as extensive student drop-out rates. The small-state approach to education also made control over evaluation irrelevant for policymakers and trumped attempts to centralize school inspection. National inspectors had unstable positions, were politicized, and were unable to enforce central decisions in schools (Helg, 1987). Shortly put, policy feedback of the existing governance model in the country was incompatible with the state-centered character of MEP recommendations.

Third, unlike Argentina and Chile, the high levels of education privatization in Colombia and the lack of coordination of the educational system gave private providers ample autonomy and greater influence on education policy (Duarte & Restrepo, 2003). Between 1945 and 1957, enrollment doubled in the public sector and quadrupled in the private sector. Although the predominance of the private sector was more evident in academic secondary education, private schools served 80% of enrolled children in some areas of vocational education (e.g., commerce), and enrollment in private technical schools also quadrupled during this period (Helg, 1987). With the support of policy elites and the Church, private schools established powerful organizations, such as the National Confederation of Teaching Centres (Confederación Nacional de Centros Docentes—CONACED) and the National Association of Private School Principals (Asociación Nacional de Rectores de Colegios Privados— ANDERCOP)—both of which advocated against state intervention in provision, curriculum, and control of the private sector (Helg, 1998). Compared to Chile and Argentina, policy legacies of a strong privatization prevented an early development of influential constituents of a state-run education system and were therefore incompatible with MEP recommendations—with the exception of the coordination problems and the expansion of vocational education—as summarized in Table 2.9.

COALITIONS AND ACTIVITIES: ALLIANCE BETWEEN POLICY ELITES AND THE CHURCH AGAINST MEP

Compared to Chile, MEP ideas found fewer advocates in Colombia, despite strong coercive and mimetic diffusion pressures in the country. Similar to Argentina, training of education planning experts in Colombia was inconsistent, further preventing a decisive support for a stronger role of the state in Colombian secondary education. The few scholars trained in planning ideas went to the National Planning Department (Departamento Nacional de Planeación—DNP), an agency formally established in 1958. However, these experts had to compete with a larger cadre of economists more inclined toward classical economics (Alvarez, 2005). Although a few education officials had strong ties with UNESCO and other international organizations advocating for MEP ideas, they often had short tenure, did not develop strong networks of education planning experts, or were tightly connected to the Church. For instance, Gabriel Betancourt was appointed twice as education ministry, but only for a couple of years (1955–1956 and 1966–1968). Before these appointments, Betancourt had served in different UNESCO positions, including the

Table 2.9. Incompatibility of Colombian Policy Legacies with MEP Ideas

Policy Area	Inherited Problems	Inherited Beliefs	Inherited Power Distribution	Compatibility Outcome
Provision	Semi-anarchic provision plus relatively low demand for secondary education as elementary school was not massive.	Predominance of subsidiary role in education provision.	Dominance of the Church, private actors', and subnational governments in education provision.	Incompatible with expansion of public secondary schooling.
Curriculum	Lack of national curriculum coordination.	Limited capacity and state interest to formulate centralized curriculum.	Autonomy of private schools to define their curriculum.	Incompatible with centralized curriculum.
VOCSED*	Uncoordinated provision of technical education.	Technical education as the state priority for poor people.	Private and state interests in of technical schools.	Compatible with expansion of VOCSED.
Evaluation	Overlapping systems of school inspection.	Small state in control of education with reduced capacity to supervise.	Autonomy of private schools over evaluation.	Incompatible with testing to monitor reforms.

Author's elaboration.

*Although VOCSED is a part of curriculum policy, this policy dimension is highlighted here as a separate one due to differences in policy legacies.

chair of the Education Planning Commission for Latin America and the general vice director of the Education Office in Paris (J. O. López, 2002), and was likely the most influential education planning expert in Colombia. Yet, his first educational plan in 1955 reflected a preference for a small state (Betauncourt Mejía, 1984). His successor, Octavio Arizmendi, implemented several planning-inspired projects (Helg, 1998), but his connections with the Catholic Church also made him a promoter of private schooling (Arizmendi Posada, 2001). The influence of the policy elite and the Church moved education planning experts away from a centrally controlled expansion of secondary education provision in Colombia.

By contrast to provision, training of education planning experts was stronger in the areas of evaluation and curriculum. On the one hand, by 1962, sponsored by the Ford Foundation, a group of education ministry officials received training from the US by the Educational Testing Service (ETS) to develop standardized tests similar to the Scholastic Aptitude Test (Grupo de Investigación sobre Pruebas Masivas en Colombia, 2008). These officials, however, worked with a higher-education agency, and therefore they had more interest in using these tests for university admission than for monitoring secondary education reforms (Molina Rodríguez, 2012). Consequently, these assessments quickly received the support of numerous important universities in the country as they provided valuable information that would be expensive to collect by their own means (Grupo de Investigación sobre Pruebas Masivas en Colombia, 2008). On the other hand, important teacher colleges in the country incorporated solid programs on curricular planning and promoted experimentation and testing of educational innovations (Martinez et al., 2011). Likewise, UNESCO and OAS provided short courses and in-service training on educational planning to middle-level bureaucrats in the education ministry (Ministerio de Educación Nacional, 1974). A former senior advisor of curriculum reform explained that these efforts consolidated a group of curricular planners in academia and government that actively advocated for the centralized and scientific elaboration of the curriculum—but mostly for primary education, as policy elites had little interest in secondary schools (personal communication #7). Briefly put, the consolidation of greater planning expertise in curriculum and evaluation was not accompanied by the support of powerful actors.

Colombian teacher unions developed late support for a stronger role of the state in education provision and were not considered an important political actor by policy elites during the National Front[5] (Chambers-Ju, 2017). Although teacher strikes often pushed the government to transfer funds to subnational units (Duarte & Restrepo, 2003), teacher organization also reflected the semi-anarchic character of the Colombian education system. Each department had its own union, and teachers had very heterogeneous labor conditions across the country (Helg, 1998). The expansion of primary education in the 1940s and 1950s alongside the quest for harmonization of contracts across the country motivated primary public-school teachers to organize a national federation known as the Colombian Federation of Teachers (Federación Colombiana de Educadores—FECODE) in 1962 (Bocanegra, 2008, p. 118). However, it was not until the late 1970s that secondary-school teachers joined the Federation. Thus, FECODE was only motivated to use its power resources with massive national strikes to force the government to centralize fiscal responsibility for primary schools, as a former union leader explained (personal communication #18).

Moreover, FECODE's support for a centralized provision of education was not transferable to the area of curriculum. Two union leaders indicated that scientific, centralized curricular design was considered highly technocratic and treated teachers as education operators only in charge of applying predesigned and pretested programs. By contrast, the union demanded the participation of teachers in the elaboration of curricula and the recognition of their pedagogical knowledge in educational planning (personal communications #14 and #18). Building on these demands, FECODE promoted the "Pedagogical Movement," which also convened prominent national scholars increasing the influence of the opposition to centralized curriculum planning in the 1980s (Bocanegra, 2010).

In addition to the limited organizational capacity of advocates of MEP ideas and the opposition they received from policy elites and teachers, the arrival of these global recommendations to Colombia happened in the institutional context of the National Front that prevented profound reforms. The traditional support of policy elites for a small state and the mutual veto between parties typical of the National Front blocked the few proposals that some Liberals and education planning experts timidly promoted to increase the role of the state in secondary education, as the next sections explains (Duarte & Restrepo, 2003). Table 2.10 summarizes the actors and strategies that led to a weak support and a strong opposition to MEP recommendations in Colombia.

OUTCOMES: DEFIANCE AND AVOIDANCE OF MEP IDEAS

Despite the strong diffusion pressures to adopt MEP ideas that Colombia experienced, the incompatibility of foreign recommendations with policy legacies raised the opposition of domestic actors. Financial and technical

Table 2.10. Coalitions' Actors and Activities During MEP Ideas in Colombia by Policy Area

Policy Area	MEP Supporters	MEP Opponents
Provision	Actors: Some Liberals, some educational planners, and FECODE. Activities: Enhanced organizational capacity: limited. Access to decision-making: limited. Mobilized of power resources: limited.	Actors: Church, Conservatives, subnational governors, some Liberals. Activities: Enhanced organizational capacity: strong. Access to decision-making: strong. Mobilization of power resources: strong.
Curriculum	Actors: Educational planners. Activities: Enhanced organizational capacity: weak. Access to decision-making: limited. Mobilization of power resources: weak.	Actors: FECODE, influential academics. Activities: Enhanced organizational capacity: strong. Access to decision-making: limited. Mobilization of power resources: strong.
VOCSED*	Actors: Educational planners, Liberals and Conservatives. Activities: Enhanced organizational capacity: limited. Access to decision-making: limited. Mobilization of power resources: limited.	Actors: The Church. Activities: Enhanced organizational capacity: limited. Access to decision-making: limited. Mobilization of power resources: limited.
Evaluation	Actors: Educational planners Activities: Enhanced organizational capacity: strong. Access to decision-making: limited. Mobilization of power resources: limited.	No engagement of domestic actors against evaluation as it was not part of secondary education reform.

Author's elaboration.

*Although VOCSED is a part of curriculum policy, this policy dimension is highlighted here as a separate one due to differences in coalitions.

aid from UNESCO, the UNDP, USAID, and the WB led Colombia to the creation of the Colombian Pedagogical Institute (Instituto Colombiano de Pedagogía—ICOLPE) in the education ministry and an education planning office inside the DNP, agencies similar to Chilean CPEIP and Argentinean CONADE. Colombian planning agencies indeed elaborated the first five-year educational plan in 1957. Yet, beliefs on a minimal state in education and the influence of the Church led education planning experts to establish that public secondary schools should be provided only for those who were unable to pay for private institutions (Ministerio de Educación Nacional, 1957). Later, in 1967, the government officially eliminated tuition-free public secondary education; hence, even public schools charged fees (Helg, 1998), which defied MEP recommendations regarding a massified secondary school. Although enrollment grew to 14% in the mid-1960s, it was still highly privatized and far from being under the state's control.

Similarly, in 1971, the coalition of policy elites and the Church prevented a Liberal reform that sought to strengthen the role of the education ministry in local schools, increase control on private education, and raise the national government expenditure on education to 20% (Duarte & Restrepo, 2003). With this reform, the Liberal minister expected to nationalize private schools and force them to enroll low-income students, which raised substantial opposition from private providers, the Church, Conservatives, and other smaller parties of a broader political spectrum (Helg, 1998). Conservatives used the veto power provided by the National Front and their influence on the education ministry to quickly dismiss any form of control over private schools, arguing that nationalization would provide free education to the more affluent classes and enrollment of low-income students would disrupt the school climate of private schools (Ministerio de Educación Nacional, 1971). Consequently, the reform was reduced to only control and assume financial responsibility over public secondary schools, as well as to establish the upper limit for public teachers that subnational units could appoint (Ley 43, 1975). But this measure was also resisted by local governors who responded by quickly appointing new teachers and increasing their salaries and benefits with the expectation that the national government would take financial responsibility over these new expenses (Hanson, 1986). Central government funds became insufficient to cover local secondary education costs, and therefore national expenditure on education was stalled, teachers' payroll and appointments were frozen, transfer of fiscal responsibility from local to central government was suspended, and the nationalization of secondary education was not completed (Avellaneda & Rodríguez, 1993).

By 1977, MEP recommendations on a state-coordinated secondary education provision were clearly avoided. Although enrollment in secondary education grew substantially to 37%, 53% of students attended completely autonomous private schools (Helg, 1998). Additionally, the country still had a mix of funding schemes, including national schools paid by the national government, department schools (similar to province) subsidized by national and local governments, municipal schools funded by all three levels, and private schools also receiving financial resources from both national and subnational jurisdictions (Hanson, 1986). The strong coalition between the Church, Conservative political elites, and local governors drove the country to ritually implement MEP recommendations on provision by expanding secondary education but retaining the uncoordinated, highly privatized governance model.

In the area of curriculum planning, the country defied MEP ideas despite stronger normative diffusion. The training of curriculum planning experts in 1975 helped the Liberal government embark on a reform called "Curricular Renovation" (Martinez et al., 2011). Following MEP ideas, this reform sought to elaborate a scientific curriculum, relevant to the country's economic needs (Ministerio de Educación Nacional, 1976). According to a former senior curriculum advisor of the education ministry involved in this reform, the process of curricular renovation was successfully completed for primary education by 1984. However, the lack of interest in secondary education by policy elites delayed the reform for this educational level, which only started in the mid-1980s (personal communication #7). Nevertheless, by this time, the influence of FECODE on curriculum had grown stronger through the Pedagogical Movement, which contested the scientific, nonparticipatory approach of curricular planning through the mobilization of the academic community and teachers preventing the government's imposition of a curriculum for secondary education, as explained by a former senior curriculum advisor and a former union leader (personal communications #7 and #14). Since this was not a priority for policy elites, the government gave in to teachers' demands and never enforced curricular renovation for secondary education (Molano, 2011).

While MEP recommendations on provision and curricular planning were dismissed, the expansion of VOCSED was only compromised because such a change did not threaten powerful interests. Concretely, the WB delivered a loan to Colombia in 1967 to establish VOCSED through schools with both vocational and academic tracks within the same organization (Helg, 1998; Zuñiga, 1979). The implementation of VOCSED schools (called INEM in Colombia) expanded the number of teacher positions, which likely prevented FECODE's opposition. Likewise, VOCSED schools were not expected to replace or compete with the existing technical schools managed by the Church (Helg, 1998; Ministerio de Educación Nacional, 1976). Thus, the administrations between 1968 and 1974 had greater motivations to use international funding to build 44 INEM schools and reach the goals proposed by the WB (Diaz-Rios & Urbano-Canal, 2023). These schools, however, were only used to expand access to low-income children without substantially increasing the role of the state in secondary education. Put differently, instead of being coerced by international organizations, policy elites filtered recommendations about VOCSED through domestic interests and compromised global ideas with the elitist model of secondary education.

Finally, as in the other two countries of this study, student evaluation was not part of the education reform debate in Colombia. Yet, by the 1950s, Gabriel Betancourt promoted the acquisition of international tests to provide vocational orientation to higher school graduates. Later, the country started developing its own exams through the National Testing Service, and by 1968, this service served as the foundation for the creation of the Colombian Institute for the Promotion of Higher Education (Instituto Colombiano de Fomento de la Educación Superior—ICFES), an agency independent from the education ministry (Grupo de Investigación sobre Pruebas Masivas en Colombia, 2008). ICFES and its testing service nurtured strong supporters in the higher-education sector but not in secondary education. Thus, rather than informing the reform as MEP recommended, testing experts emphasized the use of the exam in Colombia to select students for university studies (Ortiz, 2012; Peña, 2008). Yet, although tests as a means of monitoring educational reform attracted very little interests and were therefore avoided, these assessments helped introduce a tradition of standardized testing in the country that would have consequences in the following decades. Table 2.11 summarizes the translation processes in each policy area.

Table 2.11. Translation of MEP Ideas in Colombia

Policy Area	Compatibility with Policy Legacies	Support	Opposition	Translation
Provision	Incompatible	Moderate	Strong	Avoidance: Expansion of secondary education but without centralized planning.
Curriculum	Incompatible	Weak	Moderate	Defiance: Rejection of scientific curriculum.
VOCSED*	Relatively compatible	Moderate	Strong	Compromise: VOCSED expansion only for the poor and accommodating Catholic schools.
Evaluation	Incompatible	Moderate	Weak	Avoidance: Testing only for university admission.

Author's elaboration.

*Although VOCSED is a part of curriculum policy, this policy dimension is highlighted here as a separate one due to differences in policy legacies and coalitions.

Conclusion

Although MEP ideas did not radically challenge the traditional global template of state-run governance of secondary education that was dominant until the 1950s, they introduced important modifications to their elitist character. These global ideas recommended the massification of secondary education, the expansion of VOCSED, the centralization of a scientific curriculum that should respond to the country's economic needs, and the slight emergence of standardized tests to inform reforms. All three countries received different coercive, mimetic, and normative pressures, the latter being instrumental for the introduction of MEP ideas in domestic agendas. Nevertheless, variation in diffusion channels is insufficient to explain the translation of MEP recommendations. Compatibility between global policy ideas and the problems, beliefs, and power distribution that domestic policy legacies generated are also important.

In Chile and Argentina, the predominance of a state-run governance model lent support to MEP recommendations, but the problems that previous arrangements generated and the distribution of power varied across these two countries. Chile needed to expand secondary education after the massification of primary school, and the Church, a powerful actor, did not oppose statist proposals because political elites had typically accommodated its interests. Such conditions made MEP ideas a suitable solution for the Chilean situation. By contrast, Argentina had relatively overcome the problem of education massification and instead had not fully resolved the conflict for authority over schools between the state and the Church—also a powerful actor in the country. The statist character of MEP ideas did not promise to solve this protracted conflict; on the contrary, it seemed to undermine the Church's interests. Unlike these two countries, Colombian legacies were incompatible with MEP recommendations. The weak role the state typically had in Colombian education was internalized by political elites who therefore did not find MEP ideas entirely attractive, despite the fact that they promised to solve the governance problems of the country's educational system. Moreover, powerful actors who received the increasing returns of the uncoordinated character of Colombian education governance, including the Church, Conservatives, and subnational political leaders, prevented every attempt to strengthen the role of the state in secondary education.

Differences in policy legacies produced different responses in coalitions advocating for or opposing reforms based on MEP recommendations. In Chile, these foreign ideas received support as a result of the accommodation of the Church's interests. Although teacher unions did not support reforms, they advocated for inconsistent policy preferences even when they neared decision-making with Allende's government. In contrast, MEP ideas in Argentina attracted little domestic support, not only because of the scarcity of education planning experts, but also because of the reluctance of the Church and other anti-Peronist sectors to give more power to the state. Thus, although both countries

continued the expansion of the "teaching state" in secondary education, Chile embraced an educational planning model for its governance
while Argentina continued with a traditional bureaucratic model. By
contrast, foreign recommendations in Colombia were barely pursued
by governments uninterested in a centralized governance model. Timid
attempts to implement MEP-inspired reforms by Liberal governments
were consistently blocked by the Church and Conservatives through the
veto power provided by the National Front. Later, teachers also rejected
these recommendations and demanded authority on educational issues.
Thus, MEP ideas did not help to consolidate a bureaucratic model of
secondary education in Colombia but rather set the ground for a dualist
system with public schools serving the poor while the private sector
served the better-off population.

The combination of policy legacies and the realignment of coalitions
during the predominance of MEP ideas produced three different paths
of reinterpretation of global ideas (Table 2.12): (1) selective conformity
in Chile by accommodating policy legacies, (2) avoidance and some
compromise in Argentina that reflected the conflict between the Church
and Peronists, and (3) defiance, avoidance, and some compromise in
Colombia that concealed the continuation of an uncoordinated education
system with enormous benefits to private providers and local politicians.

The analysis of the MEP period also shows that even though
global recommendations usually bundle prescriptions for different policy
areas, translation can separate them because they may affect differently
domestic interests and beliefs producing diverse conflicts. In Chile and
Argentina, coalitions did not vary across education provision and curriculum. In Chile, center- and right-wing political parties along with
the Church defended the participation of this Catholic organization in

Table 2.12. Summary of Translation Outcomes by Country and Policy
Area During MEP Ideas

Policy Area	Chile	Argentina	Colombia
Provision	Conformity	Avoidance	Avoidance
Curriculum	Conformity	Avoidance	Defiance
VOCSED	Conformity	Compromise	Compromise
Evaluation	Conformity	Avoidance	Avoidance

Author's elaboration.

the expansion of secondary education and the centralized planning of a scientific curriculum. This coalition was faced by a weak opposition from teachers and left-wing parties. These similar dynamics in the two areas resulted in conformity to MEP recommendations in both provision and curriculum. In Argentina, educational planners were trapped in the conflict around education provision and curriculum between right-wing authoritarian governments and the Church on the one hand, and Peronists on the other. The secondary importance that these two coalitions attributed to scientific educational planning produced the avoidance of MEP recommendations in both provision and curriculum.

By contrast, in Colombia, coalitions varied across provision and curriculum. On the one hand, teacher unions joined the Liberals pursuing the nationalization of secondary education but were defeated by a powerful coalition composed of the Church and national and local policy elites. The influence of this opponent coalition avoided recommendations of state-led control of education provision and only permitted a disorganized expansion of secondary education. On the other hand, teachers became the main government opponents for the implementation of a scientific, national curriculum for secondary education. Since educational planners were left alone in this fight, these teachers managed to defy MEP curriculum recommendations. These developments suggest that when coalitions engage differently with diverse policy areas, the result of the translation may also vary across these areas.

Finally, student evaluation was not a relevant part of MEP recommendations and was barely present in the policy debates in each country. A small-scale implementation of tests was possible in Chile due to the wide acceptance of the scientific character of educational planning. By contrast, this implementation in Colombia was done outside secondary education reforms and to solve an admission problem in higher education. Lastly, in Argentina, the lack of interest in educational planning prevented any implementation of standardized tests. Although marginal, the development of assessments during the 1960s and 1970s—or the lack thereof—operated as a policy legacy that shaped the translation of future global policy ideas, as I will explain in the following chapters.

Chapter 3

Varieties of State Retrenchment

Market-Based and Active-State Ideas

In the late 1970s, global ideas on education shifted away from MEP's state-centered recommendations toward a reduction of state intervention in secondary education governance. These new ideas emerged when prominent economists criticized the relevance of manpower forecasts. These forecasts usually extrapolated standards of advanced economies to other countries due to the scarcity of data required to establish optimal ratios of manpower (e.g., impact of technical change in the labor market, time series on the productivity of labor). These economists also argued that even though there is a positive correlation between schooling and national income, different and cheaper skill combinations might lead to the same growth, which suggested that rigid forecasts of the manpower perspective would induce efficiency loss (Blaug, 1967; Bray, 1990; Psacharopoulos & Hinchliffe, 1973). Critics also pointed out that the strong role of state in education without result-based incentives for schools caused inefficiency, low education quality, and underinvestment of the private sector (Psacharopoulos, 1986). For other education analysts concerned with the democratization of the educational systems, the centralized nature of educational planning was prone to be co-opted by authoritarian regimes and was incapable of responding to diverse needs of an increasingly heterogeneous school population (Eisner, 1983; Lewy, 1977; Tedesco, 1989). These criticisms paved the way for new ideas in which the state had a limited role.

These criticisms converged with two major changes in the socio-economic and political context of Latin American countries. On the one hand, a striking economic crisis fueled massive public debt, and structural adjustment programs were portrayed as the most appropriate solution (Mundy & Verger, 2015). These programs restricted financial resources for schools despite the increasing demands for enrollment expansion and quality education (Mundy & Verger, 2015; Oliveros, 1978). This situation forced governments to look for alternative solutions to education problems beyond the state. On the other hand, demands for greater participation in education policy decisions emerged as a response to nondemocratic regimes in the region and challenged top-down approaches, such as MEP ideas (Astiz & Wiseman, 2005; Mundy & Verger, 2015). All these changes brought two different but not mutually exclusive perspectives into the educational policy debate: the market-based and the active-state approaches.

This chapter demonstrates that the interaction between these two global perspectives, the domestic policy legacies, and the responses of coalitions in Chile, Argentina, and Colombia produced different translation paths. Augusto Pinochet's authoritarian regime (1973–1990) strongly supported market-oriented ideas, which forced Chile into a path of conformity. Later, after the transition to democracy, the country compromised both market-oriented and active-state approaches, although, in general, Chile conformed to state retrenchment due to the weak domestic opposition to global recommendations. Argentina received a stronger influence of active-state ideas compared to the market-oriented perspective, but active-oriented recommendations were nevertheless compromised and avoided due to legacies of a strong state and tensions with domestic market-oriented advocates. By contrast, Colombia was only influenced by market-oriented ideas as they were highly compatible with the domestic educational model, but the opposition of the teacher unions sent the country through the path of compromise and avoidance of the market-oriented perspective.

Market-Based Approach to the Governance of Secondary Education

Inspired by New Public Management proposals, education economists and lending international organizations were the most important advocates of the market-based approach. This perspective focused on individual benefits of educational attainment, namely salaries, assuming that different types and levels of education produced dissimilar salary increases. By comparing these salary differentials, governments identified the education level that might produce higher rates of individual salary return. In a context of restricted public expenditure, higher rates of return would determine the educational levels at which public investment would be more efficient and equitable (Psacharopoulos, 1972, 1981a; Psacharopoulos & Hinchliffe, 1973). This rationale challenged the role of the state as the main provider of education and instead proposed school fees for affluent populations, scholarships and education loans for the less affluent, and voucher programs, which were intended to solve the lack of incentives for education quality by encouraging choice and competition between private and public schools (Psacharopoulos, 1986; The World Bank, 1980, 1995, 1999). School competition and vouchers had strong consequences for the centralized curriculum proposed by MEP. A rigid curriculum was framed as an obstacle for quality improvement, and therefore the WB recommended that the government set broad guidelines in core subjects and delegate the decisions over supplementary contents, teaching methodology, and textbooks to teachers and principals (The World Bank, 1980, 1995). To complement school autonomy and competition, recommendations also emphasized evaluation—an area that gained priority for the first time in global policy recommendations. The development of standardized assessments would allow governments to provide parents with information for them to choose the schools with higher performance (Friedman, 1955; World Bank, 1995).

The market-oriented perspective was disseminated in Latin American countries by coercive, mimetic, and normative mechanisms. Coercive pressures were reflected in loan conditionalities imposed by the IMF and the WB that forced highly indebted Latin American countries to reduce the role of the state and implement a free-market model in which non-subsidized industries should openly compete in the global market (Bonal, 2002, p. 4). In the area of education, coercion included reductions in the WB's investment on secondary school from 68% in 1969 to 17% in 2000 (Psacharopoulos, 2006), redirection of loans toward primary schooling, support for voucher programs for secondary education (e.g., Bangladesh, Colombia, Dominican Republic, Mexico; see Patrinos & Lakshmanan, 1997), and the promotion of national evaluation systems (Kamens & McNeely, 2010). Since the WB was arguably the largest contributor to international education aid during this period (Chabbott, 1998; Psacharopoulos, 1981b), this reorientation of its investments had a significant impact on domestic policy agendas. Mimetic mechanisms included global policy reports and technical assistance, the promotion of studies that aimed at demonstrating the inefficiency of MEP ideas, and the endorsement of the cost-analysis or rate-of-return approach to education policy (e.g., Carnoy, 1967; Psacharopoulos, 1972, 1981a; Psacharopoulos & Loxley, 1985; The World Bank, 1995). Nonetheless, evidence indicates that normative pressures often preceded other diffusion channels. In the 1950s, even before the boom of market-based ideas, the USAID initiated a program providing grants and financial aid for economists from different Latin American countries to be trained in different US universities, primarily the Chicago School of Economics—an important promoter of these new global ideas. These economists were expected to return to their countries and made a significant impact by helping market-oriented policies to permeate domestic policymaking (Biglaiser, 2002; Montecinos & Markoff, 2010).

Like in the previous period, these diffusion channels varied across countries. Coercion and mimesis were strong in Argentina and Colombia, but not in Chile. Argentina's harsh financial conditions due to the debt crisis paved the way for WB's coercion through conditional loans (Teichman, 2004). In the area of education, this funding aimed at enhancing provincial capacity for decentralization, promoting curricular reform, and establishing standardized assessment systems (The World Bank, 1994a). According to a former senior official of the education ministry, mimetic pressures were exercised using Chilean standardized tests and the advice of Chilean experts to formulate Argentinean exams (personal communication #60). In Colombia, coercive pressures included the cancellation of the WB loans for VOCSED schools in 1984, the reorientation of funding to primary education (The World Bank, 1982, 1988), a voucher program for secondary school (The World Bank, 1994b), and the consolidation of a national evaluation system of quality education (Ministerio de Educación Nacional & Departamento Nacional de Planeación, 1991). Mimetic pressures involved the WB's studies in the country showing VOCSED's inefficient rates of return (e.g., Psacharopoulos & Loxley, 1985; Vélez & Psacharopoulos, 1987). These types of cost-benefit studies were replicated by domestic experts with similar results (e.g., Ortega, 1999), which diminished VOCSED's legitimacy. Likewise, domestic assessment experts used the Trends in International Mathematics and Science Study (TIMMS) of Boston College and the Regional Comparative and Explanatory Studies of the Quality of Education conducted by UNESCO in Latin America as references for ICFES to expand standardized assessments (personal communications #10 and #12).

By contrast, all three countries experienced normative pressures, but they were stronger in Chile and Colombia. USAID financially supported Project Chile, an agreement to train Chilean economists in the US under the influence of market-oriented ideas (Castiglioni, 2005, p. 130). These generations of market-minded economists, also known as the "Chicago Boys," reached important government positions during Pinochet's authoritarian regime (Biglaiser, 2002; Montecinos & Markoff, 2010). In the 1960s, USAID, Rockefeller, and Ford Foundations also funded graduate programs for Colombian economists to be trained in the US and brought visiting professors from US universities to collaborate with the School of Economics in the most prestigious Colombian private university, Los Andes University. Like in Chile, these economists were strategically positioned in the government during the 1990s reforms (Uribe, 2014). Although Argentina also received USAID's support for a similar training project (Project Cuyo), this effort was not equally successful, as the labor conditions in the country did not attract these US-trained Argentine economists (Beech & Barrenechea, 2011; Biglaiser, 2002; Montecinos & Markoff, 2010). Thus, Argentina did not develop the critical mass of market-oriented technocrats that Chile and Colombia achieved in the 1970s and 1990s, respectively (Biglaiser, 2002; Uribe, 2014).

Active-State Approach to the Governance of Secondary Education

In contrast to the market mechanisms advocated by neoclassical education economists and lending international organizations, UN-associated agencies like UNESCO and CEPAL promoted decentralization within the context of an "active state." CEPAL advocated for the integration of Latin American economies in global markets by developing competitiveness based on technical innovation, high-skilled human resources, and the inclusion of the most vulnerable population in the production system (CEPAL & UNESCO, 1992; M. Torres, 2006). Unlike the market-based perspective, this approach considered that secondary and higher education had a crucial role in the development of competitiveness and equity; it also regarded the state not as a burden, but as a key actor for the coordination of education governance (McGinn & Welsh, 1999). This coordination, however, involved discontinuing tasks that were often conducted directly by the state, like education provision and curriculum decisions.

The active-state approach proposed the decentralization of education provision as a means to devolve decisions to lower government levels including subnational units, communities, and schools to promote democratization and prevent the authoritarian use of the education system (Picazo, 2013). Similarly, this perspective also suggested curricular autonomy. While the state should still promote a basic curricular agreement between education stakeholders, such curriculum should be flexible enough to include cultural diversity, adapt to regional needs, and emphasize adequate skills for science, technology, and innovation (Coombs, 1985; Tedesco, 1989). The state was also expected to coordinate decision-making, ensure fair distribution of resources and technical capacity, and compensate for inequalities among autonomous geographical jurisdictions and schools for them to deliver good-quality education (CEPAL & UNESCO, 1992; McGinn & Welsh, 1999; Tedesco, 1989; UNESCO, 1989). CEPAL and UNESCO recommendations suggested that the decentralization of provision and curriculum should be complemented by centralized assessment mechanisms, not to inform parental school choices as in the market-oriented approach but to enable the identification of low-performing schools and regions that required the state's assistance (CEPAL & UNESCO, 1992; McGinn & Welsh, 1999; Tedesco, 1989). With this recommendation, these international organizations also engaged in the evaluation policy debate for the first time. Finally, CEPAL and UNESCO regarded VOCSED as unresponsive to local and global skills needs. However, instead of eliminating it, they proposed its modernization by integrating general and practical knowledge to nurture soft labor skills for a knowledge economy (CEPAL & UNESCO, 1992; UNESCO/OREALC, 2002). Table 3.1 summarizes differences in the propositions of state-retrenchment approaches.

CEPAL and UNESCO, however, had a smaller leverage to disseminate their policy ideas. Coercive pressures were not feasible because

Table 3.1. Varieties of State Retrenchment in Education

	Provision	Curriculum	Evaluation
Market-Oriented Ideas	Privatized, competition between schools.	Curricular autonomy for school competition.	Standardized tests to make schools accountable to parents.
Active-State Ideas	Delegated to subnational units, financially compensated by state.	Guidelines agreed among education stakeholders coordinated by state; subnational and school autonomy for adaptation.	Standardized tests to define education policy that alleviates inequality.

Author's elaboration.

their financial capacity became compromised once several prominent state donors decided to channel their aid through bilateral programs rather than through UN organizations (Chabbott, 1998; Galarza et al., 2007). Therefore, the active-state perspective was mainly disseminated by mimetic and normative channels. A former CEPAL's executive secretary explained that UN agencies used UNESCO's Major Project of Education, policy reports and seminars, and public talks for education decision-makers and teachers to persuade key stakeholders on the benefits of an active-state approach (personal communication #28). Mimesis also included technical assistance provided by UNESCO's Latin American Laboratory for Assessment of Education Quality (Laboratorio Latinoamericano de Evaluación de la Calidad de la Educación—LLECE) as a means of developing or refining countries' assessments (Kamens & Benavot, 2011).

While mimetic pressures were relatively similar across countries, normative diffusion was stronger in Chile and Argentina, and practically absent in Colombia. During their exile caused by authoritarian regimes in both countries, Chilean and Argentinean education experts were hosted in private think tanks and UN organizations, where they drew lessons from the negative experience of authoritarianism and power concentration in their countries and collaborated in the critical assessment of preceding education reforms (Braslavsky & Cosse, 2006; Suasnábar, 2014). These experts directly participated in the preparation of CEPAL and UNESCO's report titled "Education and Knowledge: Basic Pillars of Changing Production Patterns with Social Equity," a very influential document in education policy of the 1990s. Later, these experts occupied important positions in education ministries of their respective countries (Braslavsky & Cosse, 2006; Picazo, 2013). By contrast, although CEPAL and UNESCO conducted some policy dialogues and seminars in the country, Colombian education experts did not participate in the formulation of UN global recommendations, and governments were not receptive to increasing its responsibility over secondary education, as a former CEPAL executive secretary explained (personal communication #28). Table 3.2 summarizes the presence of diffusion channels and the timing of dissemination of state-retrenchment ideas in the selected countries.

In the next sections, I explain how the strength and timing of diffusion of both market-oriented and active-state ideas influenced education policy in Chile, Argentina, and Colombia. Yet, I also show that these differences do not fully account for domestic policy decisions. We need to examine domestic politics of education to understand the translation of these state-retrenchment approaches on education policy in the 1980s and 1990s.

Table 3.2. Diffusion Channels and Timing of State-Retrenchment Ideas in Chile, Argentina, and Colombia

	Coercion	Mimesis	Norms
Market-Based Ideas	Argentina and Colombia (1990s)	Argentina and Colombia (1990s)	Chile (1970s–1980s); Colombia (1990s)
Active-State Ideas		Argentina and Chile (1990s)	Argentina and Chile (1990s)

Author's elaboration.

Chile: The Sequential Translation of Market-Based and Active-State Ideas

Despite incompatible policy legacies, Chile conformed to market-oriented ideas during the 1980s due to the strong influence of an alliance between Pinochet's regime and the Chicago Boys that prevented any opposition to their reforms. Pinochet's education policies then generated favorable legacies for further state-retrenchment reforms in the 1990s when active-state recommendations reached the country. Advocates of active-state ideas who reached important government positions were either convinced of the benefits of Pinochet's reforms or forced to compromise their preferences for a state as a coordinator of secondary education governance. This country analysis shows how a strong domestic support and a weak opposition to global norms are necessary to break policy legacies that are incompatible with global recommendations. While such conditions might be rare, they likely lead to conformity to global ideas.

Policy Legacies: Difficulties of Centralized Governance and Fear of Indoctrination

Before the coup d'état in 1973, the Chilean secondary education still followed MEP ideas with a state-coordinated governance of a mixed education provision; marginal participation of VOCSED; and a centrally defined, national curriculum. MEP-inspired reforms in the 1960s created new problems for the educational system. Significant enrollment increases that promoted the universalization of primary education and the massification of secondary school presented a challenge for a centralized management of the education system incapable of providing timely and fair responses to the needs of numerous schools across the country (PIIE, 1984). Nevertheless, two situations created disagreements on the appropriate course for decentralization. First, the polarization of the country during Allende's presidency made the authoritarian regime believe the education system could be used as a means of leftist indoctrination. Consequently, a centralized control of the curriculum to eradicate Marxist ideology from schools became a priority for Pinochet's regime (Cox, 1988; PIIE, 1984). Second, the economic crisis that hit Chile in 1975 fueled the idea that the goal of decentralization in social services was to deal with fiscal constraints instead of moving decision-making closer to communities (PIIE, 1984). Thus, while market-oriented ideas seemed promising to address financial constraints in education and stimulate education results, curriculum autonomy was incompatible with some of the problems the regime expected to solve. Unlike the areas of provision and curriculum in which previous decisions created different governance problems, the decisions during the MEP era in the area of evaluation did not generate new challenges beyond the inconsistency in the application of tests and the persistent insufficiency of information to make centralized decisions.

Concomitantly, inherited beliefs were partially unfavorable to market-oriented reforms. Tensions in the ideological orientations of policy elites shaped competing perceptions on how to solve inherited problems. Although the military junta agreed on the need for reforms, a faction led by General Gustavo Leigh preferred Keynesian, gradual reforms for social policy while another faction led by Augusto Pinochet was gradually persuaded on the benefits of more radical changes (Biglaiser, 1999; Castiglioni, 2005). A former education secretary during the authoritarian regime explained that at the beginning of the dictatorship, the education ministry staff preferred gradual education reforms that promoted decentralization while diminishing the social cost of policy changes. Yet, this situation changed over time, favoring rapid market-oriented reforms (personal communication #32). In other words, MEP ideas were still alive, but they were challenged by new market-oriented recommendations. On the other hand, previous educational planning reforms nurtured a state capacity and acceptance of standardized tests that also favored a transition to use exams as an instrument for governance, as suggested by state-retrenchment ideas (Diaz-Rios, 2020). Nevertheless, inherited beliefs on curriculum were not as compatible with new global recommendations. The previous notion of scientific educational planning was displaced by nationalist beliefs that sought to transform education into a tool to "promote moral and spiritual values consistent with our Chilean, Christian tradition" (*Declaración De Principios del Gobierno de Chile*, 1974, p.11) and prevent "the proselytizing dissemination of any doctrine or idea that threatens the tradition or national unity" (*Objetivo Nacional Del Gobierno de Chile*, 1975). These nationalist ideas were at odds with a curriculum autonomy that could open room for teachers and supporters of Allende to decide on curricular matters (PIIE, 1984).

Evidently, the coup d'état radically disrupted power distribution in the education system. Nevertheless, power struggles within the military junta initially prevented a clear direction for a specific reform. Originally, the military established a junta government with equal power and distribution of the cabinet's positions for each service branch (Valenzuela, 1995). Therefore, the first economic team and the education policymakers were not dominated by the Chicago Boys but by advocates of state-led education governance (personal communication #32). Yet, a disagreement about who had the right to rule changed the incentives and alliances of the military junta members, as the next section explains. In general, while legacies of MEP-inspired reforms were mostly inconsistent with state-retrenchment ideas, some inherited problems and the desire for more power of a section of the military junta paved the way for the arrival of market-oriented recommendations (Table 3.3).

Table 3.3. Relative Incompatibility of Chilean Policy Legacies with Market-Oriented Ideas in the mid-1970s

Policy Area	Inherited Problems	Inherited Beliefs	Inherited Power Distribution	Compatibility Outcome
Provision	Fiscal constraints to sustain an increasing number of schools.	Dominance of MEP ideas challenged by market-oriented advocates.	Power struggles in the military junta between state-oriented and market-oriented advocates.	Relatively incompatible with privatization and fiscal decentralization.
Curriculum	Fear of leftist indoctrination.	Predominance of scientific curriculum planning challenged by nationalist ideology.	Predominance of advocates of nationalist ideology due to the coup d'état.	Incompatible with curriculum autonomy.
Evaluation	Inconsistent evaluation and lack of information to inform policies.	Development of expertise on standardized tests.	Displacement of education planning experts from government.	Relatively compatible with tests for informing school choice.

Author's elaboration.

COALITIONS AND ACTIVITIES: PINOCHET'S ALLIANCE WITH THE
CHICAGO BOYS, CONVERSION OF ACTIVE-STATE ADVOCATES

The market-oriented ideas internalized by the Chicago Boys helped Pinochet defeat his rivals in the military junta. The fiscal adjustments initially undertook by the regime negatively impacted aggregate demand and were insufficient to cope with the 1975 economic crisis (Caputo & Saravia, 2018). These results discredited Keynesian orientations, a situation that was used by Pinochet to diminish Leigh's standing through an alliance with the Chicago Boys—ideological opponents of Leigh's proposals—and other factions of the junta (Biglaiser, 1999). These alliances forced Leigh to resign in 1978 (Biglaiser, 1999; Castiglioni, 2005; Teichman, 2001). Consequently, the Chicago Boys finally gained full access to decision-making and immediately aimed at implementing the Plan for Economic Recovery, more commonly known as the "shock treatment," which included a series of liberalizing and privatization measures that reduced inflation and fiscal deficit, while also fueling a short-lived economic boom. This plan initiated the erosion of the centrality of the state in social services, including education—a trend reinforced by the debt crisis that hit the country in 1981 (Teichman, 2001). Without Leigh in the military junta, supporters of gradual reforms in education also lost any possibility to influence future education decisions. A former education secretary and a former deputy secretary during Pinochet's regime explained that within the ministry, the tensions between supporters of gradual reforms and the market-oriented ideas of the Chicago Boys were finally solved with the replacement of the education minister, which gave the advantage to state-retrenchment advocates (personal communications #32 and #37).

The alliance between the Chicago Boys and Pinochet radically challenged the existing governance arrangement of the Chilean education system. In terms of provision, this market-oriented coalition argued for a voucher system that encouraged competition between schools and devolved school choice to parents (Jofré, 1988; A. Prieto, 1983). Likewise, these market-oriented advocates suggested the use of standardized tests to inform parental school choices, which was expected to promote improvement of education quality (Jofré, 1988). Although this coalition was cohesive in their goals regarding provision and evaluation, curricular preferences were the exception. The Chicago Boys had very little interest in vocational education and recommended curricular autonomy based on minimal required contents and optional subjects that schools could tailor to fit students' expectations (A. Prieto, 1983). Nevertheless, concerned about national security and engaged with the eradication of any form of Marxist ideology within the schools, the military was reluctant to give up control over the curriculum (Cox, 1988; PIIE, 1984). Although the coalition was not supported by relevant actors like the Church, which opposed vouchers due to the risk of delegating schools to the "wrong hands" and their potential effects on inequality (Picazo, 2013; PIIE, 1984), market-oriented supporters still had strong power resources, especially through the violence and repression of the regime that crushed any opposition (Aedo-Richmond, 2000; Castiglioni, 2005). Thus, despite some disagreements regarding curriculum, this coalition became extremely influential in policy decisions.

By contrast, their opponents were weakened and unable to form a coalition. Despite Leigh's preference for state intervention in social services, an alliance with state-oriented advocates of former administrations was unrealistic because the junta, with Leigh's support, persecuted and isolated supporters of a state-run model who worked for either Frei-Montalva's or Allende's governments (Picazo, 2013; PIIE, 1984). Likewise, the teacher union was dismantled in 1973, and many teachers were also persecuted, tortured, forced to disappear, or executed by the regime (Aedo-Richmond, 2000). Although Pinochet replaced the teacher union with a professional association (Colegio de Profesores aka Colegio), two former union leaders explained that this Colegio was under the control of the military, and therefore it was no longer possible for this organization to criticize reforms (personal communications #35 and #47). In brief, opposition to the radical education reforms proposed by the market-oriented coalition lacked organizational capacity, was isolated from the decision-making process, and was incapable of mobilizing power resources (Table 3.4).

After seventeen years, the transition to democracy in 1990 only brought small changes to this influence imbalance. First, the authoritarian regime and an emergent center-left party coalition called Concertación negotiated the Chilean transition to democracy. Negotiations occurred under circumstances that highly constrained the leeway of the first democratic government to undertake policy changes (Hunter, 1997). The Concertación was composed of parties that had supported Allende (MAPU, Socialist, Radicals), and other center and center-left parties (CDP, Democratic party, and Liberal party). After the democratic

Table 3.4. Coalitions' Actors and Activities During Pinochet's Regime

Policy Area	Market-Oriented Ideas: Supporters	Market-Oriented Ideas: Opponents
Provision	Actors: Sections of the military junta led by Pinochet, Chicago Boys. Activities: Enhanced organizational capacity: strong. Access to decision-making: strong. Mobilization of power resources: strong.	Actors: Sections of the military junta led by Leigh, teacher union, education planning experts. Activities: Enhanced organizational capacity: weak. Access to decision-making: weak. Mobilization of power resources: weak.
Curriculum	Actors: Chicago Boys. Activities: Enhanced organizational capacity: limited. Access to decision-making: strong. Mobilization of power resources: weak.	Actors: Military junta. Activities: Enhanced organizational capacity: limited. Access to decision-making: strong. Mobilization of power resources: strong.
Evaluation	Actors: Sections of the military junta led by Pinochet, Chicago Boys. Activities: Enhanced organizational capacity: limited. Access to decision-making: strong. Mobilization of power resources: limited.	Actors: Former educational planners with expertise on evaluation. Activities: Enhanced organizational capacity: limited. Access to decision-making: limited. Mobilization of power resources: weak.

Author's elaboration.

transition, Pinochet was still the commander in chief of the military, and thus the fear of a new coup d'état made the Concertación averse to overt conflict. Consequently, this coalition abandoned any attempts to reverse policy changes (Delannoy, 2000). Additionally, according to the Pinochet's Constitution of 1980, all changes to constitutional laws, including the Organic Constitutional Education Law (Ley Orgánica Constitucional de Enseñanza—LOCE), required a supermajority threshold of 4:7 in both chambers of the legislature (Heiss & Navia, 2007, p. 182). A former senator and a former advisor of the education ministry during the democratic transition explained that since right-wing parties (traditional allies of the military) held more than a third of the Congress, significant legislative transformations were highly unlikely and locked the LOCE with insurmountable institutional constraints (personal communications #30 and #33). Thus, despite the new government, the market-oriented coalition kept close access to decision-making power and mobilized significant power resources to oppose any attempt at reform.

Second, by the 1990s, education policymakers of subsequent democratic governments had already shifted away from a state-run education model and were now closer to state-retrenchment ideas. They were aware of the excessively bureaucratized nature of the centralized model of governance, even before the coup d'état (Nuñez, 1990). Moreover, during their exile, they realized the high concentration of power of such a model, which moved them to formulate and embrace active-state recommendations (Burton, 2011; Picazo, 2013). These policymakers positively assessed some transformations undertaken by the military regime as necessary steps toward decentralization and quality improvement (Cariola, 2003; Cox, 2005; Latorre et al., 1991; Nuñez, 1993), but they were also aware of the problems inherited from Pinochet's education reforms, including the inequality produced by the exclusive reliance on market mechanisms to regulate funding (Burton, 2011; Picazo, 2013). Thus, as explained by two former advisors of the education ministry during the democratic transition, once in their position as policymakers, they built on their internalized ideas about an active state in education to focus their decisions on compensating for the shortcomings of the existing system rather than on substantial transformations (personal communications #30 and #50). To push their ideas forward, these experts prepared several policy papers with recommendations for education reform (e.g., Cox & Bravo, 1985; PIIE, 1989; Vera & Nuñez, 1983) that, as a former

CEPAL president and advisor of the education ministry explained, were later globalized through the 1992 CEPAL and UNESCO report (personal communication #28).

However, preferences of the coalition that supported active-state ideas were not consistent across policy areas. On the one hand, preferences toward curriculum and evaluation were rather uniform. A former senior advisor of the education ministry stated that these topics were not a priority of the first democratic governments (personal communication #50). Additionally, both teachers and active-state education experts opposed curriculum autonomy despite recommendations of active-state ideas. Teachers associated this autonomy with the elimination of subjects and the deregulation of vocational contents as it was reinterpreted during Pinochet's regime, and thus they refused to adopt it (Gysling, 2005). The coordinator of the curriculum reform explained that education policymakers were also dubious about the capacity of schools to formulate curricula, and therefore they preferred to control curricular design (personal communication #50). Likewise, active-state experts paid little attention to standardized exams as a mechanism to inform parental school choices and rather regarded them as a tool that could be used to inform policy—a legacy of MEP ideas (personal communication #30). On the other hand, the coalition had conflicts regarding education provision. The CDP and the Church reconsidered their opposition to vouchers, since this system proved to bring them substantial corporate and financial benefits (Espínola & De Moura Castro, 1999). In contrast, two former union leaders explained that under the influence of the Communists, a segment of the Colegio—now freed from military influence—expected to reverse the transfer of schools to municipalities, abolish the voucher system, and restore the former governance model (personal communications #35 and #47). While cohesiveness around curriculum and evaluation permitted greater influence on decisions in these areas, conflicts undermined the influence of the active-state coalition in decisions over education provision. Table 3.5 summarizes the changes in coalitions after the Chilean transition to democracy.

OUTCOMES: FROM CONFORMITY TO MARKET-ORIENTED IDEAS TO ACCOMMODATION OF THE ACTIVE-STATE APPROACH

Despite the relative incompatibility with domestic policy legacies, Chile became an early adopter of market-oriented recommendations due to the

Table 3.5. Coalitions' Actors and Activities After the Transition to Democracy in Chile

Policy Area	Market-Oriented Coalition	(Active)-State Advocates
Provision	Actors: Right-wing parties, CDP, the Church, CONACEP. Activities: Enhanced organizational capacity: strong. Access to decision-making: strong. Mobilization of power resources: strong.	Actors: Socialists, Communists, some sections of the Colegio. Activities: Enhanced organizational capacity: limited. Access to decision-making: limited. Mobilization of power resources: limited.
Curriculum	Actors: Right-wing parties, the military. Activities: Enhanced organizational capacity: limited. Access to decision-making: strong. Mobilization of power resources: strong.	Actors: Concertación, teacher unions, education planning experts. Activities: Enhanced organizational capacity: limited. Access to decision-making: strong. Mobilization of power resources: strong.
Evaluation	Actors: Right-wing parties, CDP, the Church, some education planning experts. Activities: Enhanced organizational capacity: strong. Access to decision-making: strong. Mobilization of power resources: limited.	Actors: Left-wing parties within the Concertación; some education planning experts. Activities: Enhanced organizational capacity: strong. Access to decision-making: strong. Mobilization of power resources: limited.

Author's elaboration.

powerful alliance between the Chicago Boys and Pinochet. However, the authoritarian regime's interests shaped this conformity. Reforms in the area of provision were implemented earlier and faster with the initiation of a voucher system and the municipalization in 1980. To be sure, as explained in the previous chapter, subsidies to private schools had a long tradition in Chile, but the application of the same funding formula on a competitive basis for both public and private schools was only initiated with the rise of market-oriented ideas.

The combination of municipalization and the voucher system created an education quasi-market composed of three types of schools: public voucher municipal schools, private voucher schools, and paid private organizations. This new structure was locked in by the 1990 LOCE. With this new model of provision, enrollment in private secondary schools increased from 20% to 32% between 1981 and 1987 (Cariola, 2003). A former secretary of the Association of Chilean Private Schools (Colegios Particulares de Chile—CONACEP) explained that this structure nurtured new constituents of private voucher schools (non- and for-profit) facilitating the creation of CONACEP to represent the interests of private education in the government (personal communication #53). The presence of these new constituents facilitated the continuation of the provision reforms after the transition to democracy in 1990, once active-state supporters joined the government.

Reforms in VOCSED provision slightly deviated from conformity to market-oriented ideas. Before the establishment of the voucher system, industrial associations were contracted to manage VOCSED schools (Decreto Ley 3166, 1980). Once the voucher system and the municipalization process were initiated in late 1980, the industrial associations did not accept the competitive-based voucher system. Three factors helped these associations to keep a fixed, noncompetitive funding. First, there were only 71 schools that were already delegated to allied industrial associations (PIIE, 1984). Second, Pinochet had already offered to transform or close other "non-feasible" VOCSED schools, which was consistent with rates-of-return recommendations (Directiva Presidencial sobre la Educación Nacional, 1979, p. 5). Third, new VOCSED schools were to be created within the voucher system (Sevilla, 2012). A former education secretary and a former deputy education secretary during Pinochet's regime explained that the Chicago Boys agreed on a different funding arrangement for these 71 schools so they could maintain their allies and because these organizations were not numerous enough to become relevant (personal communications #32 and #37).

A former senior advisor of the education ministry explained that with the transition to democracy, active-state officials in the ministry introduced several programs to compensate for the inequalities in student learning produced by the education quasi-market (personal communication #30). Two of these programs focused on secondary education: (1) a program for the improvement of quality and equity (MECE-media) that provided funding and technical assistance for all secondary schools to develop improvement plans, and (2) "Liceo para Todos" ("High School for All"), which aided secondary schools with the lowest-performing students (Cox, 2005). Although the WB provided loans for MECE-media, these loans cannot be interpreted as coercion. A former senior advisor of the WB indicated that these loans were requested by the Chilean government to secure additional resources and lock in reforms in case of government change (personal communication #52). Indeed, the WB's funding only accounted for 16.9% of MECE-media, and 33.7% of this funding was canceled at the borrower's request without sacrificing any project goals (The World Bank, 2001a, p. 13). Nevertheless, the effects of these programs on inequality were limited because negotiations with the market-oriented coalition pushed MECE-media and Liceo para Todos to equally benefit public and private voucher schools (personal communications #30 and #55).

The need to negotiate with the market-oriented coalition and divisions within active-state advocates drove the new democratic government to continue and strengthen the provision structure inherited from the authoritarian regime. To appease teachers' demands for change in the funding system, in 1991, the Concertación proposed new job regulations that restored teachers in public schools as public servants, granted them life tenure, and banned discretional transfers. Although recruitment remained delegated to municipalities, teachers' salaries became centrally negotiated, forcing the state to financially support municipalities unable to manage this expenditure (Delannoy, 2000). While this proposal seemed at odds with the preferences of the market-oriented coalition, this group accepted these reforms because principals appointed by the military regime were granted tenure, and because the right-wing party coalition requested in return the expansion of a shared-funding system created during Pinochet's regime. This shared-funding system allowed private voucher schools to collect a top-up payment from families beyond the state's subsidy (Mizala, 2007). A former education minister explained that the Concertación also agreed on the shared funding due to the need for additional resources to support education reforms, including the promised teachers' salaries (personal communication #33). With the shared funding and the new job regulations for teachers, public schools were left with relatively less funding and higher restrictions to manage personnel, which arguably restricted their options to attract students (Mizala, 2007). By the mid-1990s, private enrollment in secondary education already reached 48%, and shared funding in private voucher schools experienced rapid growth (García-Huidobro, 2007). These measures further nurtured robust constituencies of market-oriented ideas compromising the state's capacity to compensate for inequalities.

Reforms in evaluation also initially conformed to market-oriented ideas. Yet, this conformity was gradual as it became inconsistent with the interests of the authoritarian regime. Chilean policy legacies in evaluation facilitated the adoption of standardized exams recommended by market-oriented ideas. A senior advisor of the education ministry explained that, to develop the Program for Performance Assessment in 1982, Pinochet's regime commissioned experts from the Catholic University of Chile who had actively participated in assessment design back in the 1960s (personal communication #48). The technical expertise of the team that conducted the program permitted the development of well-designed evaluation instruments and rigorous interpretation of the results (Himmel, 1997). For the first time, these tests would be used to hold schools accountable for their performance (Himmel, 1997; Ortiz Cáceres, 2012). However, these assessments showed poor results in both public and private voucher schools (Eyzaguirre & Fontaine, 1999). By 1985, Pinochet had agreed to call for a plebiscite to ratify his mandate (Garretón, 1995), and the regime worried that unfavorable educational results would affect electoral outcomes (Delannoy, 2000, p. 12). Therefore, the Program for Performance Assessment was discontinued from 1985 to 1988, and the work of the Catholic University was suspended (Eyzaguirre & Fontaine, 1999; Himmel, 1997). After Pinochet lost the plebiscite, the regime resumed the work on assessments in 1988 with the introduction of the System for Measurement of Education Quality (Sistema de Evaluación de la Calidad Educativa—SIMCE) (personal communication #48). Nevertheless, a former deputy education secretary during Pinochet's regime and two former senior SIMCE advisors explained that the regime refrained from widely publishing results. Only with the LOCE and the transition to democracy in 1990 did publication became mandatory (personal communications #34, #37, and #51). While the regime actually tried to emulate market-oriented ideas of evaluation, conformity was delayed for future governments to transfer political costs of poor results to their opponents (Diaz-Rios, 2020).

With the transition to democracy, evaluation decisions in Chile compromised market-oriented and active-state recommendations. A former senior advisor of the education ministry indicated that, following active-state ideas, the government initially used tests to compensate for inequalities by identifying low-performing schools, designing focalized policies, and evaluating programs (personal communication #30). Moreover, two senior SIMCE advisors explained that test results were published in newspapers with limited circulation just to fulfill LOCE's mandate (personal communications #48 and #51). However, this trend was interrupted in 1994 when the government appointed a commission to settle differences between market-oriented and active-state advocates, especially over curricular issues (Delannoy, 2000; Mizala, 2007). Reflecting changes in beliefs of active-state advocates, the National Commission for the Modernization of Education (Brunner Commission) compromised the idea of using tests to inform policy. Instead, the Commission recommended the association of SIMCE with expenditure focalization and incentives for improvement (Comisión Nacional para la Modernización de la Educación, 1994). Two factors contributed to these changes. First, the rigidities induced by the 1991 teachers' job regulations required new incentives to increase public teachers' efforts (Mizala, 2007). Second, as a former SIMCE director explained, active-state advocates regarded incentives associated to test results as a suitable way to enforce curriculum reforms (personal communication #51). Consequently, in 1996, the government established the National System for Performance Assessment (Sistema Nacional de Evaluación del Desempeño—SNED). With the SNED, teachers were able to earn salary bonuses based on student performance on SIMCE (Mizala & Romaguera, 2000). Test results became regularly and widely published to reinforce the legitimacy of the recently created teachers' incentives. In this way, standardized tests became instruments to inform policy as active-state policymakers preferred, but exams also kept the market-oriented logic of competition between schools not only for students but also for additional government resources. The bargaining of two similarly influential coalitions finally settled a compromise or hybridization of both sets of global recommendations.

Contrasting the other two areas, curricular reforms did not conform to market-oriented ideas due to the military's lack of support. Discussions during the formulation of the 1980 Constitution and the 1990 LOCE reflected how curricular autonomy and the idea of "freedom of education" was not openly rejected but rather was perceived as dangerous for the regime due to their fear of leftist indoctrination (Biblioteca del Congreso Nacional de Chile, 1980, 1990). To ease these tensions, in 1981, the government established a core curriculum with mandatory subjects and granted some marginal autonomy for schools to select optional subjects and school schedules (Aedo-Richmond, 2000; Cox, 1988). Nevertheless, four years later, the education ministry further restricted this small autonomy by specifying the types and content of the "optional" subjects for secondary school (Planes y Programas de Educación Media, 1985). Schools were also authorized to eliminate subjects from their curricula if they did not have the correspondent teachers or resources to deliver the courses (Cox, 1988). Two former senior advisors for vocational education at the education ministry argued that this measure resulted in VOCSED schools tailoring their vocational specializations according to their resources, which once more made their curriculum heterogeneous and uncoordinated, as it was in the 1950s (personal communications #36 and #45). Ultimately, the authoritarian regime used its power to avoid market-oriented curricular reforms and instead created a situation for schools to operate at minimal costs without giving them any real authority to decide on learning contents.

With the promulgation of the LOCE, the military retained its authority over the curriculum. The LOCE established a Superior Education Council to determine broad fundamental learning objectives and decentralized curricular decisions by delegating the elaboration of specific curricular programs to schools (Ley No. 18.962, Orgánica Constitucional de Enseñanza, 1990, preprint 18). Although this change seemed to open the door for curricular autonomy, a former Concertación's Senator explained that the LOCE also granted the military veto power in this Superior Education Council (personal communication #33). Following LOCE's mandate for curricular reform, the education ministry of the first democratic government elaborated a proposal in 1992, which included topics such as gender equity, human rights, environmental protection, and so on. Some of these contents, however, stoked heated opposition, and the military used its veto power in the Superior Education Council to ban the proposal (Cox, 2006). The frustrated attempt and the requirement of curricular reform that LOCE established prompted the appointment of the Brunner Commission, which recommended the creation of two task forces to elaborate new curricular proposals for both general and vocational secondary education (Cox, 2005; Gysling, 2005; Lemaitre María José et al., 2005). As the former coordinators of these task forces indicated, these venues of discussion facilitated the development of a consensus-based centralized curriculum (personal communications #45 and #50), which included consultations with different education stakeholders such as students, parents, teachers, principals, education experts, the Church, and all political parties (Gysling, 2005; Lemaitre María José et al., 2005). The former coordinators of the curriculum task forces also explained that the education ministry elaborated optional course designs for secondary education to discourage the curricular autonomy formally granted by LOCE (personal communications #45 and #50). Indeed, by 2011, less than 20% of all secondary schools had established their own programs (Cox, 2011). In addition, the task force that reformed VOCSED suggested delaying vocational education to the last two years of secondary education, following active-state ideas on avoiding early tracking of students (personal communication #30). Briefly put, instead of promoting curricular autonomy, the support for a centralized curriculum by the military encouraged some ritual implementation of active-state recommendations with national curriculum guidelines, but also with more detailed curriculum designs that constrained local authority on curriculum decisions. Table 3.6 summarizes the translation outcomes of state-retrenchment ideas in Chile.

In sum, the education reforms proposed by the Concertación did not reverse Pinochet's policies. However, my analysis shows that continuity of market-oriented policies in Chile was not the result of pressures imposed from abroad, but rather the product of the domestic legitimacy of ideas and legacies inherited from the authoritarian regime. A strong domestic coalition of the authoritarian regime, right-wing parties, and foreign-trained economists used its power resources of repression and veto power on decision-making to weaken opponents to state retrenchment and impose reforms that radically changed the country's policy legacies. At the same time, exposition to UN recommendations changed the beliefs of these opponents, and thus they continued market-oriented ideas with a mix of active-state recommendations.

Table 3.6. Translation of State-Retrenchment Ideas in Chile

Policy Area	Compatibility with Policy Legacies	Market-Oriented Ideas' Support	Active-State Ideas' Support	Reinterpretation
Provision	Relatively incompatible	Strong	Weak	Conformity to market-oriented ideas: quasi-market of education.
Curriculum	Incompatible	Moderate	Moderate	Avoidance of both market-oriented and active-state recommendations: consensus-based centralized curriculum with shorter VOCSED.
Evaluation	Relatively compatible	Moderate	Moderate	Compromise of both active-state and market-oriented ideas: standardized tests to monitor reform and inform parental decisions. Early development of test-based accountability.

Author's elaboration.

Argentinean Overlapping of Market-Oriented and Active-State Ideas

Unlike Chile, where the influence of market-oriented and active-state ideas was sequential, Argentina experienced a simultaneous arrival of market-oriented and active-state recommendations. Incompatibilities of policy legacies with state retrenchment along with inconsistent alliances between advocates of the two sets of global ideas facilitated the advance of a moderate opposition of teacher unions and provincial governors, which ultimately compromised the translation of global recommendations. Therefore, Argentina moved closer to an active-state model with a decentralization of the education system but retained a significant role of the state in the governance of secondary education.

POLICY LEGACIES: MILITARY REGIME AND PERSISTENT CONFLICTS BETWEEN THE CHURCH AND STATE ADVOCATES

Compared to Chile, the arrival of state-retrenchment ideas in Argentina found relatively similar policy legacies regarding inherited problems. First, primary schooling in Argentina was practically universalized, and gross enrollment rates in secondary education had grown from 44% to 54% between 1966 and 1976. This situation complicated the management of numerous schools across the country and fueled a growing bureaucracy that was perceived as a problem for which decentralization seemed to be a promising solution (Kisilevsky, 1990). Nevertheless, when the regime transferred primary schools to provinces without a corresponding fiscal decentralization, provinces started facing a new problem of fiscal pressures and insufficient resources that activated struggles over the decentralization model the country needed (Falleti, 2005). In addition, decentralization was also appealing to solve tensions between pro- and anti-Peronists, as transferring provision and curriculum decisions could give more power to Catholic and Conservative actors who dominated the provincial governments (Sironi, 2018).

Although inherited problems seemed relatively compatible with state-retrenchment ideas, a market-oriented approach was not predominant within the regime. The military junta was divided between nationalists who advocated for a strong state and supporters of state retrenchment who were not tightly connected with market-oriented ideas because likeminded economists were scarce in the country (Biglaiser, 2002). Likewise, the regime was not supportive of curricular autonomy for schools. Students' and workers' mobilization in 1969 known as El Cordobazo had instilled a fear for "subversive ideologies" in the military, the Church, and right-wing sectors. Therefore, like in Chile, the 1976–1982 Argentinean authoritarian regime perceived the eradication of these so-called dangerous ideas from the educational system as an urgent need and advocated for curricular contents that promoted traditional values, trained workers, and gave provinces authority to decide on curricular matters only under the strict control of the federal level (De Luca, 2013). Finally, student evaluation and testing were not part of the concern of the military regime. This regime was more interested in controlling what teachers taught in the classroom through the inspection system in charge of authorizing (and banning) school textbooks (Vassiliades, 2006). Moreover, Argentina did not develop domestic testing expertise that could have furthered standardized assessments as in Colombia and Chile (Diaz-Rios, 2020).

Compared to Chile, the distribution of power inclined the balance for the preferences of the authoritarian regime. However, this distribution was not entirely favorable to state retrenchment. The Argentine dictatorship also used violence and repression to weaken its opponents. This regime dismissed around 3,000 teachers, university professors, researchers, and education bureaucrats. Some of them went into exile fearing for their safety as their colleagues disappeared from schools and universities (Hanson, 1996). Violence and fear dismantled any opposition from teacher unions, education experts, or other social or political forces (Tedesco et al., 1983). Two union leaders explained that the impact of the regime on opponents remained until the early years of the democratic transition, and therefore influence from groups such as teacher unions was limited (personal communications #66 and #72). Unlike unions and other advocates of a state-run education system, the Church was the only actor that kept its influence. Their preferences focused on the promotion of state subsidies for private provision and decentralization that boosted its provincial influence (Aguerrondo, 1989; Minteguiaga, 2009). Nevertheless, during the authoritarian regime, the rules for power-sharing in the military junta limited the leverage of both factions, the supporters of a strong state, and the advocates of state reduction (Biglaiser, 1999). In addition, the Argentine authoritarian regime had a shorter time to implement reforms since it ruled for only seven years, compared to Pinochet's seventeen years in government. Also, the democratic transition in Argentina was preceded by a defeat of the regime instead of a bargain between parties, as in the Chilean case. Such defeat opened more room for contestation and, more importantly, created conditions for a more balanced power distribution. In sum, as Table 3.7 shows, policy legacies in Argentina were relatively incompatible with market-oriented ideas. First, although decentralization was viewed as necessary to solve inherited problems, there was no consensus on what needed to be transferred. Second, ideas of a strong role of the state were still influential in education policy. Finally, opponents of state retrenchment were weakened by the authoritarian regime, but the

Table 3.7. Incompatibility of Policy Legacies with State Retrenchment at the Time of Democratic Transition in Argentina

Policy Area	Inherited Problems	Inherited Beliefs	Inherited Power Distribution	Compatibility Outcome
Provision	Difficult centralized management of a large and growing secondary education. Financial pressures over provinces due to underfunded decentralization of primary schools.	Decentralization as the option to give more power to conservative groups. Scarcity of market-oriented advocates.	Weakened advocacy of statist model due to regime's repression, but with potential to grow in democracy. Weakened influence of the military's reforms due to regime's defeat.	Relatively compatible with decentralization of provision.
Curriculum	Tensions between Peronists and anti-Peronists over the control of learning contents.	Support for national curriculum based on traditional values and urge to eradicate "subversive" ideologies.	Large influence of the Church not affected by the military regime.	Relatively incompatible with curriculum autonomy.
Evaluation	No discussion about student evaluation.	Inspection needed to keep ideologies under control. No expertise on testing.	Inspection authority under the dominance of military regimes.	Incompatible with standardized tests.

Author's elaboration.

transition to democracy opened opportunities to reposition themselves in the political arena.

COALITIONS AND ACTIVITIES: CONFLICT AND ALLIANCE BETWEEN MARKET-ORIENTED AND ACTIVE-STATE ADVOCATES

With the transition to democracy, preferences over secondary education governance were multiple and dispersed. The Peronist Party was divided between those who expected administrative deconcentration and fiscal transfer of education to subnational units and those who wanted delegation of education decisions to subnational units. Meanwhile, the Radicals preferred devolution of decision-making authority to local communities, and the Church expected authority to be devolved to provinces (Minteguiaga, 2009). In such contexts and considering the weakness of political parties and other organizations after the authoritarian regime, coalitions between these multiple groups were hard to achieve. This struggle became evident during the National Pedagogical Congress (NPC) of the first democratically elected government of Raúl Alfonsín (1983–1989), which was called to build a consensus around education reform (Comisión honoraria de aseguramiento, 1987). A former education minister, a Church representative, two education experts, and a former government senior official coincided on the existence of a clear agreement on the need for decentralization among NPC participants, but they also explained that conflicting interpretations and preferences prevented a consensus on how decentralization should be implemented (personal communications #59, #64, #65, and #76). Additionally, the unresolved macroeconomic crisis inherited from the military regime, hyperinflation, striking increases of foreign debt, and reduction of real wages displaced education from the policy agenda of the first democratic government and made it impossible to implement any reform (Corrales, 2004).

Reforms only came in the 1990s and they focused initially on education provision. By this time, market-oriented advocates had reached crucial positions in the ministry of economy during the government of Carlos Menem (Corrales, 2004). These advocates were strongly connected to several organizations that promoted market-oriented reforms and privatization (Teichman, 2001), including the Foundation for Latin American Economic Research (Fundación de Investigaciones Económicas Latinoamericanas—FIEL), an Argentine think tank and strong proponent of school vouchers and demand-driven funding for schools (FIEL & CEA, 1993; FIEL, 2000). Nevertheless, these policymakers focused exclusively on reducing federal responsibility and the fiscal transfer of secondary schools to provinces (Corrales, 2004). These officials isolated economic policy decisions through Menem's patrimonial style of granting privileges to break down opposition to policy and by threatening to use presidential decrees to impose measures (Teichman, 2001). Menem's administration sought the support of the IMF and the WB, which was essential for a rapid implementation of market reforms and privatization in most areas of social policy. Yet, the area of education is an exception to this trend. A former education minister explained that neither market-oriented domestic policymakers in the ministry of economy nor the WB suggested implementing vouchers or school choice (personal communication #58). Explanations about the lack of support for education privatization in Argentina are divided. A former education ministry and two education experts indicated that the strong symbolic tradition of public education in Argentina prevented the development of privatization proposals (personal communication #58, #64, #76, and #81). By contrast, a senior official of UNESCO in Argentina and a former provincial education minister argued that education privatization did not promise significant savings for the federal government or revenues for private actors, and therefore Menem's government was not incentivized to push such proposals forward (personal communications #61 and #62). Yet, another explanation suggests that the WB understood that Argentina already had "a strong tradition of subsidizing the private sector [with] more than 75% of private sector institutions receiv[ing] financial support from the government to pay teacher salaries" (The World Bank, 1994a, p. 7). Regardless of whether the beliefs of policymakers in public education were too strong or the benefits of privatizing education did not exceed the political costs, Argentina's policy legacies limited the reception of market-oriented ideas.

Meanwhile, opponents to the reduction of federal responsibility and the rationalization of education expenditures were rather weak in 1990. Active-state champions were still dispersed in universities, private think tanks, and international organizations, and they had limited links to the decision-making process (Braslavsky & Cosse, 2006). The Confederation of Education Workers of Argentina (Confederación de Trabajadores de la Educación de la República Argentina—CTERA)—a national alliance of teacher unions—was still undermined by the effects of the authoritarian regime, had a reduced membership (Corrales, 2004), and did not have close ties to any political party (Chambers-Ju, 2021). However, when discussions about education policy extended beyond fiscal matters and included decentralization of curriculum and authority over education, concentrated negative effects helped the consolidation of a stronger opponent coalition. While the ministry of economy was mostly interested in fiscal decentralization, the education minister, Antonio Salonia—also the former minister of education under Frondizi's administration—pursued two additional goals. First, due to the Church's influence on the minister, Salonia expected the decentralization of the curriculum to provinces and proposed that secondary education would be reduced from six to three years. Second, still following education planning ideas, the minister also wanted to develop tests to monitor reforms. Since the transfer and reduction of secondary schools threatened to increase financial pressures for provinces, further weaken teacher unions, diminish the number of required teachers, and deteriorate teachers' job conditions (Tedesco & Tenti, 2004), unions and provincial governors avoided splits within their ranks using their party networks to engage in collective negotiations and influence on Congress (Corrales, 2004). The coalition also increased its power resources through significant support of civil society organizations—many of them keen on active-state ideas—and a public opinion that feared that the rapid and striking privatization of other public services could also be applied to education (Decibe, 2000; Nardacchione, 2011b). The strengthening of this coalition changed the balance of power and challenged the predominance of market-oriented advocates.

Nevertheless, once an agreement was reached on decentralization rules, the government disrupted the opponent coalition by co-opting some of its members. First, Menem appointed Jorge Rodríguez, the main negotiator of decentralization rules as the education minister, and this minister in turn brought Susana Decibe on board, a Peronist politician who was also trained in FLACSO under active-state ideas (Nardacchione, 2011a). Second, Rodríguez reactivated the Federal Education Council, which provided provincial education ministers with access to education policymaking. With this reactivation, the federal level was able to bypass potential opposition of provincial governors (Corrales, 2004). Consequently, provincial actors and active-state experts abandoned the opposition and joined the ministry of economy in an inconsistent market-oriented active-state coalition. As a former education minister explained, this coalition increased the government's power resources for reform implementation, but reform ideas were also constrained by the government's tensions between retrenchment of federal education expenditures advocated by the ministry of economy and the active-state core education policies supported by the education ministry (personal communication #58).

With the alignment between market-oriented and active-state advocates, CTERA was left alone in their advocacy for a state-run education governance model. The union federation still expected a greater fiscal role of the federal government, but it also opposed curriculum reforms. Since teachers were not appointed to schools and were instead instructors of a particular subject with a specific number of hours, curricular reforms could reduce the number of required instructors and change their job conditions (Terigi, 2008). In addition, the reduction of technical school duration meant a substantial decrease in the demand of technical teachers (Gallart et al., 2003). Nevertheless, CTERA's influence was seriously weakened, not only because it was left alone in its opposition but also because decentralization moved negotiations to the provincial level while the union federation still operated at the federal level (G. Nardacchione, 2011b). Later, however, initial education reforms created profound provincial financial crises, restimulating alliances between provincial teacher unions, other unions, and opposition parties. These alliances gave teachers renewed strength and activated significant provincial conflicts (G. A. Nardacchione, 2015). Overall, changes in the Argentine coalitions during the 1990s (see Table 3.8) illustrate how advocates of different branches of state-retrenchment ideas and their opponents may join forces or engage in conflict according to their opportunities to define education governance.

OUTCOMES: COMPROMISE AND AVOIDANCE OF STATE-RETRENCHMENT IDEAS

By contrast to Chile, where market-oriented and active-state advocates generated a stable coalition, the inconsistencies and conflicts between champions of these global ideas compromised their translation into Argentina's education policy. Regarding provision, while policy lega-

Table 3.8. Coalitions' Actors and Activities in Argentina in the 1990s

Policy Area	State-Retrenchment Supporters	State-Retrenchment Opponents
Provision	Actors: Market-oriented officials in the ministry of economy. Activities: Enhanced organizational capacity: limited. Accessed to decision-making: strong. Mobilization of power resources: strong.	Actors: Teacher unions, provincial governors, active-state advocates. Activities: Enhanced organizational capacity: strong. Access to decision-making: limited. Mobilization of power resources: strong.
Curriculum and Evaluation	Actors: Active-state officials in the education ministry. Activities: Enhanced organizational capacity: limited. Access to decision-making: strong. Mobilization of power resources: limited.	Actors: Teacher unions, some provincial governors. Activities: Enhanced organizational capacity: strong. Access to decision-making: limited. Mobilization of power resources: strong.

Author's elaboration.

cies filtered out voucher recommendations, Menem's government took advantage of the weakness of supporters of a state-run education system by including the federal reduction of expenditure on education and the transfer of secondary schools to provinces in a budget law preventing opponents from organizing (Falleti, 2003). This action was reinforced with patrimonial strategies, including offering separate funding bargaining to provinces (Corrales, 2004; Repetto, 2001). Consequently, a predominant market-oriented coalition was able to pass the 1991 Transference Law that delegated financial responsibility over secondary education to provinces.

Nevertheless, when the government tried to further regulate this decentralization through a new education law, it faced a more organized opposition. By 1992, the teacher union and provincial governors pressured the Senate to formulate a counterproposal for the government's education bill that increased federal responsibility to 6% of the GDP, increased free mandatory education, and maintained the existing structure of secondary education (Corrales, 2004). This opposition forced negotiations in the government and facilitated the mediation of Peronist congressman Jorge Rodríguez, who had links to active-state advocates (G. Nardacchione, 2011a). Rodriguez's proposal appealed to both market-oriented and statist coalitions. One of Rodríguez's senior staff members explained that this proposal maintained fiscal decentralization, subsidies for private schools, decentralization of curriculum, and secondary school reductions. However, it also forced the federal government to strengthen its commitment to education provision by doubling education investment over the following five years, subsidizing provinces with deficits in education expenditures, and expanding mandatory education to ten years (personal communication #58). Rodríguez built enough support to enact his bill by conducting meetings to promise provincial governors, teacher union leaders, and civil society organizations a stronger fiscal responsibility of the state. With these strategies, his bill ultimately became the Federal Education Law (FEL) in 1993 (Corrales, 2004). Briefly put, the organization of a more consistent opposition managed to compromise the domestic version of market-oriented reforms in the provision of secondary education.

Negotiations in curriculum for FEL seemed to be consistent with active-state ideas with a decentralized curriculum based on common federal guidelines that provinces should use to design their specific curricula, while schools were given autonomy to tailor them in educational projects (Gvirtz, 2002). Likewise, the FEL merged general and technical secondary streams in a unique track divided into into two levels: (1) a compulsory, lower, general secondary education of three years and (2) an upper secondary school called Polimodal of another three years oriented to the development of soft labor skills (Dussel, 2004). Nevertheless, the inconsistencies between market-oriented advocates and pressures from teachers helped to avoid the translation of these recommendations. A curriculum expert indicated that due to the negotiated character of the FEL and the reluctance of the federal government to increase their fiscal responsibilities, the law made provincial compliance with the curricular reform mainly voluntary, which provided more room for teachers to resist implementation (personal communication #77). In addition, fiscal constraints in provinces and difficulties to pay teachers' salaries increasingly spurred teachers' strikes against curricular changes in the late

1990s, forcing provincial governments to refrain from further pushing for reform implementation (Nardacchione, 2011a; Rivas, 2004). Moreover, a former education minister explained that funding from the WB was used to stimulate provinces to advance reforms, but the reluctance of the ministry of economy to assume further responsibilities over education limited this effort (personal communication #58). A former senior official of the education ministry added that the federal government refused to provide provinces with the required technical capacity to assume the new task of formulating their own curricula (personal communication #77). Consequently, only two provinces—Buenos Aires and Córdoba—fully implemented the Polimodal and the curricular reforms. Three provinces refused to accept changes—Buenos Aires City, Neuquén, and Rio Negro—and the remaining provinces tried a gradual and slow implementation that minimized the conflict with teachers (Dussel, 2004; Gallart et al., 2003; Rivas, 2004). By 2000, only 985 schools out of 8,607 had implemented the reform, 2,497 had just initiated the process without completing it, and 3,055 remained unchanged (Gallart et al., 2003).

Evaluation also reflects the inconsistencies of the market-oriented, active-state coalition and teacher resistance. The FEL initially leaned toward active-state ideas through the establishment of a National System for Education Quality Assessment (Sistema Nacional de la Evaluación de la Calidad—SINEC) to monitor the progress of the reform, identify populations with disadvantaged learning conditions, and determine mechanisms for the government to address inequalities (Ley Federal de Educación, 1993, art. 48–50). However, the education ministry soon shifted to a market-oriented use of assessments by providing incentives to high-performing schools and publishing test results to encourage benchmarking. These measures were expected to create awareness among parents of unsatisfactory learning outcomes at the school level (Benveniste, 2002, p. 103; Gvirtz et al., 2006). A former SINEC senior official also indicated that this change was a signal of soft coercion as it was likely motivated by the technical assistance of the WB and the countries of reference for this policy, which included Chile and Colombia (personal communication #60). Yet, a former education minister explained that these new ways to use assessments were adopted to compensate for the lack of federal tools to enforce curriculum reforms (personal communication #58). Thus, while foreign coercion cannot be completely discarded, consequences of domestic decisions were crucial to make the government change its initial orientations regarding evaluation.

Changes in the use of standardized assessments increased teachers' opposition to education reforms and raised provincial backlash for the negative political effects of test results (Nores, 2002). According to a former senior SINEC official and two assessment experts, the lack of assessment tradition in Argentina and the subsequent absence of technical expertise delayed the implementation of SINEC and made it highly vulnerable to technical shortcomings in test application, analysis, and subsequent result-based incentives, which undermined the legitimacy of the national assessment system (personal communications #60, #71, and #80). In addition, test results and other indicators showed that the provinces that initiated early and went further with reform implementation had a striking decline in educational attainment and student achievement (Rivas, 2004). These results transmitted a sentiment of reform failure, and therefore the federal government scaled back assessment by changing test applications from annual to triannual, dismantling incentives for high-performing schools (Oelsner, 2012), and publishing results by geographical regions without jurisdictional responsibility (Beech & Barrenechea, 2011). Ultimately, the implementation of SINEC was merely ritual and illustrates that incompatible policy legacies, combined with a weak support for global norms and a stronger opposition, facilitated the avoidance of foreign recommendations (Diaz-Rios, 2020). Table 3.9

Table 3.9. Translation of State-Retrenchment Ideas in Argentina

Policy Area	Compatibility with Policy Legacies	Support	Opposition	Reinterpretation
Provision	Relatively compatible	Moderate	Moderate	Compromise: delegation of secondary schools to provinces.
Curriculum	Relatively incompatible	Moderate	Moderate	Avoidance: implementation not fully developed by provinces.
Evaluation	Incompatible	Moderate	Moderate	Avoidance: ritual, consequence-free testing.

Author's elaboration.

summarizes translation outcomes in all three policy areas during state retrenchment in Argentina.

Colombia:
The Unexpected Modification of Market-Oriented Ideas

By contrast to Chile and Argentina, Colombian political elites had always been supportive of a small state to govern education. Thus, when market-oriented ideas arrived in the country through US-trained economists appointed in the government, one would expect an easy policy conformity to these foreign recommendations, as both policy legacies and domestic politics seemed favorable to them. Yet, as the following analysis will show, the Colombian process of democratization in the early 1990s opened access to a strengthened teacher union federation that compromised global ideas on provision and curriculum, and even avoided market-oriented recommendations regarding evaluation.

POLICY LEGACIES: PERSISTENT BELIEFS OF A MINIMAL STATE

Unlike Chile and Argentina, by the 1980s, secondary education in Colombia was not under the control of the state and rather reflected a dualist system. Although primary education became universalized, secondary school only reached an enrollment ratio of 42%, with half of the students coming from middle and upper classes and attending private schools (Helg, 1998). Since nationalization was not completed, the public provision of secondary education was still uncoordinated with different types of schools dependent on several administrative levels (Diaz-Rios, 2019). Likewise, curricular guidelines were ill defined and constantly changing (Velasco Peña, 2018). While these problems might have demanded greater centralization, which was at odds with state-re-trenchment ideas, it was also possible to argue that the state had not been capable of steering the educational system, thus rendering market mechanisms a better governance option.

Indeed, inherited beliefs encouraged the market solution. As explained in the previous chapter, domestic political elites in Colombia had typically believed that the action of the state in education should be minimal. Likewise, they were barely interested in curricular matters while teachers increasingly demanded participation and greater autonomy. Finally, although standardized tests had not been used to govern education like in the Chilean case, according to a senior curriculum advisor of the education ministry and a former ICFES director, the assessment developed by the National Testing Service unintentionally became the only curricular guideline for secondary schools because a deliberate elaboration of a national curriculum for secondary education had been unsuccessful (personal communications #7 and #10).

Likewise, the inherited power distribution relatively favored the reduction of the state role in education. The National Front was over in 1978, and demands for further democratization of political decisions rose in the country through continuous protests, mobilization, and civil unrest (Aldana, 2002). This situation drove political elites to establish democratic elections for municipal mayors in 1986 and to initiate a participatory constitutional process in 1991 (Lowden, 2004). The new Constitution did not immediately alter the dominance of the Liberals and Conservatives and their ideas on a limited role of the state in social policy. In addition, the Constitution declared Colombia as "a legal social state organized in the form of a unitary republic, decentralized, with the autonomy of its territorial units, democratic, participatory and pluralistic" (CPRC, 1991, sec. 1, art.1), which gave local and nonstate actors greater influence on decision-making. Yet, increased participation also granted actors who disagreed on market-oriented recommendations more influence on decision-making, including teacher unions and a growing number of VOCSED constituents. Briefly put, democratization opened opportunities for a more participatory debate on the role of the state in secondary education governance. Table 3.10 summarizes how policy legacies and the political and social environment of the country were mostly compatible with the reception of market-oriented ideas in the country.

COALITIONS AND ACTIVITIES: THE RISE OF ADVOCATES FOR A STRONGER STATE

While policy legacies created a favorable environment for marketoriented ideas that the WB promoted, power distribution also opened opportunities for the participation of opponent coalitions. Like Chile, US-trained, market-minded economists were very influential in the

Table 3.10. Compatibility of Policy Legacies with Market-Oriented Ideas by the End of the National Front (mid-1970s)

Policy Area	Inherited Problems	Inherited Beliefs	Inherited Power Distribution	Compatibility Outcome
Provision	Sizeable private participation in secondary education without state control. Lack of state coordination of education policy.	Persistent ideas on a minimal state role in education governance.	Persistent dominance of political parties keen on a small state. Decision democratization, including other nonstate and subnational actors due to constitutional changes.	Compatible with decentralization and privatization.
Curriculum	Ill definition of curriculum guidelines.	Limited attention to curricular matters from policy elites. Demands for autonomy from teachers.	Increased influence of unions and Pedagogical Movement.	Compatible with curriculum autonomy.
VOCSED*	Limited secondary education provision for the poor.	VOCSED as an adequate option for poor population.	Increased influence of VOCSED constituents (working-class families, subnational politicians).	Incompatible with elimination of VOCSED.
Evaluation	No significant problems identified around student evaluation.	Development of testing expertise. Tests as informal curriculum guidelines for secondary education.	Ample acceptance of tests in the country.	Compatible with standardized tests for school choice.

Author's elaboration.

*Although VOCSED is a part of curriculum policy, this policy dimension is highlighted here as a separate one due to differences in policy legacies.

Colombian national planning agency (Departamento Nacional de Planeación—DNP) and the finance ministry beginning in the 1970s. Yet, the pervasive patronage in the country drove these economists to focus mainly on macroeconomic policy, leaving social and education sectors to be used as political job banks that benefited particular regional and partisan interests (Alvarez, 2005; Díaz, 1986; Hanson, 1986). Nevertheless, the 1980s global economic crisis pushed domestic macroeconomic policies further and granted opportunities for additional structural adjustment in other policy areas—a trend that was reinforced by the 1991 Constitution and its subsequent environment of "openness" in the country (Alvarez, 2005; R. Forero et al., 2007; Uribe, 2014). Consequently, the DNP and the finance ministry committed to transforming education policy in the country, ultimately becoming very influential market-oriented champions of reforms (Montenegro, 1995). These supporters found strong allies in the municipal mayors, not because these mayors believed in market-oriented solutions but because they regarded the devolution of authority as a source of fiscal and political gains (Falleti, 2010).

Although influential, this coalition of two government bodies and mayors was not entirely cohesive, as their members pursued different interests. Regarding provision, the DNP and the finance ministry pushed for a model similar to the Chilean one, including the devolution of fiscal responsibilities to municipalities (municipalization), vouchers, and school autonomy for hiring, managing, and firing personnel (Montenegro, 1995). Nevertheless, mayors were simply interested in receiving and having authority over the fiscal transfers for all public primary and secondary schools in their jurisdictions (Falleti, 2010). All three actors were less invested in curriculum and evaluation reforms. Nevertheless, the DNP and the finance ministry advocated for curricular autonomy to promote school choice and the elimination of VOCSED, which they considered an inefficient form of secondary education (Ministerio de Educación Nacional & Departamento Nacional de Planeación, 1991). By contrast, mayors had little interest in curricular decentralization (Falleti, 2010). In addition, the new local elections created in the 1980s by the Constitution made mayors and governors pay more attention to local constituents. Thus, they were reluctant to eliminate VOCSED, since these schools were highly regarded among low-income communities, as a former education vice minister explained (personal communication #10). Likewise, the DNP and the finance ministry pushed the use of standardized tests as a means to inform school choice (Montenegro, 1995). However, as the distribution of responsibilities of different government levels was unclear, mayors and governors did not see testing as a potential gain (Diaz-Rios, 2020). Moreover, by contrast to Chile and Argentina, the Church and private providers were not part of any coalition because they typically had ample autonomy, received state subsidies, and had freedom to establish tuition fees. Therefore, they perceived few benefits in the transformation of their status quo (M. M. López, 2001; Montenegro, 1995; Sarmiento, 1998).

Although the market-oriented coalition had direct access to the decision-making process, its influence in education policy was relatively constrained. While a segment of the Liberals—the party in power during Cesar Gaviria's presidency (1990–1994)—was keen on market-oriented ideas, another segment rather favored a Keynesian approach (Uribe, 2014). According to one of the education ministers of this administration, he was part of this Keynesian segment and preferred a more centralized governance model. The minister also explained that he did not want to fuel civil unrest in the country due to numerous social policy reforms and political violence, so he decided to negotiate reform proposals with FECODE rather than impose the solutions of the DNP and the finance minister (personal communication #13). The DNP's chair pointed at the absence of likeminded policymakers in education by stating that "most of the top education experts migrated to the US and the WB, and other multilateral organizations. The available personnel were incapable of supporting any serious, ambitious process of modernization" (Montenegro, 1995, p. 12). This ideological division within the government limited the influence of the market-oriented coalition in decision-making. Similarly, although this coalition had multiple studies to back up the elimination of VOCSED (Psacharopoulos & Loxley, 1985; Vélez & Psacharopoulos, 1987) and had the assistance of the WB for a pilot of a voucher program called PACES (E. King et al., 1997), the decline in the government's popularity from 79% to 20% between 1992 and 1993 due to increasing violence, a profound energy crisis,[1] and numerous privatization reforms limited its power resources to push for market-oriented changes in education (Lowden, 2004).

Additionally, to respond to constitutional participation demands, Gaviria's government gave FECODE veto power through a seat in the discussion of a new national education bill (Rodriguez, 2001). FECODE advocated for the completion of the nationalization of school funding and the continuation of centralized negotiations on teachers' salaries and job conditions, while also looking for the creation of government-independent, teacher-led municipal councils with curricular and pedagogical autonomy and the discretion to determine the number of teachers required by each municipality (M. M. López, 2001; Montenegro, 1995).

Along with direct access to decision-making, FECODE had increased its organizational capacity to over 200,000 teachers (Bocanegra, 2010). Yet, the union federation had some internal disagreements in their preferences. Members of the Pedagogical Movement within FECODE demanded curricular autonomy for schools. However, another sector of the federation feared that such autonomy could give schools the authority to hire and fire personnel, which would threaten the stability of teachers' jobs and the political leverage of the union, as a former union leader and a former education minister explained (personal communications #14 and #19). Likewise, another former FECODE leader indicated that a segment considered VOCSED schools an inequitable option for poor students, but other union members preferred to avoid VOCSED changes that might hurt the employment stability of vocational teachers (personal communication #18). By contrast, FECODE achieved greater agreement in evaluation as teachers did not openly oppose standardized assessments that have typically been used in the country, but they rejected their use as a means of parental school choice (Diaz-Rios, 2020). Despite these differences, FECODE's demands were pushed forward, not only in negotiations with the education ministry, but also with national teachers' strikes—the union's main power resource (Lowden, 2004; Montenegro, 1995). In sum, the influence of both coalitions was mostly balanced, as indicated in Table 3.11.

OUTCOMES: COMPROMISE AND AVOIDANCE OF MARKET-ORIENTED IDEAS

A strong domestic opposition compromised the translation of global market-oriented ideas despite the compatibility of policy legacies and the significant influence of market-oriented advocates. Similar to the unfolding of events in Argentina, the initial struggle in Colombia also focused on fiscal responsibility for provision. In 1992, the DNP and the finance ministry presented the Decentralization Bill that reflected their market-oriented preferences and resembled the Chilean model (Montenegro, 1995). In response, as a former FECODE member and a former education ministry explained, the union federation employed its discussions with the education ministry to present another bill that challenged the

Table 3.11. Coalitions' Actors and Activities in Colombia in the 1990s

Policy Area	Market-Oriented Supporters	Market-Oriented Opponents
Provision	Actors: Finance ministry, DNP, mayors. Activities: Enhanced organizational capacity: strong. Access to decision-making: strong. Mobilization of power resources: limited.	Actors: Education ministry, FECODE. Activities: Enhanced organizational capacity: strong. Access to decision-making: strong. Mobilization of power resources: strong.
Curriculum	Actors: Finance ministry, DNP. Activities: Enhanced organizational capacity: limited. Access to decision-making: strong. Mobilization of power resources: strong.	Actors: FECODE, education ministry. Activities: Enhanced organizational capacity: limited. Access to decision-making: strong. Mobilization of power resources: strong.
VOCSED*	Actors: Finance ministry, DNP. Activities: Enhanced organizational capacity: limited. Access to decision-making: strong. Mobilization of power resources: limited.	Actors: FECODE, education ministry, governors and mayors. Activities: Enhanced organizational capacity: strong. Access to decision-making: strong. Mobilization of power resources: strong.
Evaluation	Actors: Finance ministry, DNP. Activities: Enhanced organizational capacity: weak. Access to decision-making: limited. Mobilization of power resources: weak.	Actors: Education ministry, FECODE. Activities: Enhanced organizational capacity: limited. Access to decision-making: strong. Mobilization of power resources: limited.

Author's elaboration.

*Although VOCSED is a part of curriculum policy, this policy dimension is highlighted here as a separate one due to differences in coalitions.

proposal of the market-oriented coalition (personal communications #13 and #18). Along with this strategic use of their access to decision-making, the union federation started a national 15-day teacher strike against the Decentralization Bill. The strike also pushed for the adoption of the General Education Bill, which reflected FECODE's preferences such as the fiscal nationalization of schools and the creation of municipal councils chaired by teacher unions (Proyecto de ley 44, 1992). Along with the strike, the division between the government's market-oriented economists and FECODE's allies in the education ministry forced renegotiations of both the Decentralization and the General Education Bills.

In these negotiations, both coalitions focused on the exclusion of the propositions that were furthest from their preferred outcome. On the one hand, the market-oriented coalition managed to eliminate the municipal councils proposed by FECODE as the government feared that these councils would give the unions significant authority over teachers' appointments, thereby diminishing the autonomy of subnational governments (Montenegro, 1995). On the other hand, pressure from the federation excluded municipalization that, according to a former FECODE leader, would undermine the union's political strength, create geographical inequalities in teachers' job conditions, and leave teachers vulnerable to corruption, clientelism, and lack of technical capacity at the municipal level (personal communication #18). Both sides also accepted compromises in certain outcomes. First, schools were only delegated to departments (similar to states or provinces), which are bigger subnational units compared to municipalities. Moreover, teachers' job conditions remained centralized (Lowden, 2004; Montenegro, 1995). Second, vouchers were transformed into government subsidies exclusively for poor students to be used for private schools only where public supply was insufficient, thus preventing competition and school choice (Ley 60, 1993, art. 8). Consequently, the WB was forced to transform its voucher program called PACES into a bursary program for poor students to "adapt the implementation mechanisms and procedures [of its program] to the new legal context, as well as to the new institutional and education policies of the country" (The World Bank, 2001b, p. 3). Later, the decentralization scheme adopted in 1993 complicated the transfer of resources to participating private schools, and the distribution of funds became politicized and were used to gain political clientele (Calderón, 1996; The World Bank, 2008). A former education vice minister explained that due to these problems, the government of Ernesto Samper (1994–1998), a Liberal of the Keynesian segment, decided to cancel PACES (personal communication #10).

The compromise of market-education ideas in provision affected the area of curriculum. Although FECODE supported school autonomy for pedagogical and curricular decisions, the federation did not accept that schools recruited and fired their own personnel (Lowden, 2004; Montenegro, 1995; Sarmiento, 1998). Thus, in the final version of the General Education Law, the federation accepted the delegation of the responsibility over curriculum design mostly to departments, while schools only received autonomy to formulate Institutional Educational Projects (Diaz-Rios, 2017). These projects formally allowed schools to define their specific education goals, the pedagogical means and resources to achieve them, the teaching methods, the management principles, and school regulation for teachers' and students' code of conduct (Ley General de Educacion 115, 1994, Art. 73). Yet, management of resources were only delegated to departments, thus leaving schools without control over their own budgets to operate their pedagogical projects (personal communication #14). Two former FECODE leaders explained that this reduced school autonomy reflected internal divisions in the federation, as well as the priority the unions ultimately gave to the stability of teachers' job conditions (personal communications #14 and 18).

Recommendations on provision and curricular autonomy were compromised by the balanced influence of supporters' and opponents' coalitions. However, the translation of global ideas on VOCSED and evaluation reflects avoidance due to weaknesses of the market-oriented coalition in these areas. Although the WB discontinued funding for vocational secondary schooling and used research to persuade the education ministry of VOCSED's inefficient rates of return (personal communication #26), a former FECODE leader and a former education vice minister explained that in addition to the unions' opposition, mayors and governors pressured against these measures due to the political costs of eliminating a program that was extremely popular among low-income families (personal communications #10 and 18). To retain the support of mayors and governors, the government only reduced VOCSED from four to two years and delegated the responsibility for funding the vocational component to the national agency for job training (Servicio Nacional de Aprendizaje—SENA), as a former SENA senior official and a former SENA union leader indicated (personal communications #2 and #4). With these decisions, the Colombian government attempted to downplay VOCSED but ultimately did not eliminate it as global norms recommended.

While pressures of mayors and governors facilitated the avoidance of VOCSED elimination, insufficient support and inconsistent institutional arrangement helped the avoidance of recommendations on evaluation. According to a former education ministry and a former FECODE leader, the tradition of standardized tests in the country since the 1960s prevented any objection to the expansion of these exams and facilitated the transformation of ICFES into the Colombian Institute for Education Assessment (personal communications #13 and #18). Nevertheless, beyond some discussions within the DNP, the market-oriented coalition barely pushed for the transformation of existing tests into a mechanism for accountability (Montenegro, 1995). Moreover, with the exclusion of school choice proposed in the Decentralization Bill, standardized assessments for informing parental school choices became meaningless, although exam results were widely published (Diaz-Rios, 2020; Lowden, 2004). Therefore, performance on tests remained mostly inconsequential for public schools and teachers. Table 3.12 summarizes the translation processes and outcomes in Colombia during market-oriented ideas.

Table 3.12. Translation of State-Retrenchment Ideas in Colombia

Policy Area	Compatibility with Policy Legacies	Support	Opposition	Reinterpretation
Provision	Compatible	Moderate	Strong	Compromise: decentralization without vouchers.
Curriculum	Compatible	Moderate	Strong	Compromise: curriculum autonomy.
VOCSED*	Relatively incompatible	Moderate	Strong	Avoidance: continuation of VOCSED outside of the education ministry.
Evaluation	Compatible	Weak	Moderate	Avoidance: persistence of testing but not for parental choice.

Author's elaboration.

*Although VOCSED is a part of curriculum policy, this policy dimension is highlighted here as a separate one due to differences in policy legacies and coalitions.

Conclusion

Since the 1980s, two sets of global ideas transformed the centrality of the state in the governance of secondary education. Market-oriented ideas regarded the state as a source of inefficiency and proposed privatization, vouchers, school choice, curricular autonomy, elimination of VOCSED, and tests as a means of activating market mechanisms and increasing school quality and efficiency. In turn, active-state ideas suggested a decentralized provision, the delegation of some authority over the curriculum, and the transformation of VOCSED, with the state compensating for potential financial and technical inequalities between subnational units and/or schools while using assessments to inform the coordination of secondary education governance. The timing and channels through which these two versions of state-retrenchment ideas traveled to Chile, Argentina, and Colombia varied across countries. The analysis of the timing and channels confirms the impact of normative diffusion on the acceptance of global ideas, but again, dissemination channels are not enough to explain different translation pathways.

In Chile, active-state ideas arrived once the country had already conformed to the market-oriented approach. Before this arrival and despite relatively incompatible legacies of a state-led secondary education, the alliance between Pinochet's dictatorship and the Chicago Boys, as well as the violent repression of opponents, radically changed the governance of the entire education system, including secondary education. These reforms transformed the beliefs of former planning experts who became active-state advocates. Policy changes also nurtured powerful constituents of private education that later, once in democracy, compromised the translation of active-state ideas, thus enhancing a quasi-market of education. By contrast, both market-oriented and active-state approaches arrived in Argentina at the same time in a democratic context that opened more opportunities for opposition. Moreover, active-state advocates were more numerous and stronger in the country's policymaking scenario. Thus, the relative incompatibility of foreign recommendations with the Argentinean teaching state, the disagreements between different factions of state-retrenchment approaches, and the mobilization of opposition, particularly teacher unions and local policy elites, prevented the conformity experienced by Chile and instead produced compromise and avoidance of active-state formulas that led to a quasi-state monopoly of education with greater participation of subnational governments. Unlike these two countries, Colombia was practically influenced only by market-oriented ideas through different channels and particularly through the socialization of market-oriented experts. Although compatible policy legacies suggested a smooth conformity to these foreign prescriptions, the democratization process of the 1990s opened opportunities for the resistance of Colombian teachers that compromised market-oriented recommendations, thus reproducing the dualist character of the education system. Table 3.13 summarizes these translation outcomes by country and policy area.

The comparative analysis of secondary education provision, curriculum, and evaluation further shows that the constitution and the actions of coalitions supporting and opposing global ideas in a country do not operate equally in all policy areas. For instance, despite the strong support for state-retrenchment ideas in Chile, curricular autonomy never attracted advocates as it did not produce clear benefits for either powerful or peripheral actors. Therefore, these recommendations were mostly avoided. Likewise, active-state advocates in Argentina made alliances with teacher unions and subnational politicians in order to force market-oriented officials in the government to strengthen federal fiscal responsibility. Yet, when these active-state experts proposed curricular reforms that involved local autonomy and changes to the structure of both general and secondary education, they faced CTERA'S opposition and resistance from some provinces, which forced a ritual implementation of active-state policy preferences in curriculum and evaluation. Finally, while Colombian teacher unions advocated for a centralized governance of secondary education, they also demanded curricular autonomy. This demand provided room for the government to delegate curricular respon-

Table 3.13. Summary of Translation Outcomes by Country and Policy Area During State-Retrenchment Ideas

Policy Area	Chile	Argentina	Colombia
Provision	Conformity	Compromise	Compromise
Curriculum	Avoidance	Avoidance	Compromise
Evaluation	Compromise	Avoidance	Avoidance

Author's elaboration.

sibilities to subnational governments and schools, a situation harder to reach in other policy areas in which the opposition of FECODE forced the government to more substantial compromises.

In addition, this chapter shows that the sequence and way in which reforms are conducted in a specific policy area affect the translation of global ideas in other areas. In all three countries, provision reforms were undertaken before policy changes in curriculum and evaluation. Yet, only Chile conformed to state-retrenchment ideas, facilitating a smoother translation in evaluation. By contrast, Argentina's compromise of market-oriented ideas constrained the chances of conforming to curricular and evaluation recommendations coming from active-state advocates. Similarly, Colombia's failure to implement vouchers made standardized tests to inform parental school choice irrelevant, leading the country to avoid these recommendations.

The consequences of reforms in provision, curriculum, and evaluation, as well as the contestation and bargaining between coalitions, produced different legacies that shaped the ways in which new global ideas in the 2000s and 2010s were reinterpreted in each country, as I will analyze in the next chapter.

Chapter 4

The Translation of Education for All
in the Era of Accountability

Although ideas of state retrenchment in education were still very popular in the early 2000s, they had already faced significant criticisms. Cuts to public spending on secondary and higher education were inconsistent with the demands in middle-income countries to expand these educational levels after the universalization of elementary education (Heyneman, 2012; Mundy & Verger, 2015). In addition, policy instruments associated with school competition and school choice had an ambiguous impact on quality and were often associated with increased inequality (Ball et al., 1996; Gordon, 2005; Hsieh & Urquiola, 2006). Likewise, the decentralization of education governance, coupled with expenditure cuts, did not improve education quality and actually worsened geographical inequality (Gvirtz, 2008; Prawda, 1993; Tedesco & Aguerrondo, 2005).

Similarly, education experts in countries where VOCSED was consolidated argued that the elimination of vocational content from secondary schools reduced the opportunities of the poorest students. These students were unable to attend higher education, and they did not receive any preparation for the labor market (personal communications #10, #45, and #50). Curricular autonomy was also criticized due to poor coordination and lack of technical capacity at schools and subnational units (Ferrer, 2004; Vegas & Petrow, 2008). Experts suggested that if this autonomy was not guided by standards and accountability, it would become a source of inequality since schools would not be encouraged to improve and equip students with the needed basic skills (Patrinos, 2015; Woessmann, 2007; Woessmann et al., 2009). These criticisms supported the expansion of standardized exams and recommended additional uses beyond parental school choice.

Criticisms to state-retrenchment recommendations did not suggest a return to a state-centered education system, but they demanded modifications to the role played by the state in the governance of secondary education. Already in the 1990s, prominent international organizations such as UNESCO, UNICEF, and the WB started the promotion of the Education for All (EFA) framework that reconfirms education as a human right, thus reinforcing the state's responsibility in its governance. According to a senior official in the WB, EFA's demands for broader, high-quality youth education brought secondary school back to the global policy agenda (personal communication #27). Yet, it was not until 2000, with EFA's relaunch through the Dakar framework, that specific targets and monitoring instruments were recommended to ensure countries' real commitment to EFA's goals (Chabbott, 2003, p. 62). This framework reoriented global ideas to a softer version of the 1990s state-retrenchment models with increased state control.

Recommendations on the secondary education provision experienced minor modifications. On the one hand, the WB minimized its advocacy for expenditure rationalization (Chabbott, 2003; Mundy & Menashy, 2014; Mundy & Verger, 2015) and instead suggested the implementation of public-private partnerships (PPPs) as tools to expand education access for the poor, improve quality, and give greater participation to communities (Patrinos et al., 2009; The World Bank, 2004, 2011). Voucher recommendations were relatively downplayed—though not eliminated—and various kinds of PPPs were promoted, such as charter[1] and contract[2] schools, as well as school-based management.[3] On the other hand, although international organizations still supported the devolution of decision-making close to the domain where actions were undertaken, UNESCO called for a balance between centralization and decentralization when subnational units or communities did not meet the technical conditions to assume the responsibility of managing schools (Abu-Duhou, 2005; McGinn & Welsh, 1999).

Ideas about curriculum and evaluation perhaps experienced more substantial modifications. EFA's promoters highlighted the importance of curricular diversification, shifting away from the rates-of-return analyses predominant in the 1980s and 1990s. Yet, this diversification was also different from the 1960s manpower approach, as it emphasized the need for deferring vocational specialization until upper-secondary or postsecondary education; rather, it called for a focus on the development of socioemotional abilities and soft labor skills, such as communication, problem-solving, critical thinking, networking, and so on (Banco Mundial, 2005; Braslavsky, 2001; UNESCO, 2000; UNESCO/OREALC, 2002). At the same time, curricular autonomy was relatively displaced by an emphasis on curricular standards. These standards were expected to define a common or national curriculum based on core competencies, complemented with optional skills customized to the particular needs and aspirations of subnational units and communities (De Moura Castro et al., 2000; UNESCO, 2005b). This ideational change implied a recentralization of authority through centralized curriculum standards and evaluation (Astiz & Wiseman, 2005). Governments were responsible for defining standards or acceptable levels of learning acquisition for all students, as well as establishing systems of monitoring and incentives for improvement (Gropello, 2006; The World Bank, 2011; UNESCO, 2000). These systems were mainly based on standardized assessments and were expected to promote benchmarking and improve accountability of schools and subnational units (The World Bank, 2011; UNESCO, 2005a). Table 4.1 shows the mild modifications between state-retrenchment recommendations in the 1980s and 1990s, as well as the emphasis on Education for All and accountability in the 2000s.

Like in previous periods, the diffusion of these new global ideas in Chile, Argentina, and Colombia varied substantially. Two factors need to be considered to understand this variation. First, the influence of a new actor, the OECD, became crucial for Chile (mid-2000s) and Colombia (mid-2010s) as these countries started processes of accession to this organization. These processes were expected to drive applicant countries to follow OECD values and policy standards (Bachelet, 2009; Gehring & Koch, 2016), which can be considered an exercise of mimetic pressures on countries aspiring to accede. Regarding education, the OECD follows UN-established goals but also has significant influence through the Programme for International Student Assessment (PISA), which has become a global reference for standardized tests and education policy recommendations (H.-D. Meyer & Benavot, 2013; Rivas, 2015). Second, since Chile, Argentina, and Colombia were already classified as middle-income nations by the 2000s, there was less room for coercive pressures from international organizations.

Table 4.1. Changes in Global Ideas Between the 1980s and the 2010s

	State Retrenchment Varieties (1980s–1990s)	Education for All and Accountability (2000s–2010)
Provision	Market-oriented approach: Decentralization, privatization, and competition. Active-state approach: Decentralization.	Public-private partnerships and controlled decentralization.
Curriculum	Market-oriented approach: Elimination of VOCSED; curricular autonomy. Active-state approach: Consensual curricular framework; some curricular autonomy; softer VOCSED.	Secondary education based on socioemotional and soft job skills. Common standardized curriculum with limited autonomy to accommodate local needs.
Evaluation	Market-oriented approach: Standardized tests for parental decisions. Active-state approach: Standardized testing to inform policy decisions.	Standardized tests for centralized, government accountability and school benchmarking.

Author's elaboration.

Out of these three countries, Colombia was the only one that received coercive, mimetic, and normative pressures in the 2000s. To cope with a country's economic crisis by the late 1990s, the IMF and the WB offered loans conditioned to increasing the fiscal responsibility over education of subnational units and offering incentives for expenditure rationalization (The World Bank, 2008). The IADB also provided an $11 million USD loan for the country to elaborate curricular standards and strengthen the evaluation system (IADB, 1999). According to a former WB senior official and a consultant for the education ministry in the 2010s, the WB also promised a loan to fund a new secondary education reform with a focus on eliminating specialized VOCSED and replacing it with a soft-skilled curriculum (personal communications #1 and #8). In addition to this coercion, Colombia experienced mimetic pressures throughout the 2000s and 2010s through the WB's and EFA's country-monitoring reports that focused on two areas: (1) praising and promoting different public-private partnership experiences in the country, including vouchers, charter schools, and contracting-out (e.g., Banco Mundial, 2006, 2008; Patrinos et al. 2009); and (2) recommending curricular standards, the improvement of accountability systems, and the participation in international assessments to establish common learning goals, solve the country's educational inequality, and correct the heterogeneous interpretation that each school made of the curricular autonomy (Banco Mundial, 2007, 2008; Ministerio de Educación Nacional, 2000). Later, by 2015, two former senior officials in the education ministry explained that the WB also provided technical assistance for the secondary education reform through study visits of "exemplary" countries and advice on local studies supporting the reform (personal communications #1 and #3). Finally, normative pressures continued disseminating market-oriented ideas as the DNP was still under the influence of experts socialized in this approach, and the WB also served as a platform to nurture a group of Colombian specialists on PPPs who often published policy-relevant studies highlighting the benefits of private education provision (Barrera Osorio et al., 2012; Barrera-Osorio, 2007; Vélez, 1996). At the same time, a former ICFES director indicated that PISA experts provided training to local assessment staff to improve the technical aspects of testing design and interpretation of results (personal communication #12).

Unlike Colombia, Chile and Argentina faced increasingly limited global pressures. Since the late 1990s, and after years of positive assessments of the Chilean education reforms, prominent international organizations including UN agencies, the WB, and the OECD published reports that highlighted the inequality and segmentation of the Chilean education system (EFA Global Monitoring Report, 2015; OECD, 2004; PNUD, 1998; The World Bank, 2007). To fix this problem, these organizations, and especially the OECD, recommended stronger state incentives and sanctions for school performance (OECD, 2004). Since Chile aimed to accede the OECD, the country constantly drew lessons from PISA, as two former SIMCE senior officials explained (personal communications #34 and #48). These mimetic pressures further fueled normative channels as participation in PISA and other international tests reinforced local training of assessment experts and provided them with opportunities to update the discussion on evaluation, as a former SIMCE director explained (personal communication #51). Argentina was the only country that only experienced mimetic pressures. While market-oriented experts in Colombia and Chile were influential in their respective government, active-state advocates from FLACSO and UNESCO remained close to Argentinean decision-making, making these ideas predominant in the country's education debate, as a former education minister and a former FLACSO official explained (personal communications #81 and #64). For example, Daniel Filmus, FLACSO's director between 1992 and 2000, was appointed as the education ministry in 2003. He was succeeded by the former director of Buenos Aires UNESCO-IIEP, Juan Carlos Tedesco, in 2007. These advocates embraced EFA's "right to education" rhetoric, promoting controlled decentralization, consensual curricular standards, and VOCSED's transformation (Filmus & Kaplan, 2012).

As Colombia experienced a variety of pressures, one would expect that the country would be more likely to conform to foreign recommendations compared to Chile and Argentina. Nevertheless, this chapter demonstrates that this is not the case and identifies three different paths of reinterpretation of global ideas. Colombia conformed to ideas of controlled decentralization, expansion of public-private partnerships, and curriculum standardization, but the country avoided test-based accountability and defied the modification of vocational education. Chile originally conformed to ideas of stronger accountability and standardization but later compromised its education quasi-market as a response to increasing inequality. By contrast, Argentina centralized its control on education provision and curriculum but defied test-based accountability. The following sections demonstrate how negative effects of 1990s education reforms drove governments in all three countries to a recentralization of authority and explains how coalitions shaped the variation in this recentralization despite the influence of similar global ideas.

The Slight Compromise of the Chilean Education Quasi-Market

Since Chile jumped early into the wagon of test-based accountability and curriculum standards, new global recommendations in the 2000s found a favorable environment and very little opposition that facilitated the conformity to these ideas. Of the three policy areas analyzed here, provision was the only one that spurred conflict in the country. EFA recommended strengthening the state's role in education, which clashed with Chile's quasi-market model. Yet, the growing inequality of the quasi-market also motivated a group of actors to see EFA as a chance for change. To address the conflict between advocates of the status quo and losers of previous reforms, Chile compromised EFA recommendations by slightly reducing the emphasis on market policy instruments in education provision. This compromise shows the impact losers may have on education policy and on the translation of global ideas that raise questions on existing domestic arrangements.

Policy Legacies: Education Inequality and Persistent Predominance of Market-Oriented Ideas

By the late 1990s, the combination of vouchers, shared funding primarily for publicly subsidized private organizations, and private schools' ability to select students drove families in each socioeconomic stratum to enroll their children at the type of school they could afford. This dynamic produced education ghettos with uneven quality (Garcia-Huidobro, 2007; Mizala & Torche, 2012). In contrast to the theory supporting education quasi-markets, parents did not select schools due to their academic performance but rather according to the social class of the school's population (M. Schneider et al., 2006). Thus, 54% enrollment in municipal schools was composed of students coming from households in the first three income deciles. This figure reached only 34% in private voucher schools and 9% in fully private schools. Furthermore, SIMCE's standardized assessments showed that students from the lowest-income households had lower performance, contributing to the perception that municipal schools were of lower quality (P. González et al., 2002). While previous curriculum reforms were not blamed for this low quality, evaluation raised some discontent among the Colegio and parental organizations, which argued that standardized tests produced stigmatization of municipal schools (Falabella & Ramos, 2019). These dynamics shaped important problems of education segmentation and inequality that challenged the existing market-oriented policies in Chile and made ideas of "quality education for all" seem promising for the country.

However, these challenges to existing policies were coupled with a high external legitimacy of the 1990s Chilean education reforms. Chile was the country in the region with the greatest progress in enrollment expansion, quality improvement, and reduction of educational inequality. By 2007, the net enrollment ratio in secondary education in Chile was 92%—17 points higher than South America's average. The country also presented a larger proportion of poor students enrolled in secondary school. The percentage of repeaters in 2000 was less than 3%—2 points lower than the regional average. The dropout rate fell from 13% to 9% between 2000 and 2010, which was 6 points under the regional rate (UNESCO/OREALC, 2013). Along with this external legitimacy, a former senior official in the education ministry and a former WB senior official explained that the ministry staff implementing reforms in the early 1990s remained in office throughout the 2000s, which fueled the positive feedback of market-oriented measures and their influence on future decisions (personal communications #50 and #52). In particular, the area of evaluation in Chile had initiated test-based accountability even before these ideas were globally popular. After the implementation of SNED in the 1990s, the country experienced an increase in testing and a growing centrality of tests as tools to incentivize schools and teachers to innovate and improve performance (Falabella & Ramos, 2019). Such developments also reinforced the legitimacy of curriculum standards that had been implemented in the early 1990s. These beliefs made it difficult to dismantle the education quasi-market and made recommendations for test-based accountability more feasible as a solution to address the issues in the Chilean education system.

The continuity of education policymakers in the government signaled not only the consistency of beliefs about education policy but also the persistence of power distribution. The left-center coalition, the Concertación, had remained in power since the transition to democracy, which provided a solid support for their own measures implemented in the 1990s. Moreover, Concertación's allies had developed strong links with private paid and voucher schools. For instance, the Church was an important education provider and a traditional ally of the CDP, a member of the Concertación. Similarly, representatives of CONACEP, the association of private providers, were also Concertación's supporters, as illustrated by Rodrigo Bosch, Walter Oliva, and Alejandro Hasbún (former leaders of CONACEP and well-known members of the CDP) (Carvajal & Partarrieu, 2014) and Rodrigo Ketterer, CONACEP's secretary and a member of the Party for Democracy (another of the Concertacións' allies) (Pérez Villamil, 2014). Additionally, enrollment in private secondary schools had already reached 50%, while 71% of private voucher schools had already implemented shared funding (Garcia-Huidobro, 2007). This growth and the links of private providers with the Concertación suggested a significant increase in the number and influence of constituents or "winners" from the three-tier system and the shared funding formula.

Likewise, the results produced by SIMCE that favored private schools also transformed advocates of the three-tier system into powerful constituents of standardized tests and government performance-based incentives, with only a timid opposition of the teacher union.

Table 4.2 demonstrates that policy legacies at the arrival of renewed ideas of a stronger role of the state in education governance were compat-

Table 4.2. Compatibility of Policy Legacies with EFA and Accountability Ideas in Chilean Education

Policy Area	Inherited Problems	Inherited Beliefs	Inherited Power Distribution	Compatibility Outcome
Provision	Educational inequality and segmentation due to three-tier education system, voucher model, and shared funding.	Ingrained beliefs of the benefits of school provision based on competition among education policymakers.	Growth of constituents of three-tier education system with powerful links in decision-making spheres.	Relatively incompatible with downplaying privatization.
Curriculum	No problems linked to previous curriculum reforms.	External legitimacy of centralized curriculum due to results in quality compared to the rest of the region.	Continuity in the government of policymakers supporting curriculum standards.	Compatible with curriculum recentralization.
Evaluation	Persistent image of low performance of public schools reinforcing segmentation.	Consolidation of testing expertise in the governance of education.	Support to SIMCE by advocates of private schooling.	Compatible with test-based accountability.

Author's elaboration.

ible with test-based accountability as a form of market regulation but were at odds with recommendations on downplaying education privatization. The compatibility of these legacies with global ideas helped the initial adoption of accountability recommendations. Nevertheless, inherited problems combined with ideas about the right to education also produced important reactions from the losers of the education quasi-market. These losers triggered significant changes in education policy coalitions, as the next section will explain.

COALITIONS AND ACTIVITIES: BREAKDOWN OF THE MARKET-ORIENTED, ACTIVE-STATE COALITION

By the early 2000s, the negative consequences of the Chilean education quasi-market had initiated both the erosion of the legitimacy of this governance model and the emergence of a coalition of opponents. This coalition was facilitated by a sequence of three events. First, although by the 2000s the right-wing coalition still held 44% of the Congress, the fear of a new authoritarian regime was already dissipated, and younger generations felt they had more room to ask for changes, as a former senior official of the education ministry explained (personal communication #38). Second, throughout the 1990s, students experienced a gradual process of awareness about the negative consequences the quasi-market model brought, which certainly contributed to their mobilization in the 2000s (Rifo, 2013). Third, in 1998, the government unintentionally provided students with a venue to join forces through the creation of the Youth Parliament, an initiative that gathered 120 presidents of student councils to discuss problems and solutions affecting young people. The Youth Parliament helped the reactivation of a former student organization previously dismantled by the dictatorship, the Santiago's Federation of Secondary Students (Federación de Estudiantes Secundarios de Santiago—FESES), and the creation of new organizations, including the National Committee for Secondary Students (Coordinadora Nacional de Estudiantes Secundarios—CONES) and the Coordination Assembly of Secondary Students (Asamblea Nacional de Estudiantes Secundarios—ACES) (UNICEF, 2014). Representing more than 400 schools in almost every province or region across the country, these organizations initiated mobilizations that started with specific demands to reestablish free student transportation in 2001, followed by massive demonstrations in 2006 and 2011 asking for the abolition of LOCE and subsequent market-oriented measures (Bellei, 2014; Bellei & Cabalín, 2013; Silva, 2009).

Although the organizational capacity of the student movement was strong due to the numerous schools they represented and their agreement on demands, such as increased support to public schools, prohibition of for-profit schools, elimination of selective students' recruitment, and abolition of the shared funding system (Propuesta de Trabajo de Estudiantes Secundarios de la R.M., 2005; personal communications #38 and #40), the movement was not entirely cohesive. According to two former student leaders, while ACES asked for radical transformations, CONES accepted a gradual change as long as it promised to be transformative in the long run (personal communications #40 and #41). In addition, beyond changes in the area of education provision, students did not challenge other education policy areas (Villalobos, 2019). Students did not disagree with authority distribution for curricular decisions (Cox, 2011), and demands for changes in VOCSED were limited to qualified and supervised field experience (Propuesta de Trabajo de Estudiantes Secundarios de la R.M., 2005). This was likely because VOCSED schools were underrepresented in the student movement, as a former student leader stated (personal communication #41). Similarly, although there were some complaints on how standardized assessments reinforced inequality (personal communication #48), students did not initially challenge the existence or purposes of SIMCE, the Chilean assessment system.

Despite these differences, the student movement used significant power resources. By 2006, around 80% of secondary students mobilized through the so-called Penguin Revolution, which included school occupation and protests demanding changes in education provision (Bellei & Cabalín, 2013; Silva, 2009). According to a former leader of a parent association and a former teacher-union leader, student demands and the popularity of their mobilization quickly attracted the support of public-school parent associations and the Colegio (personal communications #42 and #47). Likewise, the Communist Party also supported student protests (Burton, 2011). The strength of the student mobilization forced the government of President Michelle Bachelet (2006–2010) to invite the student leaders to participate in the Presidential Advisory Council for Education Quality. The role of this council was to achieve a consensus over a new education law. Through this invitation, opponents of the quasi-market of education apparently gained access to decision-making.

Nevertheless, the council also gathered political elites who have promoted the existing Chilean model and who retained significant influence in policy decisions (Larroulet & Montt, 2010).

The council convened representatives of the Church, private providers, private-school parent associations, and leaders of both left- and right-party coalitions. These actors had maintained the education model inherited from Pinochet's dictatorship and supported subsequent reforms (Burton, 2011; Larroulet & Montt, 2010). By contrast, the student movement did not have allies in any major political party, which facilitated its isolation and outmaneuvering by their opponents. The plural composition of the council and their radical differences over provision prevented any agreement and drove students to withdraw from the discussion (Movimiento Estudiantil Reconoció, 2007). Consequently, Bachelet appointed a parallel commission with the exclusive participation of the left- and right-party coalitions, the Concertación, and the Alianza, all of whom were constituents of the existing education system (Burton, 2011; Pribble, 2013).

This outmaneuvering of students did not translate into a final defeat. Although reforms were formulated during Bachelet's government, it was their implementation during the right-wing administration of Sebastian Piñera (2010–2014) that reactivated student opposition. Piñera's government increased the areas and frequency of standardized tests and dismissed socioeconomic variables from SIMCE's reports. These measures increased backlash from students and teachers due to the threat of closing low-performing schools, as a former education minister and a former senior staff of the same ministry explained (personal communications #34 and #54). However, this time, opposition to Piñera's measures did not arise from secondary-education students, but rather from higher-education students. While demands of this renewed student movement focused on higher education, they also continued the agenda established by the Penguin Revolution, including a reversal of privatization through the elimination of for-profit universities (Bellei, 2014). Literature on the Chilean student mobilizations and the statement of a former senior official of the education ministry confirmed that rallying around the elimination of for-profit education gave this movement cohesiveness, thus increasing its organizational capacity (Bellei, 2014; Figueroa, 2012; Rifo, 2013; personal communication #38).

The 2011 mobilizations built on the experience accumulated by the 2001 and 2006 protests. They did this by sustaining a 36-week strike with innovative and nonviolent means of demonstrations that delegitimized the repressive response of the right-wing government and gained, once more, extensive support from the public, teacher unions, and student organizations (Bellei, 2014; UNICEF, 2014). The movement further increased its power resources by framing their demands as a call for the "right to education" and taking advantage of EFA global pressures. Specifically, student leaders undertook a campaign against market-based education provision and its effects on segregation and inequality through tours to gain support from different international organizations, including the OECD, the UN, UNESCO, and UNICEF (AFP/EMOL, 2011; Atria, 2012, p. 15; UNICEF, 2014). Prominent international organizations such as UNESCO and UNICEF seized momentum from the students' protests to publicize reports and briefs about the shortcomings of Chilean education in the promotion of the "right to education" (e.g., V. Muñoz, 2011; UNICEF, 2014). This support eroded the external legitimacy of the Chilean education model and produced changes in the existing constituents of the Chilean school system.

The coalition supporting the quasi-market of education lost cohesiveness and organizational capacity. A portion of the Concertación agreed—to some extent—with the demands of the student movement, including the elimination of for-profit schools, sharing funding, and selective students' recruitment (Consejo Asesor Presidencial, 2006; Larroulet & Montt, 2010). Senior members of the Concertación stated that another group was more moderate and favored policies to increase funding for public schools, rather than the equal treatment typically promoted by market-oriented supporters (personal communications #28 and #33). By contrast, a third segment of the Concertación, along with the right-party coalition, argued that demands from the student movement would limit school diversification and harm student choices (Camhi et al., 2011). Instead, they asked for further deregulation of education provision, more school autonomy, and more attractive incentives for school performance (Larroulet & Montt, 2010). As a former senior official of the education ministry indicated, divisions also reflected existing pressures of vested interests of the Church and private providers on the Concertación, not only due to their direct links but also because these actors represented an attractive electoral ally (personal communication #55). Driven partially by these divisions, the Concertación relaunched itself in 2013 as the New Majority coalition (Nueva Mayoría—NM), which consisted of the former parties of the Concertación and the addition of the Communist party. The NM aimed at recapturing presidency by moving to the left and including student leaders, some of whom were elected to Congress in 2013. According to a former student leader, this election gave students direct participation in the education reforms of 2015 (personal communication #40).

While coalition changes occurred primarily around issues of education provision, backlash produced by the intensification of test-based accountability policies promoted the creation of the "Stop SIMCE" Movement (Alto al SIMCE), according to two assessment experts and a former official of the education ministry (personal communications #34, #35, and #46). This movement, however, only achieved moderate influence as it lacked cohesiveness. According to a former member of this movement, a segment of it demanded only some changes to the existing test-based accountability model, including the re-inclusion of socioeconomic status in test reports, and complementary qualitative evaluation instruments that expanded the notion of education quality and provided teachers with more authority to assess student learning. Nevertheless, another segment of the movement was more radical and asked for the total elimination of testing (personal communication #46). Similarly, the power resources of Stop SIMCE were not very effective. In addition to some broad media campaigns about the negative consequences of testing, Stop SIMCE called on schools, parents, and students to boycott the examination. However, these boycotts were not supported by teachers due to the monetary incentives that SIMCE results provided to schools and the legitimacy of the tests (Diaz-Rios, 2020). Although the influence of this movement was not strong enough to change SNED and the importance of tests, it fueled discussions about the legitimacy of the Chilean test-based accountability model. Table 4.3 summarizes the coalitions and their influence on the Chilean education policy in the 2010s.

OUTCOMES: CONFORMITY TO TEST-BASED ACCOUNTABILITY AND COMPROMISE OF EDUCATION QUASI-MARKET IN CHILE

Chile's conformity to test-based accountability and curriculum standardization by the mid-2000s can be attributed to the compatibility of policy legacies with global recommendations and the stronger influence of the quasi-market advocates compared to the student movement and its allies. The international reputation of the Chilean education system fueled domestic trust and interests invested in the education quasi-market. Consequently, strengthening the existing system of government incentives for test results seemed promising for policymakers to fix problems of education

Table 4.3. Coalitions' Actors and Activities for the 2010s Chilean Education Reforms

Policy Area	Supporters of EFA-Inspired and Accountability Reforms	Opponents to Reforms
Provision	Actors: Students, teachers, some sections of the New Majority coalition. Activities: Enhanced organizational capacity: strong. Access to decision-making: strong. Mobilization of power resources: strong.	Actors: Alianza, the Church, CONACEP, CDP. Activities: Enhanced organizational capacity: limited. Access to decision-making: strong. Mobilization of power resources: strong.
Curriculum	Actors: New Majority, Alianza, the Church, CONACEP, education policymakers. Activities: Enhanced organizational capacity: strong. Access to decision-making: strong. Mobilization of power resources: strong.	No opponents to curriculum standards.
Evaluation	Actors: Concertación, Alianza, the Church, CONACEP, education policymakers. Activities: Enhanced organizational capacity: strong. Access to decision-making: strong. Mobilization of power resources: strong.	Actors: Colegio, students, some education experts. Activities: Enhanced organizational capacity: limited. Access to decision-making: limited. Mobilization of power resources: limited.

Author's elaboration.

inequality and segmentation. Although the Penguin Revolution challenged dominant ideas in the area of provision, students were marginalized from the decision-making process through two strategies. First, the government used a bill that was already under discussion without student participation to address concerns on inequality (Larroulet & Montt, 2010). This bill, referred to as the Preferential School Voucher, offered an additional subsidy to the most vulnerable students in exchange for giving up fees to these families and achieving government-set results on the national standardized tests (Ley 20.248 Subvención Escolar Preferencial, 2008). The bill was expected to make the distribution of resources more equitable and make poor students more attractive for schools (Corvalán, 2012). However, this preferential voucher was provided to both municipal and private voucher schools against the expectation of the advocates of a stronger state for preferential funding for public education. Moreover, school participation in the Preferential School Voucher was declared voluntary to appease concerns of market-oriented advocates that the program reduced their autonomy. Thus, although the Preferential School Voucher aimed to correct market failures, by 2008 nearly 40% of private voucher schools had decided not to participate, and segregation among municipal and private voucher schools persisted (Elacqua & Santos, 2013). Second, the parallel commission that excluded students focused discussions for the new General Education Law (GEL) on less contentious issues, such as curriculum and quality assessment, reduction of vocational content, authorization of merit-based selection of students, and the creation of the Agency for Quality Assurance with the authority to close schools that constantly presented low performance (García-Huidobro, 2009; Ley No. 20.529, 2011).

GEL's focus helped conformity to curriculum standardization and government-led, test-based accountability. Both the Presidential Council and the parallel commission agreed on moderate changes to the curriculum of the 1990s that included a revision of learning goals and the establishment of more precise curricular standards that better oriented teachers' performance in the classroom. Similarly, VOCSED was also further standardized and its specialized content was reduced, making it more compatible with general secondary education (Acuerdo No. 93, 2010). Indeed, later in 2013, the education ministry eliminated nine vocational specialties and replaced them with broader occupation fields ("Mineduc Anuncia Eliminación de Nueve Especialidades En Liceos Técnicos," 2013). Regarding evaluation, as a former SIMCE director explained, the Agency for Quality Assurance and its authority to close low-performing schools gave standardized assessments even more prominence (personal communication #51). This prominence was consistent with the recommendations of a national assessment commission in 2003 that suggested an increase in frequency and areas of testing (Comisión para el Desarrollo y Uso del SIMCE, 2003). Curriculum standardization and stronger accountability did not initially raise major opposition and instead consolidated the Chilean path of a stronger role of the government as an evaluator and a compensator of market failures.

Nevertheless, as the opposition of the student movement became reactivated and grew stronger in 2011, the legitimacy of the Chilean quasi-market of education further decreased. The fracture that the 2011 student movement caused to former supporters of the existing Chilean education system contributed to Bachelet's regain of presidency in 2014 (Diaz-Rios, 2019). Changes in government and the renewed strength of students forced negotiations with supporters of the market-oriented system for a new education law (Villalobos, 2016). Although the voucher system remained in place, long negotiations produced an agreement on a gradual elimination of for-profit schools, the suspension of shared funding, and the prohibition of student selection through a centralization of enrollment (Bellei, 2016; G. Muñoz & Weinstein, 2019). The new Inclusion Law (Ley No 20.845, 2015) therefore compromised both the quasi-market of education established since 1980 and a more controlled role of private actors in education. While the voucher system remained unchallenged, reforms established by the Inclusion Law have decelerated the movement from public to private voucher schools (G. Muñoz & Weinstein, 2019). According to WB statistics, between 2015 and 2018, the average annual growth of the percentage of enrollment in private secondary schools was only 0.24 percentage points, while such figures reached 1 percentage point between 2002 and 2014. There is still scarce research on the effects of the Inclusion Law, but some evidence indicates that segmentation has slightly decreased across municipal and private voucher schools. Yet, significant changes have not been observed (G. Muñoz & Weinstein, 2019).

While minor changes also happened in the area of evaluation, the conformity of the country with test-based accountability remained practically unchanged. Due to pressures of the Stop SIMCE movement and their coincidence with student protests, Piñera's government suspended the exclusion of socioeconomic status in the communication of tests to avoid additional backlash (personal communication #54). Additionally, with the priority given to education in the policy agenda of Bachelet's second administration, the government invited leaders of the Stop SIMCE Movement to join a commission assessing and recommending changes to tests. Yet, the commission's report reflected the preferences of the moderate sector of Stop SIMCE, including the expansion of the concept of learning and quality beyond tests, greater leverage and voice to teachers to evaluate student performance, a reduction of test frequency and areas, an avoidance of improper comparisons that may stigmatize schools, and the balance of the responsibility for student learning among different education stakeholders (Equipo de Tarea SIMCE, 2015). While these recommendations did not alter test-based accountability in the country, the task force lessened the need to close low-performing schools and discontinued the publication of school rankings, although aggregated results continued to be disseminated (Diaz-Rios, 2020). Ultimately, the pressure of the Stop SIMCE movement slightly downplayed the accountability discourse and forced the dismissal of the most recent changes in standardized evaluations but did not shift the country away from test-based accountability. Table 4.4 summarizes the translation processes and outcomes of the reforms in Chile during the 2000s and 2010s.

Table 4.4. Translation of EFA and Accountability Ideas in Chilean Education

Policy Area	Compatibility with Policy Legacies	Support	Opposition	Reinterpretation
Provision	Relatively incompatible	Strong	Strong	Compromise of stronger state and PPPs: dismantling of student selection, shared funding, and for-profit schools, but continuation of vouchers.
Curriculum	Compatible	Strong	Weak	Conformity: further curriculum standardization and reduction of VOCSED specialized content.
Evaluation	Compatible	Strong	Moderate	Conformity: continuation of test-based accountability.

Author's elaboration.

The Revival of a Strong Active State in Argentina's Secondary Education

The translation of global education ideas in Argentina during the 2000s was shaped by the negative consequences of the 1990s reforms and the persistent beliefs on the importance of state involvement in education. These two policy legacies led to the formation of a coalition between teachers who had suffered as a result of previous policies and a newly elected government that was receptive to the idea of an active state. In contrast to the 1990s, when attempts to combine market-oriented and active-state ideas resulted in an inconsistent scaling-back of the state's role, the discrediting of market-oriented advocates and the support of teachers for a state-led education led to a compromise of EFA recommendations that strengthened the state's authority over education provision and curriculum.

Policy Legacies: The Failures of the 1990s Reforms

Unlike Chile where previous reforms had been widely supported until 2000, 1990s education reforms in Argentina were never regarded as positive. Government inconsistencies between expenditure cuts and an ambitious 1990s education reform produced a financial crisis that left provinces with insufficient resources to respond to salary demands from teachers (Nardacchione, 2012). Likewise, the dispersion between multiple secondary-school curricula across provinces due to the inconsistent implementation of 1990s reforms made attractive the instruments that promised to improve education quality, including an emphasis on curriculum standards and soft labor skills.

While inherited problems seemed compatible with EFA recommendations, domestic beliefs were more ambiguous. As a former education minister explained, on the one hand, the decline in Menem's popularity and the poor results of his social policy eroded the acceptance of state-retrenchment ideas in the area of education and paved the way for a more decisive advocacy for a stronger state role, especially in provision and curriculum. On the other hand, the erosion of state-retrenchment ideas affected the legitimacy of standardized assessments that were associated with market-oriented policy instruments and were insufficient to address education quality problems (personal communications #81, #62, and #66). Moreover, by contrast to Chile and Colombia, the frustrated attempt to consolidate assessments in the 1990s drove Argentina to continue with its lack of testing expertise (Diaz-Rios, 2020).

Similarly, legacies that shaped power distribution also seemed compatible with controlled decentralization but incompatible with global ideas recommending an evaluator state. In general, the popularity of Menem's economic reforms, particularly privatizations, had already declined to low levels by the end of the 1990s, and even legislators of their own party diminished their support for Menem's policies (Zelaznik, 2014). In the area of education, provincial struggles to cover teachers' salaries increased the unpopularity of Menem's education reforms. While initial conflicts remained provincial (Giovine, 2003), a harsh repression of the government to a protest in the province of Neuquén permitted the nationalization of the mobilization. By 1997, Menem's government faced the most significant teachers' protest in the recent history of Argentina, the White Tent (Carpa Blanca), with the participation of more than 1,400 teachers in a 1,000-day strike between April 1997 and December 1999 (Nardacchione, 2012). A former education minister explained that this strike gained ample public support and became one of the major symbols of social discontent with Menem's policies (personal communication #81). A former teacher union leader also declared that although teachers' demands started with salary increases, like in Chile, claims quickly escalated to the abolition of the 1993 Federal Education Law and the definition of a steady formula for education funding (personal communication #72). To appease protests, the education ministry proposed a monetary incentive funded through a new vehicle tax. Nevertheless, the ministry of economy took advantage of the opposition of the transportation sector and refused to increase teacher salaries, arguing that it was a provincial responsibility (Morduchowicz, 2000, 2002). Ultimately, as a former education minister explained, financial resources remained insufficient to pay teachers' monetary incentives and the education minister resigned, expressing her support for teachers' demands (personal communication #58). Essentially, while the White Tent fractured the already weak coalition between market-oriented and active-state advocates who had supported 1990s reforms, it made teachers a more influential actor in the political arena. Table 4.5 summarizes the policy legacies that shaped education reforms in the 2000s.

Table 4.5. Compatibility of Policy Legacies with Ideas on a Stronger Role of the State in Argentinean Education

Policy Area	Inherited Problems	Inherited Beliefs	Inherited Power Distribution	Compatibility Outcome
Provision	Underfunded provinces to cover education expenditures.	Weakened market-oriented ideas of efficiency and federal expenditure cuts.	Diminished influence of Menem's supporters and growing political power of teachers.	Compatible with ideas of controlled decentralization.
Curriculum	Inconsistent implementation led to poor curriculum coordination across provinces.	Revival of ideas on national curriculum standards.	Persistent influence of supporters of a centralized curriculum.	Compatible with curriculum standardization.
Evaluation	Poor learning results in schools that implemented previous reforms.	Lack of legitimacy and expertise on testing.	Dominance of opponents to standardized tests.	Incompatible with test-based accountability.

Author's elaboration.

COALITIONS AND ACTIVITIES: ACTIVE-STATE AND STATIST ADVOCATES TOGETHER AGAIN

The failure of Menem's economic policies reached its peak in 2001 when his government ended, annual inflation grew to 70%, the banking system collapsed, and the new government imposed restrictions on bank withdrawals, severely limiting access to deposited funds. The country also experienced a drastic decline of the GDP, a dramatic increase in poverty and inequality, and the suspension of external debt payments

(Cortés Conde, 2003). This crisis drove Argentina to political instability that further eroded 1990s reforms, including but not limited to education policies (Novaro, 2002). As a response to this crisis and after the removal of 4 presidents within 12 days due to massive civil unrest, an anticipated presidential election was called in 2003. Although Menem won the first round of voting with a small margin, he withdrew from the runoff fearing a potential electoral defeat. His withdrawal diminished the legitimacy of the automatically elected and little-known Peronist president, Nestor Kirchner (Levitsky & Murillo, 2008, p. 16). In the quest for a broader political coalition, Kirchner allied with the unions including CTERA due to their political leverage and their symbolic role as opponents of Menem's policies (M. V. Murillo, 2013). This alliance gave teachers access to decision-making—something they did not have in the 1990s. It also increased power resources of this coalition as the alliance not only lent legitimacy to Kirchner, but also attracted public opinion support, signaling that the new government would restore public education and reverse the state-retrenchment education policies of the 1990s (Cao, 2011).

Kirchner's government (2003–2007) also got the support of active-state advocates. A senior faculty of FLACSO explained that Kirchner recruited a former FLACSO director to be the education minister and the former director of the International Institute for Educational Planning (IIEP-UNESCO Buenos Aires), one of the authors of the 1992 CEPAL-UNESCO report, to be vice-minister and, later, the education minister in the administration of Cristina Fernández de Kirchner (2007–2015). Moreover, during Kirchner's administration, staff from both agencies (FLACSO and IIEP-UNESCO Buenos Aires) assisted in developing and implementing the education reforms undertaken in 2005 and thereafter (personal communication #64). One of these education ministers stated that these active-state advocates shifted away from the "efficiency" discourse promoted by Menem's administration and reframed their proposals in EFA's "right to education" rhetoric, including the universal right to quality education, consensual curricular standards, and the transformation of VOCSED into soft labor skills (personal communication #81).

This coalition of Peronists in government, active-state advocates, and teacher unions was cohesive in some of their policy preferences. In terms of provision, all coalition members perceived benefits from keeping secondary schools decentralized to provinces but with a larger contribution and authority from the federal government. For Kirchner's government, greater dependence of the provinces on federal funding could provide the national education ministry with more tools to enforce provincial compliance with national policies (personal communication #81). For teachers, this stronger role of the federal government was expected to contribute to salary increases (personal communications #66 and #75). Evaluation was also an area of agreement since neither member of the coalition was interested in standardized exams. A former education minister explained that they believed testing might be an instrument to guide policy decisions, but they were more concerned with promoting pedagogical mechanisms to improve educational attainment of the poorest students, such as teaching methods, textbooks, innovative learning strategies, and so on (personal communication #81). Similarly, a country's evaluation expert, a former teacher union leader, and a former senior official of IIEP-UNESCO indicated that teachers rejected the use of test results as a tool for accountability (personal communications #62, #66, and #71). Thus, test-based accountability lacked domestic supporters during the 2000s.

Despite consistency in provision and evaluation, agreement over curriculum policy was less clear. Consistent with EFA recommendations, the education ministry wanted VOCSED to be deferred to the last three years of secondary education and wanted it to be transformed into the development of soft labor skills. By contrast, teachers demanded the reestablishment of tracking between general and technical schools and the reinstatement of the traditional six years for both general and technical secondary education (Southwell, 2010). Since Argentinian secondary education teachers in public schools were contracted to teach a particular number of hours and a subject—even in different schools—they rejected significant changes in the curriculum that could reduce the demand for specific teachers and/or the workload in particular subjects (personal communication #73). Moreover, a senior official of the education ministry and two education experts explained that teachers' demands to reverse the 1990s curricular reforms seemed reasonable considering the decline in educational attainment, and therefore the government had limited leverage to reform curriculum and replace specialized technical education with soft labor skills, as active-state advocates preferred (personal communications #64, #71, and #78).

Opposition to this version of a stronger state remained weak until the mid-2010s. Nevertheless, the government of Fernández de Kirchner struggled to keep its promises and alliances with different unions due to the effects of the 2008 global economic crisis in Argentina. Additionally, corruption scandals debilitated the government, and by 2012 civil discontent grew in the country (Natalucci, 2018). This situation reactivated a right-wing coalition that won the presidency in 2015 with a small margin. Particularly in the area of education, the government of Mauricio Macri (2015–2019) replaced the education ministry staff with officials coming from think tanks, NGOs, and other organizations who were keener on result-oriented governance (Suasnábar, 2018). Specifically, Macri's government appointed a new evaluation secretary, a former official of UNICEF, who was a strong advocate of standardized testing (personal communication #74). This appointment signaled a return to test-based accountability. But beyond an emphasis on evaluation and a concern to reduce public expenditure on education again, Macri's education agenda did not propose major changes to the 2005 reforms (Rivas & Dborkin, 2018; Suasnábar, 2018). Ultimately, the advocacy for a reconsideration of the role of the state through market-oriented instruments remained weak in the country. Table 4.6 summarizes changes in coalitions during the 2000s and 2010s in Argentina.

Outcomes: Accommodating Teachers' Interests in EFA-Inspired Education Reforms

A greater contribution from and control by the state to the provision of secondary education sounded promising to solve the inequalities attributed to the 1990s reforms and consistent with predominant ideas of a stronger state in Argentinian education. Moreover, unsatisfactory results of the 1990s reforms and the political crisis of the country prevented any strong opposition to Kirchner's education proposals, as reflected by the smooth approval of various bills between 2005 and 2006, including the Education Budget Law (Ley de Financiamiento Educativo—LFE), the Vocational Education Law (Ley de Educación Técnico-Profesional—LETP), and the National Education Law (Ley Nacional de Educación—LEN). The prompt process to pass these bills contrasted with the conflicted and lengthy negotiations of the 1990s reforms that raised more contestation (Cao, 2011).

The compatibility of inherited policy problems and policy feedback eased conformity to EFA ideas on controlled decentralization in the area of secondary education provision. Since both active-state advocates in

Table 4.6. Dominance and Compromises of a Stronger State Coalition

Policy Area	Supporters of EFA-Inspired Reforms	Opponents to EFA-Inspired Reforms
Provision	Actors: CTERA, active-state advocates, Peronists supporting Kirchners' governments. Activities: Enhanced organizational capacity: strong. Access to decision-making: strong. Mobilization of power resources: strong.	Actors*: Right-wing parties, market-oriented intellectuals. Activities: Enhanced organizational capacity: weak. Access to decision-making: strong. Mobilization of power resources: weak.
Curriculum	Actors: Active-state advocates. Activities: Enhanced organizational capacity: limited. Access to decision-making: strong. Mobilization of power resources: limited.	Actors: Teachers.** Activities: Enhanced organizational capacity: strong. Access to decision-making: limited. Mobilization of power resources: strong.
Evaluation	Actors: Advocates of standardized tests. Activities: Enhanced organizational capacity: weak. Access to decision-making: limited. Mobilization of power resources: weak.	Actors: CTERA, active-state advocates. Activities: Enhanced organizational capacity: strong. Access to decision-making: strong. Mobilization of power resources: strong.

Author's elaboration.

*Market-oriented coalition was mostly inactive from 2001 to the early 2010s.

**Teachers did not oppose curriculum recentralization but demanded accommodation of their labor conditions.

the education ministry and CTERA were interested in strengthening the role of the federal government in education provision, the LFE increased public expenditure on education from 4% to 6% and raised the fiscal commitment of the federal government from 25% to 40% of the additional funds necessary to achieve the set objectives (Ley de financiamiento educativo, 2005). A former education minister explained that the LFE pleased CTERA's interests by forcing provinces to employ additional federal funding to pay teachers' salaries. Additionally, the law favored greater control from the federal government by requiring provinces to sign contracts with goals on enrollment and retention of the poorest students in exchange for additional federal resources for infrastructure and quality (personal communication #81). Between 2006 and 2009, education expenditure increased to the 6% promised by LFE (Narodowski et al., 2023), while the percentage of enrollment in private secondary schools after 2005 remained stable, reaching nearly 26%. This stability reflected the historical legacies of public subsidies to private schools but not global recommendations of educational PPPs.

This conformity was slightly affected in the following years by a slight decline in education expenditure that became even more noticeable during Macri's government (Narodowski et al., 2023). Despite the replacement of active-state advocates in the education ministry, the popularity of Kirchner's education reforms and the limited expertise of new education policymakers prevented major changes to secondary education provision during this government. While the government actually reduced its expenditure in education as a percentage of GDP affecting provincial funding (Rivas & Dborkin, 2018), federal authority on education remained unchanged and the percentage of private enrollment in secondary school did not increase.

In contrast to conformity to controlled decentralization, global curriculum ideas on standardization and VOCSED transformation were compromised. Despite the lack of opposition to the active-state coalition, disagreements between policymakers and teachers made the government bargain a middle-ground solution. A former education minister explained that the government framed VOCSED reforms to supply human resources required for the reindustrialization of the country after the 2001 economic crisis, but such reforms also sought to meet teachers' demands for reestablishment of the country's technical education (personal communication #81). Thus, the LETP reinstituted the former six years of technical secondary school but also divided it into two levels: (1) low secondary education oriented to general academic training, and (2) upper secondary education focused on the development of soft labor skills and career exploration (Resolución No. 84, 2009). Nevertheless, curricular contents of secondary education were ultimately decided by the provinces, which aimed to accommodate existing technical teachers, as a provincial vice secretary of education explained (personal communication #75). Yet, early specialization in VOCSED was gradually displaced to postsecondary levels, as an OAS's vocational training expert and a former ILO senior official explained (personal communications #69 and #70).

Similar negotiations occurred in the area of curriculum standardization. Two former senior officials of the education ministry explained that, consistent with the controlled decentralization preference of active-state education policymakers and the tradition of centralized curriculum in Argentina, the LEN mandated the establishment of Priority Learning Cores (Núcleos de Aprendizaje Prioritario—NAP), which operated as curricular standards that every province and school had to follow if they wanted to grant degrees (personal communications #77 and #78). Nevertheless, one of these officials and an education vice secretary in the province of Buenos Aires acknowledged that this curricular recentralization was implemented under the premise that it would not affect teachers' employment security (personal communications #75 and #78). Since the appointment of teachers as instructors of specific subjects was not reformed, provincial governments were urged to tailor curricular designs and follow NAPs according to teachers' appointments (personal communication #73 and #75). A former education minister accepted that this accommodation limited the changes the secondary education curriculum actually experienced, as well as the control the federal government had on it (personal communication #81).

In the area of evaluation, however, Argentina shifted away from following accountability ideas and in fact defied them. Due to the absence of technical expertise in standardized exams and the backlash they generated among teachers, active-state policymakers were not invested in promoting test-based accountability (Diaz-Rios, 2020). Although the government decided to continue the triannual application of the standardized tests initiated in the 1990s, it explicitly prohibited the publication of results to avoid the stigmatization of schools (personal communications #61 and #71). A former member of the National Council for Education Quality, a body created by LEN to manage existing assessments, and a former education minister explained that this council was quickly dissolved once its participants failed to achieve agreements over the most appropriate way to monitor curriculum implementation, reflecting the government's lack of interest in this topic (personal communications #62 and #81). Educational evaluation experts agreed that standardized tests in the country did not have any consequences for schools or provinces, were not employed to design education policy or to monitor the achievement of curricular standards, and had limited legitimacy among Argentine education scholars (personal communications #71 and #80). Table 4.7 summarizes the translation of EFA and accountability ideas in Argentina.

Testing and test-based accountability experienced a revival during Macri's government. His evaluation secretary transformed the triannual exams into annual tests, with results published by province but not by schools. Results were not associated with material incentives for performance (personal communication #61). Nevertheless, these changes reactivated teacher opposition (Perassi, 2017). It is uncertain whether this

Table 4.7. Translation of EFA and Accountability Ideas in Argentina

Policy Area	Compatibility with Policy Legacies	Support	Opposition	Reinterpretation
Provision	Compatible	Strong	Weak	Conformity to controlled decentralization: recentralization of funding.
Curriculum	Compatible	Moderate	Moderate	Compromise: curriculum standardization accommodating teachers; VOCSED reestablishment but with soft skills contents.
Evaluation	Incompatible	Weak	Strong	Defiance: testing without accountability.

Author's elaboration.

potential revival of test-based accountability will persist, as the country changed governments again in 2019 and Peronism regained office. The new government of Alberto Fernández, elected in 2019, discontinued tests in 2020 due to the pandemic. Only by the end of 2021 did the education ministry decide to do the assessments again, along with other instruments "that are more efficient to capture the complexity of the process that we want to evaluate," as declared by the education minister ("¿Cómo Se Realizarán Las Pruebas 'Aprender' En Argentina?" 2021). Hence, it is hard to claim that Argentina will jump on the wagon of test-based accountability any time soon. Overall, the recentralization of authority Argentina experienced during the mid-2000s and subsequent policies were not sufficient to alleviate the regional disparities in education. A few provinces still concentrate students with satisfactory academic performance, while the rest of the jurisdictions struggle to improve student achievement (Observatorio Argentinos por la Educación, 2022, p. 7).

Colombia:
A More Favorable Environment for Market-Based Reforms

In contrast to Argentina, Colombian policy in the 2000s did not reject market-oriented ideas but instead embraced a reinterpretation of the state's role as one that should incentivize efficiency. A new Conservative government achieved a more cohesive support for controlled decentralization, expansion of PPPs, and curriculum standardization. Conservatives also argued that previous increases of education expenditure had not produced satisfactory results and blame FECODE for this development. This government's framing, along with a severe economic crisis, prevented FECODE from gaining the support it needed to secure additional funding. Nevertheless, following the country's legacies of a small state, policymakers did not adopt test-based accountability tasks. Instead, they focused on reforms that promoted greater fiscal rationalization and weakened the influence of teacher unions.

Policy Legacies: Failure of Previous Reforms and Decline of Teachers' Influence

The 1990s education reform in Colombia did not achieve the expected improvement in education quality. Although enrollment rates in secondary education increased from 52% to 72% between 1990 and 1997, the school dropout rate also grew from 26% to 41% in the same period, and student performance in standardized tests also declined, despite the growth of public education expenditure from 2.4% to 4.4%. By the end of the 1990s, the number of teachers had increased by 60.5%, while the total enrollment only grew 37.5% (L. Melo, 2005). A former education ministry advisor explained that due to the accelerated growth in the number of teachers, payroll became unsustainable, especially in the context of the economic crisis that hit the country by the end of the 1990s (personal communication #16). Growth in recruited teachers might be a result of an insufficient number of educators in previous decades, but subnational governments often created temporary teacher positions—a practice that was historically used for clientelist purposes—because additional costs created by these temporary contracts were often covered by the central government whenever costs exceeded central transfers (Villa & Duarte, 2002).

In addition, curricular autonomy and the continuation of VOCSED were perceived as problems. As explained by a former teacher union leader and a former advisor of the education ministry, the autonomy schools received to formulate their pedagogical projects was not accompanied by adequate government assistance or teacher training. Hence, disparities in the content and inequality of education offered to students across the country increased (personal communications #14 and #16). While autonomy over pedagogical projects generated processes of reflection and self-assessment in schools, teachers perceived that they lacked the capacity and resources to effectively run participatory pedagogical processes (P. C. Prieto, 1996). VOCSED, in turn, was still considered an expensive way to provide secondary education, as a former education minister and a former vice minister explained (personal communications #10 and #19). These problems inherited from the previous decade seemed compatible with ideas of stronger state controls over education and reduction of vocational contents.

This compatibility attracted the attention of Colombian policymakers. Yet, these officials were also keen on education expenditure rationalization following the country's tradition of a small role of the state in the governance of the school system and the influence of market-oriented ideas in the previous decade. Consequently, the Conservative government of Andrés Pastrana (1998–2002) framed the situation of the school system as an efficiency problem rather than a problem of insufficient public education funding or other educational and pedagogical issues (Presidencia de la República, 1999). This government attributed this inefficiency to the amendments of the 1993 decentralization bill produced by negotiations with FECODE (Echavarria et al., 2003; Lowden, 2004; Wiesner, 1995). Reports assessing the effects of the 1990s reforms argued that the distribution of fiscal transfers based on department education costs discouraged performance improvement, increased geographical education disparity, and limited the capacity to invest in education quality and innovation (L. Melo, 2005; Parra, 2017; Vergara & Simpson, 2001). Additionally, by this time the country had already consolidated important expertise and legitimacy of standardized assessments without significant contestation from any actor (Diaz-Rios, 2020). This policy feedback opened opportunities for global ideas that stressed the role of the state in accountability but also revived 1990s reform proposals linked to market-oriented policies.

The compatibility of inherited problems and beliefs with global ideas in the 2000s was also accompanied by changes in power distribution. With the election of Andrés Pastrana and the appointment of a Conservative education ministry in 2000, the new government settled the ideological divisions that the Liberal government of Gaviria exhibited in the 1990s. The national planning agency, the finance ministry, and the education ministry were all keen on greater accountability, expenditure rationalization in the education sector, and elimination of expensive programs like VOCSED (Lowden, 2004). A former advisor of the education ministry explained that the minister wanted to recover control over schools and make them more efficient (personal communication #16), and he favored private education provision (Espinosa, 2010). Conversely, internal tensions in FECODE had grown during the 1990s, making its leadership unstable. The divisions between those who advocated for reforms with a strong pedagogical content and those who emphasized the demand for better labor conditions increased, and turnover of FECODE's presidents became more frequent (M. M. López, 2008). Moreover, union presidents started to use FECODE's positions as an instrument to gain votes for Congress elections, displacing their goals from representing teachers' interests to using their administration as campaigns (Chambers-Ju, 2017). Therefore, by the late 1990s, the government was in a better position to support their reform proposals by taking advantage of the union's debilitation. The only area in which the government did not have notable advantages was VOCSED, which had become a highly praised education opportunity for numerous low-income families (Diaz-Rios & Urbano-Canal, 2021). Despite this exception, power distribution at the end of the 1990s favored a controlled decentralization but again centered in market-oriented instruments. Table 4.8 summarizes policy legacies and their compatibility with global ideas in the 2000s.

Table 4.8. Compatibility of Policy Legacies with EFA and Accountability Ideas in Colombia

Policy Area	Inherited Problems	Inherited Beliefs	Inherited Power Distribution	Compatibility Outcome
Provision	Growth in enrollment but paired with high dropout and budget problems despite increase of expenditure in the 1990s.	Strong market-oriented ideas link to a search for improving efficiency.	Diminished influence of FECODE and growing power of market-oriented policymakers.	Relatively compatible with ideas of controlled decentralization.
Curriculum	Lack of capacity to manage school autonomy.	Strong belief on the need for central guidelines.	Diminished influence of Pedagogical Movement.	Compatible with curriculum standardization.
VOCSED*	Uncontrolled growth of Articulation.	Perception of VOCSED as an inefficient education.	Consolidated VOCSED constituency.	Incompatible with changes in VOCSED.
Evaluation	Lack of incentives attached to educational results.	High legitimacy and consolidated expertise in standardized tests.	Growing influence of policymakers looking for increasing efficiency.	Compatible with test-based accountability.

Author's elaboration.

*Although VOCSED is a part of curriculum policy, this policy dimension is highlighted here as a separate one due to differences in policy legacies.

COALITIONS AND ACTIVITIES: A WEAKENED OPPOSITION
TO A SMALL, CONTROLLING STATE

In addition to the strengthening that market-oriented advocates achieved by the end of the 1990s, the economic crisis that hit the country at the same time also helped changes in coalitions. Despite previous constant economic growth, in 1999 Colombia experienced a harsh decline of the GDP of –4.2%, an increase in the unemployment rate to 22%, and a striking bank crisis (A. Torres, 2011). Pastrana's government sought to address serious fiscal imbalances with the assistance of the IMF using structural adjustment reforms that included modifications to the 1993 decentralization model. The segment of the Liberal party that supported neoclassic measures—which were part of the government in the finance ministry—also supported this decision (Lowden, 2004). By this time, the verified accusations about the links between the campaign of the previous presidency of Ernesto Samper (1994–1998) and drug-traffickers (Crandall, 2001) undermined the Keynesian Liberal segment. Therefore, opposition from this segment was unfeasible.

According to a former advisor of the education ministry, Pastrana's government reactivated proposals from the 1990s on school municipalization and demand-driven funding that were supposed to increase efficiency (personal communication #16). Local support for these measures was ambiguous. On the one hand, mayors welcomed the increase in authority and fiscal transfers through municipalization, but governors did not want to give up financial resources (M. M. López, 2008). On the other hand, both governors and mayors did not want to see their fiscal transfers reduced through a change to the demand-driven formula. However, in times of economic crisis, they wanted to stabilize their revenues, clarify responsibilities, and avoid the political cost of the fiscal crisis (Lowden, 2004). Despite the ambiguities in this support, market-oriented advocates took advantage of particular conditions and used specific strategies to weaken their main opponents: the teacher unions. Since a new decentralization model required a constitutional reform, discussions were restricted to Congress without the direct participation of FECODE (Espinosa, 2010, p. 57). While the union federation still had access to decision-making through its links with the left-party Democratic Pole (Polo Democrático) (Chambers-Ju, 2017), its influence was limited, as the government held the support of the majority in Congress (M. M. López, 2008). A former union leader also added that the government took advantage of the difficult economic situation in the country to attract the support of public opinion for efficiency and rationalization of education expenditures (personal communication #14). The education ministry also neutralized FECODE's protests and strikes against the new decentralization model by threatening strikers with salary deductions, framing union mobilization as an attempt to politicize education policy, and attributing poor education performance to teachers ("A Despolitizar La Educación," 2002; Miñana, 2010). With such strategies, the government further reduced FECODE's power resources to oppose decentralization reforms.

In subsequent reforms beyond decentralization, provision, and expenditure, the market-oriented coalition was not equally cohesive, although FECODE remained weak. A former education ministry who had also been the vice director of the DNP explained that during her administration, she was persuaded of the effectiveness of curricular standards (personal communication #19). Yet, a former education ministry advisor indicated that, despite the rhetoric of quality and accountability, the government was more interested in reducing educational expenditure than it was in increasing quality through standards and incentives (personal communication #16). Moreover, mayors and governors were not willing to assume responsibility for performance and the risk of being blamed for poor results (Diaz-Rios, 2020). Nonetheless, curricular standards did not face substantial opposition. A curricular education expert and a former teacher union leader accepted that the curricular autonomy granted by the 1993 General Education Law left teachers without a clear guidance on learning goals, curricular content, and appropriate teaching methodologies. Consequently, teachers demanded more specific and clear curricular orientation from the education ministry and did not see standards as an autonomy loss (personal communications #17 and #20).

The elimination of VOCSED was perhaps the area in which coalitions changed more substantially in the 2000s and 2010s. In the early 2000s, the administration of Alvaro Uribe (2002–2010) unintendedly promoted VOCSED growth despite the government's rhetoric against this kind of education. With the purpose of increasing enrollment in postsecondary education, Uribe's administration included SENA students in the statistics of higher education and raised the enrollment goals of this agency (Téllez Rico & Ramírez Guevara, 2016). Since SENA had some difficulties achieving these new goals, the agency decided to transform its assistance to VOCSED schools into an initiative called Articulation through which students initiated SENA's programs while they were still in their secondary education, as explained by a former senior official of the agency, a former SENA union leader, and a former regional director (personal communications #2, #4, and #11). Later, facing similar pressures to increase enrollment in higher education, the education ministry decided to expand technical two-year postsecondary education, which was considered more affordable than four-year programs, as a former senior official of the education ministry explained (personal communication #3). Since these two-year programs were not in high demand, the education ministry chose to replicate SENA's Articulation and converted numerous academic public secondary schools into preparatory programs for technical postsecondary education (Diaz-Rios & Urbano-Canal, 2021). These converted schools received additional human, material, and pedagogical resources. A former senior official of the education ministry, a former advisor, and a former WB senior official reported that by 2011, more than 2,000 secondary schools already participated in Articulation, which nurtured strong constituents of this program composed of SENA, higher education organizations, school principals, teachers, families, and even staff within the education ministry (personal communications #3, #5, and #8). Consequently, mayors and governors perceived the Articulation program as a source of electoral gains and strongly opposed the elimination of VOCSED. Table 4.9 shows that despite the relative weakness of opponents to 2000s global norms in Colombia, the market-oriented coalition did not equally support changes in the areas of provision, curriculum, and the evaluation of secondary education.

OUTCOMES: A STRONGER BUT SMALL STATE FOR
EDUCATION GOVERNANCE

Despite the weakness of FECODE, conformity to global norms was only achieved in the areas of provision and curriculum standardization. By 2001, the government submitted a fiscal reform proposal, which included two bills: (1) Legislative Act 001, which limited the increase of central government financial contributions for education, transferred schools to municipalities with more than 100,000 habitants, and introduced a demand-driven formula to fund schools according to the number of enrolled children instead of historical costs (Acto Legislativo 01, 2001); and (2) Law 715, which further specified the formula for school funding and created mechanisms to control expenditure at subnational

Table 4.9. Coalitions' Actors and Activities by Policy Area in Colombia (2000–2015)

Policy Area	Small, Controlling State Coalition	Statist Coalition
Provision	Actors: Education ministry, finance ministry, DNP, Liberals, Conservatives, mayors. Activities: Enhanced organizational capacity: strong. Access to decision-making: strong. Mobilization of power resources: strong.	Actors: Teacher unions, some governors. Activities: Enhanced organizational capacity: limited. Access to decision-making: weak. Mobilization of power resources: limited.
Curriculum	Actors: Education ministry, universities, education think tanks. Activities: Enhanced organizational capacity: limited. Access to decision-making: strong. Mobilization of power resources: limited.	No opposition to curriculum standardization.
VOCSED*	Actors: Education ministry. Activities: Enhanced organizational capacity: weak. Access to decision-making: limited. Mobilization of power resources: weak.	Actors: FECODE, mayors, governors, some education bureaucrats. Activities: Enhanced organizational capacity: strong. Access to decision-making: strong. Mobilization of power resources: strong.
Evaluation	Actors: Education ministry. Activities: Enhanced organizational capacity: limited. Access to decision-making: weak. Mobilization of power resources: weak.	Actors: FECODE, mayors, governors. Activities: Enhanced organizational capacity: limited. Access to decision-making: limited. Mobilization of power resources: weak.

Author's elaboration.

*Although VOCSED is a part of curriculum policy, this policy dimension is highlighted here as a separate one due to differences in coalitions.

levels, including mandatory ratios of students per teacher (Ley 715, 2001). Although these two bills were officially expected to encourage an increase in enrollment and obtain savings at the national level to invest in education quality (Banco Mundial, 2007; Proyecto de Ley 715, 2000), a former education ministry advisor explained that the finance and education ministries fixed the funding formula to favor supportive departments and municipalities.

These ministries also expected an increase in private enrollment due to the possibility opened by the bills to bargain per-student rates with private organizations lower than the rates established for public schools (personal communication #16). A former education minister also accepted that contracting-out was expected to avoid the expensive and slow building of new public schools and skip the "rigid" labor regulation of public teachers (personal communication #19). With FECODE's opposition neutralized, the support of mayors, and a majority in the Congress, the bills were easily approved, thus achieving a controlled decentralization combined with expenditure rationalization and an increase in PPPs (Espinosa, 2010; Lowden, 2004). A former education minister explained that these bills permitted the national expansion of contracting and concession schools she had initiated in the capital city in previous years (personal communication #19). Between 2004 and 2012, student enrollment in PPPs had increased by 24%, while enrollment in public schools decreased by 4%.

Curricular standardization did not need such strong support. Although the finance ministry, the DNP, mayors, and governors had little interest in this policy, teachers were willing to adopt curricular guidelines. Moreover, the education minister increased the legitimacy of curricular standardization by appointing the most influential education faculties in the country and private education think tanks to coordinate this process in consultation with teachers, as two advisors of the curriculum reform explained (personal communications #17 and #24). This alliance nurtured additional constituents of curricular standards. These standards were framed as "guidelines" that schools could adapt according to their own pedagogical projects, which formally respected the autonomy gained in the 1990s (Ministerio de Educación Nacional, 2006, p. 10). Yet, curriculum standards conformed to global ideas by centralizing the authority to define learning goals and contents. This recentralization was later reinforced—although very slowly—through the alignment between curriculum standards and standardized exams, which, according to a former ICFES director, took over 12 years to be completed (personal communication #12).

The slow pace in which curriculum standards were aligned with tests showed the lack of domestic interest in test-based accountability by contrast to global recommendations. Although the country had a strong tradition with testing, domestic actors did not have the technical expertise or the will to develop incentives and sanctions tied to test results. A former ICFES director and education vice minister explained that, on the one hand, ICFES's mandate was limited to designing, applying, and interpreting test results, but not to designing performance incentives for schools or teachers. On the other hand, the education ministry officially had the responsibility of developing such incentives, but it lacked the technical capacity to do so (personal communication #10). In addition, test-based accountability found little support among mayors and governors, and even within the national government it was not a priority. A former education ministry senior advisor explained that, rather than developing test-based accountability, the government chose to change job conditions by implementing higher educational requirements for teachers' recruitment and promotion (personal communication #16). These new requirements also permitted greater savings and further undermined unions' political support by creating divisions between senior teachers with generous social provisions and less-privileged junior teachers (Bautista, 2009). Moreover, institutions created by Law 715 encouraged privatization but not results-based accountability. The per-student funding formula established by Law 715 was used to make expenditure more efficient and avoid cost overruns, but it was not used to encourage market competition as parents were unable to choose their children's school (Diaz-Rios, 2019, 2020). Mechanisms to allocate students remained tied to residency areas to avoid school selection and oversubscription (República de Colombia, 2006).

More recent developments in the country had shown a persistent avoidance of test-based accountability in favor of expenditure cuts. In 2015, the education ministry started offering some incentives to public schools for improvement of test scores. However, by 2018, both incentives and most national tests (grades three, five, and nine) were suspended due to a budget deficit ("Persiste la incertidumbre alrededor del futuro de las Pruebas Saber," 2018). Later, in 2020, these exams were replaced by tests that schools and teachers could voluntarily apply to their students (D. Forero, 2021). These developments suggest that, despite coercive and normative pressures from international organizations and the early introduction of large-scale tests in the country, legacies of a small state and the lack of support of domestic actors avoided the consolidation of government-oriented, test-based accountability in Colombia. At best, the country has maintained a limited soft accountability by distributing information of test results at the end of secondary school. However, teachers and schools do not have a right to get rewarded nor an obligation to be sanctioned for school performance (Diaz-Rios, 2020).

While Colombian policies conformed to foreign ideas on curricular standardization and avoided global prescriptions on test-based accountability, global recommendations to eliminate VOCSED were defied. Early in the 2000s, VOCSED followed the same pattern of neglect initiated in the 1990s when the education ministry delegated the responsibility for VOCSED curriculum to SENA, as explained by a former senior official in the education ministry (personal communication #3). However, the growth of Articulation and the subsequent increase of VOCSED constituents changed this pattern. By 2011, the education vice minister requested the assistance of the WB to propose a reform for secondary education that controlled Articulation's expansion. The vice minister expected to embrace global recommendations about soft labor and socioemotional skills (personal communications #3, #5, and #24). The WB advised evaluations that showed the shortcomings of Articulation's programs, particularly their unsatisfactory results in conducing students to continue and complete postsecondary education (Econometría Consultores, 2012). Nevertheless, the expansion of Articulation had already created a bureaucracy within the education ministry that was not willing to see the elimination of the program. This bureaucracy used its access to decision-making to delay the policy process and the formulation of the WB loan project, as the task chief of this reform project explained (personal communication #1). The former chief of foreign loan projects in the education ministry also noted that even though the minister was keen on WB recommendations, staff refrained from publicly endorsing the cancellation of VOCSED due to the strength of their constituents (personal communication #3). Bureaucratic delay and the ambiguous position of the education ministry toward VOCSED coincided with a new appointment in the education ministry in 2014. The new minister, who was the former SENA chief, immediately canceled the reform process and the WB loan request (personal communications #1, #3 and #8). With this decision, Colombia defied recommendations for the transformation of VOCSED. This defiance was not the sole and individual decision of this minister, as demonstrated by the consistent growth of Articulation in every local and national reform in secondary education policy since 2014 (Diaz-Rios & Urbano-Canal, 2021). Table 4.10 synthesizes the translation processes and outcomes of EFA and accountability ideas in Colombia.

Conclusion

In the 2000s, global education governance ideas did not significantly change compared to the 1990s. Market-oriented recommendations were moderated, with the state playing a stronger role as a market regulator and evaluator. Active-state ideas continued supporting a state that was expected to compensate inequalities and coordinate different education stakeholders. The two varieties converged in suggesting a controlled

Table 4.10. Translation of EFA and Accountability Ideas in Colombia

Policy Area	Compatibility with Policy Legacies	Support	Opposition	Reinterpretation
Provision	Relatively compatible	Strong	Moderate	Conformity: decentralization and PPPs increase.
Curriculum	Compatible	Moderate	Weak	Conformity: curriculum standards.
VOCSED*	Relatively incompatible	Weak	Strong	Defiance: strengthening of VOCSED.
Evaluation	Compatible	Weak	Weak	Avoidance: persistence of testing but without incentives or sanctions.

Author's elaboration.

*Although VOCSED is a part of curriculum policy, this policy dimension is highlighted here as a separate one due to differences in policy legacies and coalitions.

decentralization, a national standardization of the curriculum, and test-based accountability as adequate tools to guarantee the right to education. Despite a more limited presence of diffusion pressures in Chile, Argentina, and Colombia, EFA recommendations promoted a recentralization of the governance of secondary education. Yet, a closer look shows that this recentralization substantially varied in all three countries. Like in previous periods, this variation is not the outcome of different international pressures over domestic decisions, but rather the product of the interaction between global ideas, policy legacies, and domestic politics.

Chile's policy elites continued to support a blend of market-oriented and active-state solutions that had proven successful compared to other Latin American countries. As the new global ideas did not significantly differ from those of the 1990s, EFA's proposals gained domestic support, leading to a path of conformity. However, those who were negatively affected by previous arrangements also utilized these suggestions to push for a minor modification in the education quasi-market. By contrast, in Argentina, results of previous reforms weakened market-oriented recommendations and gave a new boost to statist advocates like CTERA. This new scenario moved the country closer to EFA ideas, giving the state more authority over the way provinces manage secondary education. By contrast, poor results of previous policy decisions in Colombia rather discredited the statist approach of teachers, giving the government leverage to get closer to a more market-oriented version of EFA recommendations. This translation reproduced the dualist character of the education system even though the state increased its control over the public sector while delegating responsibilities to subnational units. Changes in each country did not necessarily disrupt path-dependent dynamics, but they signaled the nonlinear evolution of secondary education governance.

Table 4.11. Summary of Translation Outcomes by Country and Policy Area During EFA and Accountability Ideas

Policy Area	Chile	Argentina	Colombia
Provision	Compromise	Conformity	Conformity
Curriculum	Conformity	Compromise	Conformity
Evaluation	Conformity	Defiance	Avoidance

Author's elaboration.

This chapter also confirms that policy legacies and coalitions may vary across policy areas and that such variation shifts translations in different directions. In Chile, only EFA's recommendations on a controlled decentralization were relatively incompatible with the country's education quasi-market. This incompatibility raised strong opposition in the country but also gave students, the losers of previous reforms, a tool to strengthen their coalition for changes. The conflict between the defenders of the status quo and the advocates for changes sent the country down the path of compromising on a stronger role of the state in education delivery. While this translation did not break the Chilean education quasi-market, it reversed important policies that had been adopted and strengthened since the authoritarian regime. Conversely, curriculum and evaluation—two areas in which policy legacies were compatible with global recommendations—did not attract sufficient domestic opposition and therefore conformed to global recommendations.

In Argentina, evaluation was the only incompatible area, but it did not attract supporters because teachers, the losers of previous reforms, did not see benefits in test-based accountability. Consequently, evaluation recommendations were defied. By contrast, recommendations in the other two areas were compatible with the country's legacies, which produced conformity in provision and compromise in curriculum, only because of the need to accommodate teachers' interests.

Interestingly, the Colombian case shows that compatible policy legacies are not enough for a smooth translation. Even though policy legacies were compatible with global ideas in all three policy areas (with the small exception of VOCSED elimination), evaluation recommendations were avoided due to the weak support of domestic actors that perceived greater benefits from pursuing different policies regarding teachers' salaries. The dynamics in each area across countries ratifies that we cannot look only at one part of the mechanism—legacies or coalitions—but that we need to look at the interplay of them.

Paths of Translation

Implications for Future Research and Reforms

Global ideas on how to govern secondary education changed substantially between the 1960s and the 2000s. International recommendations in the 1960s and 1970s were dominated by Manpower Education Planning (MEP) ideas—a model that did not significantly transform the existing bureaucratic template but rather promoted the massification of secondary education, the scientific planning of its curriculum to meet human resource needs, and the use of tests to monitor reforms. Later, in the context of the global 1980 economic crisis, the massification of secondary school and its increasing fiscal pressure on governments moved global recommendations away from state-run models and toward market-oriented policies. These new ideas advised fiscal decentralization and reduction of education expenditure, privatization of the provision, curricular autonomy, elimination of VOCSED, and testing to inform parental choices about school. Concurrently, as historically marginalized populations gained access to secondary education, the active-state approach emerged as a critique of the concentration of educational power in bureaucratic governance models. The active-state approach advocated for delegating the responsibility of provision and curricular authority to subnational units, modernizing VOCSED, and utilizing tests as a means for the state to coordinate and address regional disparities in an equitable manner.

However, in the 2000s, escalating educational disparities compelled these two approaches to converge into the Education for All (EFA) framework. This shift deemphasized recommendations regarding privatization and budgetary cutbacks and instead emphasized the role of the state as a coordinator of nonstate actors through educational public-private partnerships (PPPs), as well as the enforcer of controlled decentralization through standardized curricula and test-based accountability. Despite the influence of these recommendations on Latin American countries' education systems, notable variations in education reforms have emerged, prompting scholars to delve into the influence of global ideas on policy decisions within the region.

This book explores this influence and the variation in education reforms by tracing the process through which Chile, Argentina and Colombia reinterpreted global ideas on secondary education provision, curriculum, and evaluation since the 1960s. The question of why some countries adopt education reforms that are closer to global recommendations than others is an important one—especially in Latin America where the influence of foreign prescriptions has been considered a crucial factor in the inability of education reforms to overcome education inequalities. My argument builds on the concept of translation defined as a contentious process through which foreign ideas are reinterpreted and combined with domestic practices, beliefs, and interests. While I acknowledge that global ideas have produced important similarities in reforms across Latin America and around the globe, the concept of translation reveals that these ideas do not always drive countries to policy convergence and that foreign recommendations are not always conformed but are often slightly changed or compromised, ritually implemented or avoided, or resisted or defied. Particularly, the book identifies a mechanism of translation composed by two parts. First, policy legacies define whether a global idea is compatible or incompatible with the domestic arrangement. Compatibility between these two entities creates a more favorable context for conformity, while incompatibility tips the balance to defiance. Second, domestic coalitions can either support the adoption of a global idea when it benefits their interests and is close to their ideologies, or they can oppose it when it threatens their status quo. The conflict between domestic supporters and opponents shapes the extent to which a foreign prescription is conformed or defied.

The analysis of Argentina, Chile, and Colombia suggests that a transition to postbureaucratic forms of secondary education governance has produced various outcomes that reflect different paths of translation. The paths of conformity and compromise have led to the emergence of education quasi-markets, as illustrated by almost all education reforms in Chile in every analyzed period and policy area. These paths are made viable by a strong domestic endorsement of global ideas and the successful neutralization of potential opposition. The process of neutralization is facilitated when existing policies align with global recommendations, as it allows for smoother accommodation of the interests of opponents. However, when inherited arrangements conflict with foreign prescriptions, neutralization is more likely to involve violence and repression. The Chilean case serves as an illustration of these dynamics. Education quasi-markets in Chile have shown potential for improving enrollment rates and student achievement, especially when compared to other Latin American countries. However, they have also contributed to increased educational segregation, as families enroll their children in schools they can afford, thus resulting in a concentration of low-income students in underfunded institutions. Consequently, these negative consequences have recently prompted a shift in the coalitions that once strongly supported the Chilean quasi-market system, leading to the dismantling of certain policy instruments.

The only exception to conformity and compromise in Chile was the curriculum reform in the 1980s during the predominance of market-oriented ideas. Unlike changes in provision and evaluation that were strongly supported by the military regime and the Chicago Boys, curriculum autonomy was avoided because it was at odds with the regime's quest to eradicate leftist influence from the curriculum. In other words, the dominant coalition of that moment did not have enough incentives to break the inherited model of a centralized curriculum and instead replaced autonomy with curriculum cuts to reduce expenses.

The paths of compromise and avoidance, predominantly observed in education reforms in Argentina, result in subnational, quasi-bureaucratic models with recentralized responsibilities at the national level. On the one hand, the presence of compromise in Argentina confirms the observation that compatible policy legacies, along with a strong support for global ideas, can accommodate opponents without deviating significantly from foreign recommendations. On the other hand, the Argentinean case shows that avoidance results from limited support for global ideas among domestic policy elites and their inability to effectively neutralize domestic opposition. The failure to neutralize opposition is more likely to occur when global recommendations are incompatible with existing policy legacies, thus posing a threat to the interests of influential stakeholders. Additionally, a lack of support may arise when global ideas do not directly contradict policy legacies but their implementation does not promise significant benefits for domestic actors. The Argentinean decentralization of responsibilities led to underfunded provinces and a varied implementation of education reforms across the country. These challenges prompted teachers and a significant faction of Peronism to advocate for a recentralization of authority. However, this recentralization proved insufficient in addressing the regional disparities within the education system.

Two exceptions were observed to the Argentinean path of compromise and avoidance. First, provision reforms during the predominance of EFA ideas conformed to global recommendations for a controlled decentralization. Consistent with the mechanism theorized here, this conformity emerged from legacies of a centralized education system and fiscal problems created by previous decentralization reforms that spurred strong support for recentralization. Second, evaluation policy changes during the 2000s defied predominant accountability ideas. This defiance was the result of incompatible policy legacies and a weak support from dominant groups that were not advocates of test-based accountability and did not want to upset teacher unions.

A third path oscillates between accepting global recommendations and rejecting them, thereby resulting in a dualist governance model of secondary education in which a substantial part of the authority is devolved to subnational units and private actors, as the Colombian case illustrates. While accepting or rejecting global ideas is facilitated by whether policy legacies are compatible with foreign recommendations, differences between conformity and compromise, on the one hand, and avoidance and rejection on the other, are shaped by the extent to which the adoption of global ideas affects the interest of powerful groups. The Colombian case shows that dualist systems emerge in contexts where the role of the state in secondary education has been historically weak. Oscillation between short and inconsistent centralization and decentralization efforts in the country has created a system where education policy decisions are highly centralized, but the distribution of responsibilities for implementation is unclear. Moreover, these centralized decisions barely affect private education, making it highly heterogenous regarding quality. In the next sections of this chapter, I summarize the book's main findings and underscore its theoretical and practical contributions.

Main Findings and Implications

POLICY LEGACIES

The findings presented in this book reveal three channels through which previous policy design influences the translation of global ideas. First, policy legacies shape education problems that can make global ideas (un) attractive as solutions. For example, the universalization of primary education achieved through a highly centralized education system in Chile created the need for the massification of secondary education. Thus, the government of Frei-Montalva (1964–1970) enthusiastically embraced MEP recommendations, and their suggestions changed secondary school from elite-oriented to a massified education. By contrast, the centralization of the Argentinean education system created a conflict between the Church and Peronists for the control of secondary schools. This conflict made recommendations of a state-run education governance unattractive for Catholic policymakers during Frondizi's administration (1958–1962), which sought to settle this struggle in their favor.

A second way in which policy legacies shape the translation of global ideas is through the inherited beliefs and state capacities that may enhance or diminish the acceptance of foreign recommendations. While market-oriented ideas had little resonance with 1990s reforms in Argentina due to the country's tradition of a strong state in education, they had wide acceptance in Colombia where the historically weak coordination of the educational system had nurtured a belief in a minimal state for the governance of secondary education. Similarly, market-oriented reforms in Chile during Pinochet's regime and subsequent democratic governments became highly reputable due to the relatively positive results compared to most Latin American countries. Thus, in the 2000s, global recommendations on test-based accountability were easily accepted as they reinforced previous policy designs.

Third, policy legacies influence the translation of global ideas by empowering some groups at the expense of others. In all three countries, the historical role of the Church in education provision has transformed it into a staunch advocate for private education. For instance, in Argentina and Colombia, the Church played a pivotal role in impeding state-led planning efforts during the 1960s and 1970s. Similarly, in Chile, the Church was instrumental in sustaining market-oriented reforms during the 1990s. However, groups that have been adversely affected by past policy decisions are not devoid of agency. Instead, these negative consequences may serve as incentives for them to mobilize and advocate for changes, even if they are incremental. In Colombia, teacher unions successfully compromised state-retrenchment proposals that could have further deteriorated their working conditions. In Argentina, although the unions were unable to prevent the reforms of the 1990s, they later emerged as important actors in amending decentralization policies and challenging the imposition of test-based accountability measures.

These findings suggest that conformity to foreign recommendations is more likely when all three channels through which policy legacies can influence translation are compatible with global ideas: when they look promising to solve inherited problems, when they are consistent with inherited beliefs, and when they benefit influential domestic actors. When previous policy designs and global ideas are mostly incompatible, the potential for rejection of foreign prescriptions increases. This insight emphasizes the importance for international organizations to take into account domestic policy legacies when formulating recommendations, enabling them to assess the feasibility of their proposals within diverse contexts.

However, policy legacies alone do not dictate the outcome of the translation process. Despite the considerable constraints imposed by existing policy legacies, domestic actors retain the ability to advocate for incremental changes that can have far-reaching implications for future policy decisions and the influence of particular groups. This discovery holds significance not only for international actors endeavoring to promote global ideas but also for domestic actors aiming to challenge education reforms inspired by global trends.

POLITICAL COALITIONS

Another noteworthy finding presented in this book relates to the significance of domestic coalitions in the reinterpretation of foreign recommendations. These coalitions play a crucial role in shaping the translation process of global ideas through three key activities: (1) building organizational capacity characterized by a cohesive membership base; (2) active participation in the decision-making process, either through close connections with decision-makers or direct involvement in policy formulation; and (3) mobilization of power resources, including research capabilities, media influence, and organized protests, among other strategies.

The level of engagement of these coalitions in these activities is partly influenced by the existing policy legacies. Consequently, when global ideas align with policy legacies, the beneficiaries of the prevailing domestic arrangements often lend strong support to the adoption of foreign recommendations. Given the influential status of these beneficiaries, their endorsement tends to foster conformity with global norms. This scenario was observed in eight of the cases analyzed in this book.[1] Conversely, when global norms are at odds with policy legacies, they face vehement opposition from these prevailing winners, leading to a tendency of defying the adoption of foreign recommendations. This pattern was observed in three cases.[2]

Nevertheless, my analysis also shows that the negative effects of past policies can get domestic losers enough incentives to organize, oppose, and shift the translation away from the preferences of the domestic winners. When policy legacies are compatible with global ideas, increases in the influence of opponents to domestic arrangements can lead to a compromise, as exemplified by seven cases analyzed in this book.[3] The growth of Colombian teacher unions, their organization as a national federation, and their alliance with the ministry of education of Cesar Gaviria (1990–1994) helped teacher unions prevent the implementation of a quasi-market of education, compromise decisions about the decentralization of funding, and avoid test-based accountability even against the powerful action of the finance ministry and the national planning agency. Another example is provided by the alliance President Kirchner (2003–2007) needed to establish with teacher unions in Argentina, which compromised VOCSED's reduction that active-state advocates supported. In both countries, groups of actors managed to attract support—not only from political elites but also from public opinion—thus preventing convergence with foreign recommendations.

When beneficiaries of existing arrangements cannot or are not motivated to support global recommendations, even the slight push of opponents can lead to avoidance, as illustrated by four cases in this book.[4] For instance, Argentinean beneficiaries of a bureaucratic model during the predominance of MEP ideas could not advocate for further expansion of secondary public school due to the proscription of Peronism. Likewise, their quest to continue a politically oriented curriculum discouraged them from supporting a scientific-based curriculum reform. These situations gave leverage to Catholic officials to expand the role of private schooling in the country and avoid curriculum changes. Yet, avoidance is also a likely outcome under incompatible policy legacies when supporters of global recommendations engage in activities that at least force opponents to act as if they were implementing reforms. I found five of these cases in my analysis.[5] For instance, despite strong opposition of key players like the Church, Conservative parties, and subnational politicians, Colombian reforms during MEP ideas that included a centralization of secondary education provision were passed by a Liberal government. Nevertheless, its implementation was disrupted by subnational governments that perceived further benefits from the existing lack of coordination of the education system.

Instances of radical disruption of policy legacies are very infrequent; the only example in this book are the 1980s Chilean reforms that required a totalitarian regime and extreme violence to achieve such an outcome. While these rapid shifts are rare, other cases examined in this study demonstrate that those who suffer from the existing domestic arrangement can leverage incompatible global norms to drive changes in their favor. Drawing upon the principles of the Education for All (EFA) movement and the right to education, students affected by the segregation prevalent in the Chilean education system have recently mobilized to challenge the longstanding coalitions that historically supported the quasi-market approach to education. They garnered support from influential political parties, propelling progress toward a stronger role for the state in education and achieving a compromise in the translation of EFA recommendations. As a result, certain policies were discontinued, such as the shared funding system, student selection by private voucher schools, and for-profit schools.

These findings have important theoretical and practical implications. At the theoretical level, the mechanism proposed here that links policy legacies, coalition responses, and specific translation outcomes helps resolve the question of why sometimes global ideas are fully emulated and other times they are contested and reinterpreted. At the practical level, the study underscores the need for international organizations and policymakers to analyze the potential acceptability that a foreign recommendation can have in a specific country, which may diverge from its global legitimacy. The negotiations required to adopt global ideas open room for groups seeking to influence education policy to produce small changes that can result in significant reforms in the future. While these negotiations may increase the influence of less powerful groups in education reforms, they may also produce new inequalities and forms of segregation, thus creating the need for new reforms.

Furthermore, the analysis presented in this book highlights two crucial dynamics concerning the relationship between coalitions and policy areas. First, domestic coalitions advocating for or opposing global ideas may vary depending on the specific policy area under consideration. The groups that stand to benefit from increased (de)centralization of education provision may not necessarily be the same as those that perceive advantages in (de)centralizing curriculum or evaluation processes. For example, in Colombia, teacher unions argued against market-oriented recommendations and advocated for the centralization of funding during the 1990s reforms. However, they also supported the devolution of curriculum authority to schools. Consequently, they settled for a semi-decentralized arrangement that maintained negotiations on labor conditions at the national level while granting some autonomy in curriculum decision-making at the school level. This example illustrates the complex interplay between coalitions and different policy areas, as stakeholders navigate their priorities and interests within each specific domain.

Second, the sequence in which policy areas are reformed and the outcomes they produce can have implications for other policy areas, often resulting in reforms that are inconsistent with the original recommendations. For instance, in Chile, privatization and municipalization were prioritized, while standardized testing and curriculum autonomy were delayed or resisted. This arguably resulted in limited information for parents and constrained the school innovation promised by market-oriented ideas. In Colombia, the avoidance of vouchers and school choice rendered test-based accountability irrelevant and led to its abandonment. These examples show that we cannot assume domestic responses are completely uniform and responsive to globally recommended reform packages, such as MEP recommendations, market-oriented ideas (or New Public Management), active-state recommendations, and the EFA framework.

IMPLICATIONS FOR ALTERNATIVE EXPLANATIONS

In my comparative analysis of Chile, Argentina, and Colombia, I identified diffusion pressures that align with both world society theory and traditional approaches in political economy. For instance, international organizations exercised coercion through the Alliance for Progress in the 1960s and conditional loans for structural reforms in the 1980s and 1990s. Additionally, powerful international actors applied mimetic pressures, particularly in cases where countries lacked technical expertise. Examples include UNESCO's Major Project of Education, which advocated for the establishment of educational planning offices, and the World Bank's technical reports highlighting the inefficiency of VOCSED schools and public education provision. However, the analysis presented in this book highlights the fact that coercive and mimetic pressures alone are not sufficient to drive domestic actors to adopt global ideas. Despite facing strong coercion and mimetic pressures in the 1960s and 1990s, Colombia and Argentina deviated from global recommendations due to incompatible policy legacies and/or significant domestic opposition.

In contrast, my findings indicate that normative diffusion played a role in cases of conformity and compromise. In Chile, officials with expertise in educational planning and the influence of the Chicago Boys were instrumental in adopting the recommendations of MEP and market-oriented approaches, respectively. Similarly, likeminded policymakers in Chile and Argentina embraced active-state recommendations, leading to education reforms in both countries during the 1990s and 2000s. However, while normative pressures hold greater significance compared to coercive and mimetic pressures, they alone do not dictate the adoption of global norms. Experts trained in MEP ideas were not able to prevent the defiance of the Colombian curricular reform of the 1960s. Economists trained in market-oriented ideas were also outpaced by a fierce opposition of teachers who compromised state-retrenchment in the Colombian 1990s education reforms. In Argentina, despite the advocacy of active-state proponents, there were challenges in implementing curriculum reforms at the provincial level.

The varying influence of normative pressures on secondary education governance reforms has important practical implications. The impact of normative pressures suggests that international actors should invest in training policymakers to enhance the impact of their recommendations. However, relying solely on foreign pressures and the legitimacy of recommendations is insufficient, and both international actors and domestic champions of foreign recommendations need to consider additional factors to achieve meaningful reform.

My analysis further supports and adds nuance to approaches that emphasize the significance of local factors in the globalization of education policy, such as cultural political economy, policy-borrowing, and anthropological perspectives. Consistent with these approaches, domestic policymakers seek legitimate solutions and tailor education reforms based on their own ideological frameworks. However, my findings indicate that ideology is not the sole determinant in this process of selection, as interests also play a crucial role in filtering foreign recommendations. The adoption of market-oriented ideas in the 1980s Chilean reforms, for instance, was not solely driven by the ideology of the Chicago Boys but also by Pinochet's political interests. By identifying the channels through which policy legacies influence the translation of global ideas, my analysis provides a more balanced and integrated understanding of the role of both semiosis (meaning-making) and interests in explaining the dynamics of policy adoption.

Additionally, the role of domestic coalitions underscores the challenges of disentangling processes of selection exclusively done by policymakers and retention in which nongovernment groups participate. Such processes are often intertwined in practice. For example, the formulation of the 1990s reforms in Argentina and Colombia involved ongoing contention within the government and with opponents, blurring the boundaries between selection and retention.

Finally, while my analysis supports the notion of path dependence embraced by political economic approaches, which suggests self-reinforcing effects of previous policies, it also reveals instances of self-undermining effects that create opportunities for alternative actors to participate in the translation of global ideas. This highlights the limitations of synchronic analysis that treats institutions as stable rules, such as formal veto points or forms of government. Instead, adopting a historical analysis that recognizes the centrality of evolving institutions becomes crucial, as "policy transforms policies into institutions that have significant explanatory power in and of themselves" (Béland et al., 2022, p. 4).

Implications for Secondary Education Policy

While this book's findings have broader implications for the education system as a whole, they also hold specific lessons that are particularly relevant to secondary education. The debate surrounding the purpose of secondary education has predominantly been framed as a technical discourse, focusing on factors such as aligning school curricula with the country's workforce needs, achieving cost-efficiency, developing relevant skills for the current economy, or addressing the comprehensive needs of young people. Regrettably, this discussion has largely overlooked the political dimensions that shape decisions about the type of secondary education adopted by a country.

This book addresses the gap by examining the shifting interests and ideologies that influence policy decisions in the realm of secondary education. It highlights that right-wing governments in Colombia and Argentina initially supported the expansion of vocational education as a means of segregating disadvantaged students into a less prestigious track. However, these governments later attempted to reduce funding for vocational education due to fiscal pressures. Despite these efforts, the initial expansion of vocational education had already cultivated strong constituencies for these schools. This included unions that experienced membership growth, teachers who developed a professional identity within vocational schools, low-income families who saw vocational education as the primary path for their children's job training, bureaucrats who gained expertise and achieved organizational goals through vocational education, and even politicians who recognized the electoral popularity of vocational schools. More recently, these constituencies also impeded changes in vocational education when policymakers began shifting toward a softer approach, emphasizing the development of soft labor and socioemotional skills within secondary education.

By examining the influence of policy legacies on coalitions that either support or oppose global recommendations, this book sheds light on the political challenges for secondary education reforms. These findings emphasize the need for policymakers and international organizations to go beyond technical discussions and take into account how previous decisions shape the feasibility of desired changes in secondary school provision and curriculum. Understanding the broader context and considering the impact of policy legacies and domestic coalitions are crucial elements for effectively navigating the complexities of secondary education reform and achieving desired outcomes.

Future Research

Findings in this book raise important questions that should be addressed in future studies. The analysis presented here thoroughly tested the mechanism theorized in this book in multiple cases that involve different policy areas, three historical periods, and three countries. Nevertheless, an important area of future research still involves exploring the extent to which this mechanism is portable to other Latin American cases and low- and middle-income countries in other regions. A particular question is whether lower-income countries that depend more on international actors are more likely to follow foreign prescriptions regardless of their domestic policy legacies and politics. While using Central American countries as shadow cases to test my theorized mechanism is beyond the scope of this book, these countries provide an interesting terrain to assess the impact of policy legacies and domestic coalitions in the adoption of 1990s privatization ideas. During this decade, El Salvador, Honduras, Nicaragua, and Guatemala initiated school-based management reforms strongly encouraged by the financial and technical support of the WB, USAID, the IADB, UNICEF, and UNESCO, among others (Corrales, 2006; Edwards, 2013; Morales Ulloa & Magalhães, 2013; Vargas Castro, 2020). These reforms aimed to devolve authority to local communities to manage school matters, including infrastructure, budgeting, and hiring and firing teachers. This devolution was theoretically grounded on the assumption that parental and community participation in the governance of autonomous schools would be an appropriate solution for very weak states and remote areas where citizens have limited chances to demand accountability from policymakers (Gershberg, 2012).

Along with the strong push from international organizations to implement these reforms, school-based management was also relatively compatible with inherited problems of these countries, specifically the need to expand school access quickly while being debilitated by internal conflicts that had eroded their education systems (Altschuler & Corrales, 2013; Edwards, 2015; Ganimian, 2016; Gershberg et al., 2009). In addition, school autonomy programs were relatively consistent with inherited beliefs of traditional political elites that preferred a small state and had limited resources to expand enrollment (Altschuler & Corrales, 2013; Gershberg et al., 2009). These initiatives also favored the interests of these elites in diminishing the influence of their opponents, especially in countries where teacher unions had been allies of left-wing movements (Edwards, 2018; Vargas Castro, 2022). In El Salvador in particular, similar schools already existed—a legacy that facilitated the modification of these organizations to fit the government's agenda (Edwards, 2015).

While the compatibility with policy legacies likely eased the adoption of school-based management in all four countries, their implementation was shaped by the ways in which governments dealt with the opposition of teacher unions and accommodated the interest of political elites. In El Salvador, Nicaragua, and Guatemala, competing unions were created for the school-based management initiatives, which debilitated the union organizations of teachers in traditional public schools (Altschuler & Corrales, 2013; Lemus Barahona, 2021). Additionally, the expansion of the program started in rural areas either where the influence of teacher unions and left-wing party allies was relatively undermined (Vargas Castro, 2020) or through individual teachers' contracts that prevented membership in traditional unions (Edwards, 2015). Later, however, the expansion of the program increased the opposition of teachers' unions, and once these organizations gained sufficient access to decision-making through alliances or negotiations with the ruling party, they forced the discontinuation of autonomous schools—despite the advocacy of international organizations for these programs (Altschuler, 2013; Edwards, 2018; Ganimian, 2016).

In contrast, the program took a divergent path in Honduras. It was introduced as a parallel education system, exclusively targeting areas without access to traditional public schools, primarily due to opposition from unions (Altschuler & Corrales, 2013). However, this approach had unintended consequences. The country's patronage politics allowed political elites to co-opt the program, using it as a means to appoint teachers affiliated with their own party. As a result, parents lost the authority to hire and fire teachers, significantly deviating from the original intention of empowering them (Altschuler, 2013). Among the four countries, Honduras stands alone in its continued implementation of this initiative, albeit with significant modifications compared to the original concept of parent-managed schools. These modifications have likely altered the way the schools operate. On the one hand, they ensure the policy's continuity, but on the other hand, they have strayed from its initial objective.

Another future research area involves comparative analyses on the relationship between different translations of global ideas and educational inequality. Despite the expansion of secondary education across Latin American countries, educational inequality in the region is still pervasive, although heterogenous. Comparative literature has primarily focused on factors like education expenditure, income inequality, or family characteristics to explain cross-national variations in educational attainment (Castro Aristizábal et al., 2017; Cox, 2010; Neidhöfer et al., 2018). Others have also explored the effect of certain aspects of education governance, such as privatization, as a determinant of education inequality (F. J. Murillo & Garrido, 2017; Verger, Moschetti, et al., 2017). However, the evidence provided here suggests that variation in this inequality goes beyond socioeconomic characteristics, privatization, or education expenditure and can be in more complex governance models and the politics they generate.

In Chile, the education quasi-market completed the universalization of secondary education yet produced a particular type of segregation—not only between private and public schools, but also within each sector, according to the household capacity to pay for fees (Elacqua, 2012). Future research needs to examine whether recent reforms in the Chilean education provision without transformation in other policy areas alter this pattern of segregation. The case of Argentina indicates that when the state assumes a prominent role in a quasi-state monopoly, it leads to the universalization of secondary education. However, this approach also exacerbates educational inequality across different regions when subnational governments receive unequal funding, possess uneven capacities, or face challenges in aligning policy actions with the central state. Moreover, some scholars suggest that the erosion of public schools may be motivating families to opt out of the public system and enroll in private schools (Moschetti & Verger, 2020). Finally, similar to quasi-state monopolies, dualist systems such as the one in Colombia also fuel geographical education inequalities. However, these systems also permit the growth of an educational segmentation between those who can afford high-quality and costly private schools and those who are stuck in underfunded public and low-fee private schools (Diaz-Rios et al., 2021; García et al., 2013). Overall, the analysis presented in this book suggests the need to analyze the effect of different configurations of governance models beyond isolated aspects of them in the production of various patterns of education inequality. Such research will also illuminate reforms that can be more responsive to domestic needs.

Finally, another avenue for future research involves the examination of whether the paths theorized in this book help explain the variation in the translation of global ideas associated with other policy areas and educational levels. For example, research on teacher-related policies shows that the centralization process promoted by educational planning ideas in the 1950s and 1960s helped the harmonization of teacher labor conditions, the emergence of teacher professional development regimes, and the strengthening of teacher unions. However, such trends vary substantially across countries due to differences in the expansion of education and different levels of resistance from teachers to lose their autonomy and influence on curriculum decisions (Birgin, 1999; Tiramonti, 2001).

Likewise, recent changes toward the deregulation of teacher careers and teacher performance policies have negatively affected teachers, but such effects have not been equal in all Latin American countries, vary across time, and have produced diverse resistance responses (Bruns & Luque, 2014). In the area of higher education, studies have shown convergence toward privatization (Levy, 2006), but others have pointed at resistance and evidence of the reversal of such a trend (Alcántara et al., 2013). It is possible that these responses are the product of policy legacies and interactions of rival coalitions in the countries of the region.

Secondary education reproduces pervasive educational inequality in Latin America and partially explains the classification of the region as one of the most unequal in the world. Globally disseminated ideas have motivated different reforms to distribute education authority and responsibilities with the goal to improve the access and quality of secondary education. Yet, reforms vary substantially across countries, and their achievements are mixed with an important expansion of this educational level and significant segregation. Moreover, secondary education continues to be an important "bottleneck" for many countries in the region. The theoretical mechanism proposed in this book helps explain why globally inspired reforms adopt very diverse forms in similar Latin American countries and shed light on different governance structures through which educational inequality persists. These reforms show convergences but also resistances that often produce small changes with lasting consequences for the educational systems of the region and important political implications for future reforms and generations.

Appendix

Personal Interviews

COLOMBIA

Personal Communication #1: Marcela Bautista, coordinator of the Project for the Modernization of Secondary Education, Ministry of Education (Colombia). September 11, 2014.

Personal Communication #2: Amparo Sandoval, senior official, SENA (Colombia). September 11, 2014.

Personal Communication #3: Bibiam Diaz, director of foreign loans, Ministry of Education (Colombia). September 12, 2014.

Personal Communication #4: Wilson Arias, former senior official, SENA's union (Colombia). September 12, 2014.

Personal Communication #5: Martha Laverde, education specialist, World Bank (Colombia). September 15, 2014.

Personal Communication #6: Víctor M Gómez, education expert, Universidad Nacional de Colombia (Colombia). September 15, 2014.

Personal Communication #7: Carlos Vasco, former senior official of the curriculum reform, Ministry of Education (Colombia). September 16, 2014.

Personal Communication #8: Elvia María Acuña, education independent consultant (Colombia). September 16, 2014.

Personal Communication #9: María Teresa Matijasevic, education researcher, CRECE (Colombia). September 17, 2014.

Personal Communication #10: Margarita Peña, former education vice minister and former director of ICFES (Colombia). September 18, 2014.

Personal Communication #11: Patricia Asmar, former regional director, SENA (Colombia). September 19, 2014.

Personal Communication #12: Daniel Bogoya, former director, ICFES (Colombia). September 20, 2014.

Personal Communication #13: Carlos Holmes Trujillo, former minister of education (Colombia). September 23, 2014.

Personal Communication #14: Abel Rodríguez, former senior leader, FECODE (Colombia). September 24, 2014.

Personal Communication #15: Catalina Turbay, independent education consultant (Colombia). September 24, 2014.

Personal Communication #16: Luis Piñeros, independent education consultant (Colombia). September 25, 2014.

Personal Communication #17: Juanita Lleras, independent education consultant (Colombia). September 26, 2014.

Personal Communication #18: José Fernando Ocampo, former senior leader, FECODE (Colombia). September 29, 2014.

Personal Communication #19: Cecilia María Velez, former minister of education (Colombia). October 02, 2014.

Personal Communication #20: John Avila Buitrago, former senior leader, FECODE (Colombia). October 02, 2014.

Personal Communication #21: Luisa Pizano, director, Alianza Educativa (Colombia). October 2, 2014.

Personal Communication #22: Andrés Casas, independent education consultant (Colombia). October 3, 2014.

Personal Communication #23: Liliana González, director, Qualificar (Colombia). October 3, 2014.

Personal Communication #24: Mauricio Duque, education expert, Universidad de los Andes (Colombia). October 15, 2014.

Personal Communication #25: Jorge Celis, independent education consultant (Colombia). October 15, 2014.

Personal Communication #26: George Psacharopoulos, former senior official, World Bank (online communication). November 12, 2014.

Personal Communication #27: Ernesto Cuadra, former senior official, World Bank (online communication). November 14, 2014.

CHILE

Personal Communication #28: Ernesto Ottone, former director, CEPAL (Chile). November 25, 2014.

Personal Communication #29: Dante Contreras, education expert, Universidad de Chile (Chile). November 26, 2014.

Personal Communication #30: Juan Eduardo García-Huidobro, former senior official, Ministry of Education (Chile). November 26, 2014.

Personal Communication #31: Claudio Almonacid, education expert, Universidad Metropolitana de Ciencias de la Educación (Chile). November 27, 2014.

Personal Communication #32: René Salamé, former education secretary (Chile). November 27, 2014.

Personal Communication #33: Sergio Bitar, former minister of education (Chile). November 28, 2014.

Personal Communication #34: María José Ramirez, researcher, World Bank (online communication). November 28, 2014.

Personal Communication #35: Osvaldo Verdugo, former president, Colegio de Profesores (Chile). December 1, 2014.

Personal Communication #36: Carlos Concha, former education advisor, Ministry of Education (Chile). December 2, 2014.

Personal Communication #37: Paulina Dittborn, former education vice secretary (Chile). December 2, 2014.

Personal Communication #38: Marco Cueva, former senior official, Ministry of Education. (Chile). December 3, 2014.

Personal Communication #39: Cristián Bellei, education expert, Universidad de Chile (Chile). December 4, 2014.

Personal Communication #40: Tomas Leighton, former student movement leader (Chile). December 5, 2014.

Personal Communication #41: Julio Isamit, former student movement leader (Chile). December 05, 2014.

Personal Communication #42: Eduardo Catalán, former leader of parent school association. (Chile). December 6, 2014.

Personal Communication #43: Anibal Palma, former minister of education (Chile). December 9, 2014.

Personal Communication #44: Eric Olivares, advisor, Colegio de Profesores (Chile). December 10, 2014.

Personal Communication #45 Martín Miranda, former advisor, Ministry of Education (Chile). December 10, 2014.

Personal Communication #46: Beatrice Avalos, education expert, Universidad de Chile (Chile). December 11, 2014.

Personal Communication #47: Guillermo Scherping, senior leader, Colegio de profesores (Chile). December 12, 2014.

Personal Communication #48: Iván Ortiz, senior official, Ministry of Education (Chile). December 12, 2014.

Personal Communication #49: Mariana Aylwin, former minister of education (Chile). December 13, 2014.

Personal Communication #50: Cristián Cox, former coordinator of MECE-media, Ministry of Education. (Chile). December 13, 2014.

Personal Communication #51: Lorena Meckes, former director of SIMCE (Chile). January 6, 2015.

Personal Communication #52: Luis Pisani, former senior official, World Bank (Chile). January 7, 2015.

Personal Communication #53: Rodrigo Ketterer, former general secretary, CONACEP (Chile). January 8, 2015.

Personal Communication #54: Harald Beyer, former minister of education (Chile). January 8, 2015.

Personal Communication #55: Daniel Contreras, former senior official, Ministry of Education (Chile). January 11, 2015.

Personal Communication #56: José Weinstein, education expert, Universidad Diego Portales (Chile). January 16, 2015.

Personal Communication #57: Gonzalo Durán, former student movement leader (Chile). January 16, 2015.

ARGENTINA

Personal Communication #58: Susana Decibe, former minister of education (online communication). April 15, 2015.

Personal Communication #59: Carlos Torrendell, education expert, Universidad Católica de Argentina (Argentina). April 20, 2015.

Personal Communication #60: Ana Diamant, former senior official, Ministry of Education (Argentina). April 20, 2015.

Personal Communication #61: Mariano Narodowski, education expert, Universidad Torcuato di Tella (Argentina). April 21, 2015.

Personal Communication #62: Emilio Tenti, former senior official, IIPE-UNESCO Buenos Aires (Argentina). April 22, 2015.

Personal Communication #63: Claudia Jacinto, education expert, IPES (Argentina). April 23, 2015.

Personal Communication #64: Guillermina Tiramonti, education expert, FLACSO (Argentina). April 24, 2015.

Personal Communication #65: Norberto Fernández Lamarra, former senior official, Ministry of Education (Argentina). April 27, 2015.

Personal Communication #66: Nestor Rebecchi, union leader, CTERA (Argentina). April 28, 2015.

Personal Communication #67: Dora Niedzwiecki, education expert, FLACSO (Argentina). April 29, 2015.

Personal Communication #68: Cecilia Veleda, education expert, CIPPEC (Argentina). April 30, 2015.

Personal Communication #69: Irma Briasco, senior official, OEI (Argentina). April 30, 2015.

Personal Communication #70: Pedro Weinberg, former senior official, ILO (Argentina). May 4, 2015.

Personal Communication #71: Martin Legarralde, education expert, Universidad de la Plata (Argentina). May 4, 2015.

Personal Communication #72: Luis Cabeda, union leader, CTERA (Argentina). May 5, 2015.

Personal Communication #73: Flavia Terigi, education expert, Universidad General Sarmiento (Argentina). May 6, 2015.

Personal Communication #74: Elena Duró, former senior official, UNICEF (Argentina). May 6, 2015.

Personal Communication #75: Claudia Bracchi, vice minister of education Province of Buenos Aires (Argentina). May 6, 2015.

Personal Communication #76: Myriam Southwell, education expert, FLACSO (Argentina). May 11, 2015.

Personal Communication #77: Cecilia Cresta, former senior official, Ministry of Education (Argentina). May 12, 2015.

Personal Communication #78: Adriana Vilanoba, former senior official, Ministry of Education (Argentina). May 13, 2015.

Personal Communication #79: Felicitas Acosta, education expert, Universidad General Sarmiento (Argentina). May 15, 2015.

Personal Communication #80: Silvina Larripa, education expert, Universidad General Sarmiento (Argentina). May 15, 2015.

Personal Communication #81: Juan Carlos Tedesco, former minister of education (online communication). May 12, 2016.

Notes

Introduction

1. Public Choice scholars coined the term "quasi-state monopoly" to describe educational systems that maintain hierarchical control despite some delegation of authority (Peterson, 1990). In Argentina, the term has primarily been used to illustrate the transfer of education authority from the central to the provincial level (Narodowski, 2008; Narodowski & Andrada, 2004). Although the term often carries a negative connotation, associating inefficiencies with state-run education systems, I utilize it in this book solely to emphasize minor modifications within the traditional hierarchical bureaucratic model, where centralization remains prevalent for most education responsibilities and decision-making.

2. Translation has also been labeled as recontextualization, internalization, implementation, indigenization, and appropriation, among others (Phillips & Ochs, 2003; Schulte, 2012; Steiner-Khamsi, 2014).

Chapter 2

1. By the 1950s and 1960s, although CEPAL and Alliance for Progress built on opposing policy assumptions (dependency theory vs. modernization theory), both emphasized the need for skilled workers for economic growth and the role of educational planning for their training.

2. These agencies include the Planning Office (ODEPLAN) and CPEIP.

3. Perón was a three-time president of Argentina and became the most influential political figure in the country. His party was originally a polyclass alliance of workers, sectors of the army, and industrialists, with various ideological influences (Munck, 1985, p. 51).

4. In 1962, Frondizi was overthrown by a military coup. Similarly, in 1966, a new coup deposed the democratically elected president Arturo Illia (1963–1966).

5. To settle an armed conflict between Liberal and Conservative elites, party leaders agreed on an arrangement called the National Front that involved the alternation of each party in the presidential office every four years, as well as the equal distribution of legislative, executive, and administrative positions between parties (Lijphart, 1969, p. 213).

Chapter 3

1. In 1992, Colombia experienced a dramatic power shortage that the government initially addressed with electricity rationing and blackouts, depriving cities of energy for several hours daily and introducing fees to stop power overconsumption (López Díez, 2017).

Chapter 4

1. Charter schools are public schools where management has been contracted out to a private operator.

2. Contract schools are privately owned organizations to which the government outsource the delivery of education.

3. School-based management involves schools managed by parents or communities.

Conclusion

1. Cases of conformity in which policy legacies were compatible with global ideas and their supporters were stronger than opponents include the following reforms. During MEP ideas: Chilean reforms in provision, curriculum, and evaluation. During EFA and accountability ideas: Chilean reforms in curriculum and evaluation; Argentinean provision reforms; Colombian reforms in provision and curriculum.

2. Cases of defiance in which policy legacies were incompatible with global ideas and their opponents were stronger than supporters include Argentinean evaluation reforms during EFA and accountability ideas, Colombian curriculum reforms during MEP ideas, and Colombian VOCSED reforms during EFA ideas.

3. Cases of compromise in which policy legacies were compatible but opponents were as strong as the supporters include the following reforms. During MEP ideas: Argentinean and Colombian VOCSED reforms. During state-retrenchment ideas: Chilean evaluation reforms, Argentinean provision reforms, and Colombian reforms in provision and curriculum. During EFA and accountability ideas: Argentinean curriculum reforms.

4. Cases of avoidance in which policy legacies were compatible but global norms did not achieve any domestic support include the following reforms: Argentinean provision and curriculum reforms during the predominance of MEP ideas, and Colombian evaluation reforms during the state-retrenchment and EFA periods.

5. Cases of avoidance in which policy legacies were incompatible but supporters of global norms were as strong as opponents include the following reforms: Colombian provision and evaluation reforms during MEP ideas, Chilean curriculum reforms, and Argentinean curriculum and evaluation reforms during state-retrenchment recommendations.

References

A despolitizar la educación. (2002, June 22). *El Tiempo.* http://www.eltiempo. com/archivo/documento/MAM-1339850

Abu-Duhou, I. (2005). *School-based management* (No. 62; Fundamentals of Educational Planning). IIEP-UNESCO. http://unesdoc.unesco.org/images/ 0011/001184/118487e.pdf

Acosta, F. (2011). Escuela secundaria y sistemas educativos modernos: Análisis histórico comparado de la dinámica de configuración y expansión en países centrales y en la Argentina. *História, Sociedade e Educação No Brasil,* *42,* 3–13.

Acosta, F. (2012). La escuela secundaria argentina en perspectiva histórica y comparada: Modelos institucionales y desgranamiento durante el siglo XX. *Cadernos de História Da Educação, 11*(1), 131–144.

Acto Legislativo 01, Diario Oficial de la República de Colombia 44.506, August 1, 2001. http://www.mineducacion.gov.co/1621/articles-90475_archivo_pdf.pdf

Acuerdo No. 93, Consejo Nacional de Educación de Chile, September 2, 2010. http://www.cned.cl/Transparencia/2010/ActosEfect/093-2010.pdf

Aedo-Richmond, R. (2000). *La educación privada en Chile: Un estudio histórico-analítico desde el período colonial hasta 1990.* RIL Editores.

AFP/EMOL. (2011, October 14). Líderes del movimiento estudiantil se reunieron con autoridad de la Unesco en París. *El Mercurio Online.* http://www.emol. com/noticias/nacional/2011/10/14/508015/lideres-de-movimiento-estudiantil-fueron-recibidos-en-la-unesco.html

Agency for Aid Development. (1966). *US foreign aid and the Alliance for Progress.* Agency for International Development. http://pdf.usaid.gov/pdf_docs/ pdace249.pdf

Aguerrondo, I. (1989). Los aportes de los partidos políticos al C.P. In C. De Lella & P. Krotsch (Eds.), *Congreso pedagógico nacional. Evaluación y perspectivas* (pp. 181–192). Suramericana - Instituto de Estudios de Acción Social.

Alcántara, A., Llomovatte, S., & Romão, J. E. (2013). Resisting neoliberal common sense in higher education: Experiences from Latin America.

International Studies in Sociology of Education, 23(2), 127–151. https://doi. org/10.1080/09620214.2013.790661

Aldana, L. A. M. (2002). *Poder capitalista y violencia política en Colombia: Terrorismo de estado y genocidio contra la Unión Patriótica.* Edición Ideas y Soluciones Gráficas.

Almond, B. (1991). Education and liberty: Public provision and private choice. *Journal of Philosophy of Education, 25*(2), 193–202.

Altschuler, D. (2013). How patronage politics undermines parental participation and accountability: Community-managed schools in Honduras and Guatemala. *Comparative Education Review, 57*(1), 117–144. https://doi. org/10.1086/667963

Altschuler, D., & Corrales, J. (2013). The rise of community-managed schools: Push and pull factors. In D. Altschuler & J. Corrales, *The promise of participation* (pp. 23–38). Palgrave Macmillan UK. https://doi. org/10.1057/9781137271846_3

Alvarez, J. E. (2005). Elites intelectuales y producción de política económica en Colombia. In J. E. Alvarez (Ed.), *Intelectuales, tecnócratas y reformas neoliberales en América Latina* (pp. 259–320). Universidad Nacional de Colombia.

Anderson-Levitt, K. (2003a). A world culture of schooling? In K. Anderson-Levitt (Ed.), *Local meanings, global schooling: Anthropology and world culture theory* (pp. 1–26). Palgrave Macmillan.

Anderson-Levitt, K. (2003b). *Local meanings, global schooling: Anthropology and world culture theory.* Palgrave Macmillan.

Ansell, C., Reckhow, S., & Kelly, A. (2009). How to reform a reform coalition: Outreach, agenda expansion, and brokerage in urban school reform. *Policy Studies Journal, 37*(4), 717–743. https://doi.org/10.1111/j.1541-0072. 2009.00332.x

Anyon, J. (2009). Progressive social movements and educational equity. *Educational Policy, 23*(1), 194–215. https://doi.org/10.1177/0895904808328523

Arizmendi Posada, O. (2001). El principio de subsidiariedad y el problema de las fronteras del estado y de la sociedad civil. *Dikaion, 15*(10), 13–26.

Arnove, R. (1980). Education policies in the National Front. In R. A. Berry & M. Solaun (Eds.), *Politics of compromise: Coalition government in Colombia* (pp. 381–411). Transaction Publishers.

Arnove, R., Torres, A., Franz, S., & Morse, K. (1996). A political sociology of education and development in Latin America. *International Journal of Comparative Sociology, 37*(1–2), 140–158.

Arnove, R., Torres, C. A., & Franz, S. (2012). Education in Latin America: From dependence and neoliberalism to alternative paths of development. In *Comparative education: The dialectic of the global and the local.* Rowman & Littlefield Publishers.

Astiz, M. (2006). Policy enactment and adaptation of community participation in education: The case of Argentina. In D. P. Baker & A. W. Wiseman (Eds.), *The impact of comparative education research on institutional theory*. Emerald Group Publishing.

Astiz, M., & Wiseman, A. (2005). Slouching toward a global ideology: Decentralization and devolution of Central Education Authority. In D. Baker & G. LeTendre (Eds.), *National differences, global similarities: World culture and the future of schooling* (pp. 134–149). Stanford Social Sciences.

ATEP. (1971). *La reforma educativa. Análisis crítico de todos los documentos oficiales*. Agremiación Tucumana de Educadores Provinciales.

Atria, F. (2012). *La mala educación. Ideas que inspiran al movimiento estudiantil en Chile*. Catalonia—CIPER.

Avellaneda, L. C., & Rodríguez, A. (1993). *Proyecto de ley de educación: Propuesta de articulado. Hacia una reforma educativa para la democracia y el desarrollo: una propuesta para el debate y la concertación*. Corporación S.O.S. Colombia-Viva la Ciudadanía.

Bachelet, M. (2009). Chile at the OECD. *The OECD Observer, 273*, 59.

Baker, D., & LeTendre, G. (2005). *National differences, global similarities: World culture and the future of schooling*. Stanford Social Sciences.

Balarin, M. (2014). The changing governance of education: A comparative political economy perspective on hybridity. *American Behavioral Scientist, 58*(11), 1446–1463. https://doi.org/10.1177/0002764214534672

Balduzzi, J. (1988). Peronismo, saber y poder. In A. Puiggrós, S. José, & J. Balduzzi (Eds.), *Hacia una pedagogía de la imaginación para América Latina*. (pp. 169–202). Contrapunto.

Ball, S. J., Bowe, R., & Gewirtz, S. (1996). School choice, social class and distinction: The realization of social advantage in education. *Journal of Education Policy, 11*(1), 89–112. https://doi.org/10.1080/0268093960110105

Ball, S. J., & Youdell, D. (2009). Hidden privatisation in public education. *Education Review, 21*(2), 73–83.

Banco Mundial. (2005). *Ampliar oportunidades y construir competencias para los jóvenes. Una agenda para la educación secundaria*. Banco mundial.

Banco Mundial. (2006). *Colombia: Contratación de servicios educativos* (Informe No. 31841-CO). Banco Mundial. http://datatopics.worldbank.org/hnp/files/edstats/COLesr06b.pdf

Banco Mundial. (2007). *Colombia 2006–2010: Una ventana de oportunidad. Notas de políticas presentadas por el Banco Mundial*. BIRD-Banco Mundial.

Banco Mundial. (2008). *La calidad de la educación en Colombia: Un análisis y algunas opciones para un programa de política*. Banco Mundial.

Barrera Osorio, F., Guaquetá, J., & Patrinos, H. (2012). The role and impact of public private partnerships in education. In S. Robertson, K. Mundy, & A.

Verger (Eds.), *Public private partnerships in education: New actors and modes of governance in a globalizing world*. Edward Elgar Publishing.

Barrera-Osorio, F. (2007). *The impact of private provision of public education: Empirical evidence from Bogota's concession schools* (Policy Research Working Paper Series No. 4121). The World Bank. https://ideas.repec.org/p/wbk/wbrwps/4121.html

Bartlett, Lesley. (2003). World culture or transnational project? Competing educational projects in Brazil. In K. Anderson-Levitt (Ed.), *Local meanings, global schooling: anthropology and world culture theory* (pp. 183–200). Palgrave Macmillan.

Bautista, M. (2009). La profesionalización docente en Colombia. *Revista Colombiana de Sociología, 32*(2), 111–132.

Beach, D. (2016). It's all about mechanisms—what process-tracing case studies should be tracing. *New Political Economy, 21*(5), 463–472. https://doi.org/10.1080/13563467.2015.1134466

Beach, D., & Pedersen, R. B. (2013). *Process-tracing methods: Foundations and guidelines*. University of Michigan Press.

Beckert, J. (2010). Institutional isomorphism revisited: Convergence and divergence in institutional change. *Sociological Theory, 28*(2), 150–166.

Beech, J. (2006). The institutionalization of education in Latin America. In D. P. Baker & A. W. Wiseman (Eds.), *The impact of comparative education research on institutional theory*. Emerald Group Publishing.

Beech, J. (2011). *Global panaceas, local realities: International agencies and the future of education*. Peter Lang GmbH, Internationaler Verlag der Wissenschaften.

Beech, J., & Barrenechea, I. (2011). Pro-market educational governance: Is Argentina a black swan? *Critical Studies in Education, 52*(3), 279–293.

Béland, D. (2005). Ideas and social policy: An institutionalist perspective. *Social Policy & Administration, 39*(1), 1–18. https://doi.org/10.1111/j.1467-9515.2005.00421.x

Béland, D. (2010). Reconsidering policy feedback: How policies affect politics. *Administration & Society, 42*(5), 568–590. https://doi.org/10.1177/0095399710377444

Béland, D., & Cox, R. H. (2016). Ideas as coalition magnets: Coalition building, policy entrepreneurs, and power relations. *Journal of European Public Policy, 23*(3), 428–445. https://doi.org/10.1080/13501763.2015.1115533

Béland, D., & Schlager, E. (2019). Varieties of policy feedback research: Looking backward, moving forward. *Policy Studies Journal, 47*(2), 184–205. https://doi.org/10.1111/psj.12340

Bellei, C. (2014). The 2011 Chilean student movement against neoliberal educational policies. *Studies in Higher Education, 39*(3), 426–440.

Bellei, C. (2016). Dificultades y resistencias de una reforma para des-mercantilizar la educación. *RASE: Revista de La Asociación de Sociología de La Educación, 9*(2), 232–247.

Bellei, C., & Cabalín, C. (2013). Chilean student movements: Sustained struggle to transform a market-oriented educational system. *Current Issues in Comparative Education*, 15(2), 108–123.

Bellei, C., & Pérez, C. (2016). Democratizar y tecnificar la educación. La reforma educacional de Eduardo Frei Montalva. In C. Huneeus & J. Couso (Eds.), *Eduardo Frei Montalva: Un gobierno reformista. A 50 años de la "Revolución en Libertad."* Editorial Universitaria.

Benavot, A. (1983). The rise and decline of vocational education. *Sociology of Education*, 56(2), 63–76.

Benavot, A., Archer, D., Moseley, S., Mundy, K., Phiri, F., Steer, L., & Wiking, D. (2010). International aid to education. *Comparative Education Review*, 54(1), 105–124. https://doi.org/10.1086/649052

Bengtsson, B., & Hertting, N. (2014). Generalization by mechanism: Thin rationality and ideal-type analysis in case study research. *Philosophy of the Social Sciences*, 44(6), 707–732. https://doi.org/10.1177/0048393113506495

Benveniste, L. (2002). The political structuration of assessment: Negotiating state power and legitimacy. *Comparative Education Review*, 46(1), 89–118.

Betancur, N. (2016). The "advocacy coalitions" of educational policies: Conceptual framework and its application to a country case. *Revista de Estudios Teóricos y Epistemológicos En Política Educativa*, 1(1), 150–169.

Betauncourt Mejía, G. B. (1984). *Informe del proyecto para el primer plan quinquenal de educación*. Universidad Pedagógica Nacional, Centro de Documentación Educativa.

Bianchi, S. (1992). Iglesia católica y peronismo la cuestión de la enseñanza religiosa (1946–1955). *Estudios Interdisciplinarios de América Latina y El Caribe*, 3(2), 89–103.

Biblioteca del Congreso Nacional de Chile. (1980). *Historia de la Ley. Constitución Política de la República de Chile de 1980, Artículo 19 No. 11. Libertad de Enseñanza*. Biblioteca del Congreso.

Biblioteca del Congreso Nacional de Chile. (1990). *Historia de la ley No. 18.962. Ley Orgánica Constitucional de Enseñanza*. Biblioteca del Congreso.

Biglaiser, G. (1999). Military regimes, neoliberal restructuring, and economic development: Reassessing the Chilean case. *Studies in Comparative International Development*, 34(1), 3–26.

Biglaiser, G. (2002). The internationalization of Chicago's economics in Latin America. *Economic Development and Cultural Change*, 50(2), 269–286.

Birgin, A. (1999). *La regulación del trabajo de enseñar*. Editorial Troquel.

Blat Gimeno, J. (1983). *Education in Latin America and the Caribbean: Trends and prospects 1970–2000*. UNESCO.

Blaug, M. (1967). *A cost-benefit approach to educational planning in developing countries* (No. EC157; pp. 1–44). The World Bank. http://documents.worldbank.org/curated/en/1967/12/16811060/cost-benefit-approach-educational-planning-developing-countries

202 | References

Bocanegra, H. (2008). Políticas educativas, condición social del magisterio colombiano y su constitución como organización sindical y actor político: Antecedentes históricos de la Colonia hasta 1934. *Diálogos de Saberes: Investigaciones y Ciencias Sociales, 28*, 105–120.

Bocanegra, H. (2010). Las políticas educativas y el magisterio colombiano en la década de los 80. *Diálogo de Saberes, 32*, 29–44.

Bonal, X. (2002). Plus ça change . . . : The World Bank global education policy and the post-Washington consensus. *International Studies in Sociology of Education, 12*(1), 3–22.

Boxenbaum, E., & Jonsson, S. (2008). Isomorphism, diffusion and decoupling. In R. Greenwood, C. Oliver, R. Suddaby, & K. Sahlin-Andersson (Eds.), *The SAGE handbook of organizational institutionalism* (pp. 78–98). SAGE.

Brahm, L., Cariola, P., & Silva, J. (1971). *La educación particular en Chile*. CIDE.

Braslavsky, C. (Ed.). (2001). *La educación secundaria. Cambio o inmutabilidad?: Análisis y debate de procesos europeos y latinoamericanos contemporáneos*. Santillana.

Braslavsky, C., & Cosse, G. (2006). Las actuales reformas educativas en América Latina: Cuatro actores, tres lógicas y ocho tensiones. *Revista Electrónica Iberoamericana sobre Calidad, Eficacia y Cambio en Educación, 4*(2), 1–26.

Bray, M. (1990). The economics of education. In R. M. Thomas (Ed.), *International comparative education: Practices, issues & prospects* (pp. 253–275). Pergamon.

Bruns, B., & Luque, J. (2014). *Great teachers: How to raise student learning in Latin America and the Caribbean*. World Bank Publications.

Bruter, A., Savoie, P., & Frijhoff, W. (2004). Secondary education: Institutional, cultural and social history. *Paedagogica Historica, 40*(1–2), 9–14.

Burton, G. (2011). *Policy-making and education reform in the development of Latin American social democracy: The role of the left in Brazil and Chile*. Edwin Mellen Press.

Busemeyer, M. (2009). Asset specificity, institutional complementarities and the variety of skill regimes in coordinated market economies. *Socio-Economic Review, 7*(3), 375–406.

Busemeyer, M., & Trampush, C. (2011). Comparative political science and the study of education. *British Journal of Political Science, 41*(2), 413–443.

Cacace, M., & Schmid, A. (2008). The healthcare systems of the USA and Canada: Forever on divergent paths? *Social Policy & Administration, 42*(4), 396–417.

Caiceo Escudero, J. (2012). Estado, iglesia y sistema educativo durante la república en Chile. *Revista HISTEDBR On-line, 9*(35), 3–18. https://doi.org/10.20396/rho.v9i35.8639610

Calderón, A. (1996). *Voucher program for secondary schools: The Colombian experience* (No. 16232; pp. 1–32). The World Bank. http://documentos.bancomundial.org/curated/es/1996/05/696552/voucher-program-secondary-schools-colombian-experience

Camhi, R., Troncoso, R., & Arzola, M. P. (2011). *La buena educación*. Libertad y Desarrollo.

Campbell, J. L. (1998). Institutional analysis and the role of ideas in political economy. *Theory and Society, 27*(3), 377–409.

Campbell, J. L. (2004). *Institutional change and globalization*. Princeton University Press.

Cao, C. (2011). Las reformas del gobierno y la gestión del sistema educativo: Debate parlamentario de la ley de educación nacional (2006). *Historia de La Educación—Anuario, 12*(1) http://www.scielo.org.ar/scielo.php?script=sci_abstract&pid=S2313-92772011000100005&lng=es&nrm=i-so&tlng=es

Caputo, R., & Saravia, D. (2018). *The monetary and fiscal history of Chile: 1960–2016*. Micro Finance Research Program—Becker Friedman Institute. https://www.ssrn.com/abstract=3238188

Cariola, L. (2003). Estructura y currículum de la educación media. Cambios y reformas, 1980–2000. In *Veinte años de políticas de la educación media en Chile* (pp. 27–172). IIEP-UNESCO.

Carnoy, M. (1967). Rates of return to schooling in Latin America. *The Journal of Human Resources, 2*(3), 359–374. https://doi.org/10.2307/144840

Carvajal, V., & Partarrieu, B. (2014, November 19). Sostenedores vinculados a la DC recibieron en 2013 más de $41 mil millones en subvenciones. *Centro de Investigación e Información Periodística*. http://ciperchile.cl/2014/11/19/sostenedores-vinculados-a-la-dc-recibieron-en-2013-mas-de-41-mil-millones-en-subvenciones-escolares/

Castiglioni, R. (2005). *The politics of social policy change in Chile and Uruguay: Retrenchment versus maintenance, 1973–1998*. Routledge.

Castro Aristizábal, G., Giménez, G., & Pérez, D. (2017). Desigualdades educativas en América Latina, PISA 2012: Causas de las diferencias en desempeño escolar entre los colegios públicos y privados. *Revista de Educación, 376*. https://doi.org/10.4438/1988-592X-RE-2017-376-343

Celis Muñoz, L. (2004). La reforma educacional de 1965. *Revista de Educación, 315*, 45–49.

CEPAL, & UNESCO. (1992). *Educación y conocimiento: Eje de la transformación productiva con equidad*. CEPAL.

Chabbott, C. (1998). Constructing educational consensus: International development professionals and the world conference on Education for All. *International Journal of Educational Development, 18*(3), 207–218.

Chabbott, C. (2003). *Constructing education for development: International organizations and Education for All*. Psychology Press.

Chambers-Ju, C. (2017). *Protest or politics? Varieties of teacher representation in Latin America* [Doctoral dissertation, University of California, Berkeley]. Available from ProQuest Dissertations & Theses Global (2014438135).

Chambers-Ju, C. (2021). Adjustment policies, union structures, and strategies of mobilization: Teacher politics in Mexico and Argentina. *Comparative Politics, 53*(2), 185–207. https://doi.org/10.5129/001041521X15918883398085

Chmielewski, A. K., Mundy, K., & Farrell, J. P. (2017). International educational indicators and assessments: Issues for teachers. In K. Bickmore, R. Hayhoe, C. Manion, K. Mundy, & R. Read (Eds.), *Comparative and international education: Issues for teachers* (2nd ed., pp. 361–391). University of Toronto Press.

Clavier, C. (2010). Bottom-up policy convergence: A sociology of the reception of policy transfer in public health policies in Europe. *Journal of Comparative Policy Analysis, 12*(5), 451–466.

Comisión honoraria de aseguramiento. (1987). *Congreso pedagógico. Informe sobre posibles reformas del sistema educativo.* Ministerio de Educación y Justicia.

Comisión Nacional para la Modernización de la Educación. (1994). *Los desafíos de la educación chilena frente al siglo XXI.* Editorial Universitaria.

Comisión para el Desarrollo y Uso del Sistema de Medición de la Calidad de la Educación. (2003). *Evaluación de aprendizajes para una educación de calidad.* Ministerio de Educación.

¿Cómo se realizarán las pruebas "aprender" en Argentina? (2021, June 17). *Aptus. Propuestas Educativas.* https://aptus.com.ar/como-se-realizaran-las-pruebas-aprender-en-argentina/

CONADE. (1968). *Educación, desarrollo y recursos humanos.* CONADE - Presidencia de la República.

Constitución Política de la República de Colombia, Gaceta Constitucional 116 (1991). http://www.senado.gov.co/el-senado/normatividad/constitucion-politica

Consejo Asesor Presidencial para la Calidad de la Educación. (2006). *Informe final del consejo asesor presidencial para la calidad de la educación.* Presidencia de la República.

Coombs, P. (1968). *The world educational crisis: A systems analysis.* Oxford University Press.

Coombs, P. (1970). *What is educational planning?* (No. 1; Fundamentals of Educational Planning). IIEP-UNESCO. http://unesdoc.unesco.org/images/0007/000766/076671eo.pdf

Coombs, P. (1985). *The world crisis in education: The view from the eighties* (Reprinted edition). Oxford University Press.

Corrales, J. (2004). Multiple preferences, variable strengths: The politics of education reform in Argentina. In R. R. Kaufman & J. M. Nelson (Eds.), *Crucial needs, weak incentives: Social sector reform, democratization, and globalization in Latin America* (pp. 315–349). Woodrow Wilson Center Press; Johns Hopkins University Press.

Corrales, J. (2006). Does parental participation in schools empower or strain civil society? The case of community-managed schools in Central

America. *Social Policy & Administration*, 40(4), 450–470. https://doi.org/10.1111/j.1467-9515.2006.00498.x

Cortés Conde, R. (2003). La crisis Argentina de 2001–2002. *Cuadernos de Economía*, 40(121), 762–767. https://doi.org/10.4067/S0717-68212003012100049

Corvalán, J. (2012). *La subvención escolar preferencial en Chile. Mirada a su primera fase de funcionamiento* (Serie Auditorías de Política Educativa de PREAL). PREAL.

Cowen, R. (2009). The transfer, translation and transformation of educational processes: And their shape-shifting? 45(3), 315–327.

Cox, C. (1988). *Políticas educacionales y principios culturales, Chile, 1965–1985*. Centro de Investigación y Desarrollo de la Educación.

Cox, C. (2005). Las políticas educacionales de Chile en las dos décadas del siglo XX. In *Políticas educacionales en el cambio de siglo. La reforma del sistema escolar de Chile* (pp. 19–114). Editorial Universitaria.

Cox, C. (2006). Construcción política de reformas curriculares: El caso de Chile en los noventa. *Revista de Currículum y Formación Del Profesorado*, 10(1), 24. https://revistaseug.ugr.es/index.php/profesorado/article/view/19812

Cox, C. (2010). Educational inequality in Latin America. Patterns, policies and issues. In Atewell & K. Newman (Eds.), *Growing gaps: Educational inequality around the world* (pp. 33–58). Oxford University Press.

Cox, C. (2011). Currículo escolar de Chile: Génesis, implementación y desarrollo. *Revue International de Education de Sevres*, 56, 1–9.

Cox, C., & Bravo, A. (Eds.). (1985). *Hacia la elaboración de consensos en política educacional: Actas de una discusión*. CIDE.

Crandall, R. (2001). Explicit narcotization: U.S. policy toward Colombia during the Samper administration. *Latin American Politics and Society*, 43(3), 95–120. https://doi.org/10.2307/3177145

Cucuzza, H. (Ed.). (1997). *Estudios de historia de la educación durante el primer peronismo 1943–1955*. Libros del Riel.

Czarniawska-Joerges, B., Sevon, G., & Sevón, G. (1996). *Translating organizational change*. Walter de Gruyter.

Dale, R. (2000). Globalization and education: Demonstrating a "common world educational culture" or locating a "globally structured educational agenda"? *Education Theory*, 50(4), 427–448.

Dale, R. (2012). Global education policy: Creating different constituents of interest and different modes of valorization. In A. Verger, H. K. Altinyelken, & M. Novelli (Eds.), *Global education policy and international development: New agendas, issues and policies* (pp. 287–300). Bloomsbury Academic.

Danermark, B. (2012). *Explaining society: An introduction to critical realism in the social sciences*. Taylor and Francis.

De Luca, R. (2013). La educación argentina en épocas de la última dictadura militar: Regionalización y descentralización del nivel primario de educación (1976–1983). *Contextos Educativos*, 16, 73–88.

De Moura Castro, C., Carnoy, M., & Wolff, L. (2000). *Secondary schools and the transition to work in Latin America and the Caribbean* (Sustainable Development Dept. Technical Papers Series). IADB. https://publications.iadb.org/handle/11319/4733

DeBray, E., Scott, J., Lubienski, C., & Jabbar, H. (2014). Intermediary organizations in charter school policy coalitions: Evidence from New Orleans. *Educational Policy*, 28(2), 175–206. https://doi.org/10.1177/0895904813514132

Decibe, S. (2000). Argentina: Una década sólo alcanzó para comenzar una reforma estructural de la educación. In S. Martinic & M. Pardo (Eds.), *Economía política de las reformas educativas en América Latina* (pp. 78–96). CIDE - PREAL.

Declaración de Principios del Gobierno de Chile. (1974). División de comunicación Social, Ministerio Secretaría General de Gobierno. http://www.archivochile.com/Dictadura_militar/doc_jm_gob_pino8/DMdocjm0005.pdf

Decreto Ley 3166, Diario Oficial de la República de Chile, November 17, 1980. http://bcn.cl/1uzdh

Delannoy, F. (2000). *Education reforms in Chile, 1980–98: A lesson in pragmatism*. The World Bank. http://siteresources.worldbank.org/EDUCATION/Resources/278200-1099079877269/547664-1099080026826/Ed_reforms_Chile_EN00.pdf

Díaz, E. (1986). *El clientelismo en Colombia: Un estudio exploratorio*. Ancora Editores.

Diaz-Rios, C. (2017). La traducción de las ideas globales en la gobernanza de la educación secundaria en Colombia. *Universitas Humanística*, 83, 31–56.

Diaz-Rios, C. (2019). Domestic coalitions in the variation of education privatization: An analysis of Chile, Argentina, and Colombia. *Journal of Education Policy*, 34(5), 647–668. https://doi.org/10.1080/02680939.2018.1460494

Diaz-Rios, C. (2020). The role of policy legacies in the alternative trajectories of test-based accountability. *Comparative Education Review*, 64(4), 619–641. https://doi.org/10.1086/710767

Diaz-Rios, C., & Urbano-Canal, N. (2023). The World Bank and education policy in Colombia: A comparative analysis of the effects of international organizations' learning on domestic policy. *Journal of Comparative Policy Analysis: Research and Practice*, 25(1), 1–17. https://doi.org/10.1080/13876988.2021.1991796

Diaz-Rios, C., Urbano-Canal, N., & Ortegón-Penagos, N. (2021). How do national regulations for publicly subsidized private schools work in a decentralized context? *International Journal of Educational Development*, 84, 102437. https://doi.org/10.1016/j.ijedudev.2021.102437

DiMaggio, P., & Powell, W. W. (1983). The iron cage revisited: Institutional isomorphism and collective rationality in organizational fields. *American Sociological Review*, 48(2), 147–160.

Dion, M. (2008). International organizations and social insurance in Mexico. *Global Social Policy*, 8(1), 25–44.

Directiva Presidencial sobre la Educación Nacional. (1979). *Cuaderno Del Profesor Rural*, *4*(17), Separata.

Djelic, M.-L. (2004). Social networks and country-to-country transfer: Dense and weak ties in the diffusion of knowledge. *Socio-Economic Review*, *2*(3), 341–370.

Djelic, M.-L., & Quack, S. (2008). Institutions and transnationalization. In R. Greenwood, C. Oliver, & R. Suddaby (Eds.), *The SAGE handbook of organizational institutionalism* (pp. 299–323). SAGE.

Dobbin, F., Simmons, B. A., & Garrett, G. (2007). The global diffusion of public policies: Social construction, coercion, competition, or learning? *Annual Review of Sociology*, *33*, 449–472.

Dobbins, M., & Busemeyer, M. R. (2015). Socio-economic institutions, organized interests and partisan politics: The development of vocational education in Denmark and Sweden. *Socio-Economic Review*, *13*(2), 259–284. https://doi.org/10.1093/ser/mwu002

Dolowitz, D. P., & Marsh, D. (2000). Learning from abroad: The role of policy transfer in contemporary policy-making. *Governance*, *13*(1), 5–23.

Drori, G. S., Meyer, J. W., & Hwang, H. (Eds.). (2006). *Globalization and organization: World society and organizational change*. Oxford University Press.

Duarte, J., & Restrepo, M. C. (2003). *Educación pública y clientelismo en Colombia*. Editorial Universidad de Antioquia.

Dussel, I. (2004). Los cambios curriculares en los ámbitos nacional y provinciales en la Argentina (1990–2000). In BID, Ministerio de Educación Argentina, Ministerio de Educación Chile, & Ministerio de Educación Uruguay (Eds.), *Las reformas educativas en la década de 1990*. BID.

Dussel, I. (2006). Currículum y conocimiento en la escuela media argentina. *Anales de La Educación Común*, *2*(4), 95–105.

Dussel, I., & Pineau, P. (1995). De cuando la clase obrera entro al paraíso: La educación técnica estatal en el primer peronismo. In A. Puiggrós (Ed.), *Discursos pedagógicos e imaginario social en el peronismo (1945–1955)*. Galerna.

Echavarria, J. J., Rentería, C., & Steiner, R. (2003). *Descentralización y salvamentos (bail outs) en Colombia*. Fedesarrollo. http://lacer.lacea.org/handle/11445/1066

Eckstein, M., & Noah, H. (1993). *Secondary school examinations: international perspectives on policies and practice*. Yale University Press.

Econometría Consultores. (2012). *Evaluación de la estrategia de Articulación de la Educación Media con la Educación Superior y la Formación para el Trabajo* [Informe final]. DNP.

Editorial. (1973, March 14). *El Mercurio*, 2.

Edwards, D. B. (2012). Researching international processes of education policy formation: Conceptual and Methodological Considerations. *Research in Comparative and International Education*, *7*(2), 127–145. https://doi.org/10.2304/rcie.2012.7.2.127

Edwards, D. B. (2013). International processes of education policy formation: An analytic framework and the case of plan 2021 in El Salvador. *Comparative Education Review*, *57*(1), 22–53.

Edwards, D. B. (2015). Rising from the ashes: How the global education policy of community-based management was born from El Salvador's civil war. *Globalisation, Societies and Education*, *13*(3), 411–432. https://doi.org/10.1 080/14767724.2014.980225

Edwards, D. B. (2018). *The trajectory of global education policy: Community-based management in El Salvador and the global reform agenda*. Palgrave Macmillan. http://myaccess.library.utoronto.ca/login?url=https://link.springer. com/10.1057/978-1-137-50875-1

EFA Global Monitoring Report. (2015). *Education for All 2000–2015: Achievements and challenges*. UNESCO.

Eisner, E. (1983). Educational objectives: Help or hindrance? *American Journal of Education*, *91*(4), 549–560.

Elacqua, G. (2012). The impact of school choice and public policy on segregation: Evidence from Chile. *International Journal of Educational Development*, *32*(3), 444–453.

Elacqua, G., & Santos, H. (2013). Preferencias reveladas de los proveedores de educación privada en Chile. El caso de la Ley de Subvención Preferencial. *Gestión y Política Pública*, *22*(1), 85–129.

Elkins, Z., Guzman, A., & Simmons, B. A. (2006). Competing for capital: The diffusion of bilateral investment treaties, 1960–2000. *International Organization*, *60*(4), 811–846.

Ellermann, A. (2015). Do policy legacies matter? Past and present guest worker recruitment in Germany. *Journal of Ethnic and Migration Studies*, *41*(8), 1235–1253. https://doi.org/10.1080/1369183X.2014.984667

Elster, J. (1998). A plea for mechanisms. In P. Hedström & R. Swedberg (Eds.), *Social Mechanisms: An Analytical Approach to Social Theory* (pp. 45–73). Cambridge University Press.

Equipo de Tarea para la Revisión del Sistema Nacional de Evaluación del Aprendizaje. (2015). *Informe Ejecutivo*. Ministerio de Educación.

Espínola, V., & De Moura Castro, C. (1999). *Economía política de la reforma educacional en Chile. La reforma vista por sus protagonistas*. BID.

Espinosa, J. (2010). *Análisis de las relaciones entre FECODE y el estado frente a las reformas educativas entre 1990 y 2006* [Bachelor's thesis]. Universidad del Rosario. https://doi.org/10.48713/10336_1795

Eyzaguirre, B., & Fontaine, L. (1999). ¿Qué mide realmente el SIMCE? *Estudios Públicos*, *75*, 107–161.

Falabella, A., & Ramos, C. (2019). La larga historia de las evaluaciones nacionales a nivel escolar en Chile. *Cuadernos Chilenos de Historia de La Educación*, *11*(0), 66–98.

Falleti, T. G. (2003). *Governing governors: Coalitions and Sequences of Decentraliza-tion in Argentina, Colombia, and Mexico* [Doctoral dissertation]. Northwestern University. https://www.proquest.com/docview/305315176

Falleti, T. G. (2005). A sequential theory of decentralization: Latin American cases in comparative perspective. *American Political Science Review, 99*(3), 327–346.

Falleti, T. G. (2010). *Decentralization and subnational politics in Latin America.* Cambridge University Press.

Falleti, T. G., & Lynch, J. F. (2009). Context and causal mechanisms in polit-ical analysis. *Comparative Political Studies, 42*(9), 1143–1166. https://doi.org/10.1177/0010414009331724

Fan, S., & Rao, N. (2003). *Public spending in developing countries: Trends, deter-mination, and impact* (EPTD Discussion Paper No. 99). International Food Policy Research Institute (IFPRI). https://ideas.repec.org/p/fpr/eptddp/99.html

Farrell, J. P. (1986). *The National Unified School in Allende's Chile: The role of education in the destruction of a revolution.* University of British Columbia Press: Centre for Research on Latin America and the Caribbean, York University.

Ferrer, G. (2004). *Las reformas curriculares de Perú, Colombia, Chile y Argentina: Quién responde por los resultados?* GRADE.

Figueroa, F. (2012). *Llegamos para quedarnos: Crónicas de la revuelta estudiantil* (Primera edición). LOM Ediciones.

Filmus, D., & Kaplan, C. (2012). *Educar para una sociedad más justa. Debates y desafíos de la Ley de Educación Nacional.* AGUILAR.

Finnemore, M. (1993). International organizations as teachers of norms: The United Nations Educational, Scientific, and Cutural Organization and Science Policy. *International Organization, 47*(4), 565–597. https://doi.org/10.1017/S0020818300028101

Finnemore, M. (1996). Norms, culture, and world politics: Insights from sociol-ogy's institutionalism. *International Organization, 50*(2), 325–347.

Finnemore, M. (1998). International norm dynamics and political change. *International Organization, 52*(4), 887–917.

Fischer, K. B. (1979). *Political ideology and educational reform in Chile, 1964–1976.* UCLA Latin American Center, University of California.

Forero, D. (2021, November 15). A evaluar para avanzar. *Portafolio.* https://www.por-tafolio.co/a-evaluar-para-avanzar-opinion-de-david-fernando-forero-558537

Forero, R., González, L., & Gómez, V. M. (2007). Formación de élites y educación superior: Meritocracia y reclutamiento en el Departamento Nacional de Planeación. *Revista Colombiana de Sociología, 28,* 161–180.

Friedman, M. (1955). The role of government in education. In R. A. Solo (Ed.), *Economics and the public interest* (p. 124). Rutgers University Press.

Fundación de Investigaciones Económicas Latinoamericas (FIEL). (2000). *Una educación para el siglo XXI. Propuesta de Reforma*. FIEL-CEP.

Fundación de Investigaciones Económicas Latinoamericas (FIEL), & Consejo Empresarial Argentino, C. (1993). *Descentralización de la escuela primaria y media: Una propuesta de reforma*. FIEL-CEA.

Galarza, D., Suasnábar, C., & Merodo, A. (2007). Los organismos intergubernamentales e internacionales. In C. Suasnábar, D. Galarza, & M. Palamidessi (Eds.), *Educación, conocimiento y política: Argentina, 1983–2003* (pp. 67–97). Ediciones Manantial.

Gallart, M. A., Miranda, M., Peirano, C., & Sevilla, M. (2003). *Tendencias de la educación técnica en América Latina. Estudios de caso en Argentina y Chile*. IIPE-UNESCO. http://unesdoc.unesco.org/images/0013/001360/136066s.pdf

Ganimian, A. J. (2016). Why do some school-based management reforms survive while others are reversed? The cases of Honduras and Guatemala. *International Journal of Educational Development, 47*(Complete), 33–46.

García, M., Espinosa, J., Jiménez, F., & Parra, J. (2013). *Separados y desiguales. Educación y clases sociales en Colombia*. DeJusticia.

Garcia-Huidobro, J. (2007). Desigualdad educativa y segmentación del sistema escolar. Consideraciones a partir del caso chileno. *Pensamiento Educativo, 40*(1), 65–85.

García-Huidobro, J. (2009). ¿Qué nos dejó la movilización de los pingüinos? *Nomadias, 9*, 205–207.

Garretón, M. (1995). *Hacia una nueva era política. Estudios sobre las democratizaciones*. Fondo de Cultura Economica.

Gauri, V. (1998). *School choice in Chile: Two decades of educational reform*. University of Pittsburgh Press.

Gehring, H., & Koch, M. C. (2016). *On the path from failed state to OECD member? Colombia's way towards a brighter future* (International Reports 1; The Globalisation of Terrorism, pp. 95–110). Konrad Adenauer Stiftung. https://www.jstor.org/stable/resrep10109.9

Gerring, J. (2008). The mechanismic worldview: Thinking inside the box. *British Journal of Political Science, 38*(1), 161–179. https://doi.org/10.1017/S0007123408000082

Gershberg, A. I. (2012). Understanding and improving accountability in education: A conceptual framework and guideposts from three decentralization reform experiences in Latin America. *World Development, 40*(5), 1024–1041.

Gershberg, A. I., Meade, B., & Andersson, S. (2009). Providing better education services to the poor: Accountability and context in the case of Guatemalan decentralization. *International Journal of Educational Development, 29*(3), 187–200. https://doi.org/10.1016/j.ijedudev.2008.08.002

Gill, C. (1966). *Education and social change in Chile*. US Department of Health, Education and Welfare.

Giovine, R. (2003). *Sindicalismo y gobierno* (Proyecto Sindicalismo Docente y Reforma Educativa En América Latina). FLACSO-PREAL.

González, H. (1976). Tecnología educativa: ¿Hacia una "optimización" del proceso de subdesarrollo? *Revista de Tecnología Educativa*, 2(4), 445–480.

González, J. (1971). Nueva estructura del sistema educativo Argentino. El nivel intermedio. In A. Villaverde (Ed.), *La Escuela Intermedia en Debate*. Humanitas.

González, P., Mizala, A., & Romaguera, P. (2002). Recursos diferenciados a la educación subvencionada en Chile. In *Documentos de Trabajo* (No. 150; Documentos de Trabajo). Centro de Economía Aplicada, Universidad de Chile. https://ideas.repec.org/p/edj/ceauch/150.html

Gordon, L. (2005). School choice and the social market in New Zealand: Education reform in an era of increasing inequality. *Educational Administration Abstracts*, 40(1), 0143.

Griffiths, T., & Arnove, R. (2015). World culture in the capitalist world-system in transition. *Globalisation, Societies and Education*, 13(1), 88–108.

Grindle, M. S. (2004). *Despite the odds: The contentious politics of education reform*. Princeton University Press.

Gropello, E. D. (2006). *Meeting the challenges of secondary education in Latin America and East Asia: Improving efficiency and resource mobilization*. The World Bank.

Grupo de Investigación sobre Pruebas Masivas en Colombia. (2008). El surgimiento del servicio nacional de pruebas del ICFES en las voces de sus protagonistas. *Magistro*, 2(3), 115–134.

Gvirtz, S. (2002). Curricular reforms in Latin America with special emphasis on the Argentine case. *Comparative Education*, 38(4), 453–469.

Gvirtz, S. (Ed.). (2008). *Equidad y niveles intermedios de gobierno en los sistemas educativos*. Aique.

Gvirtz, S., Larripa, S., & Oelsner, V. (2006). Problemas técnicos y usos políticos de las evaluaciones nacionales en el sistema educativo argentino. *Archivos Analíticos de Políticas Educativas*, 14(18), 1–22.

Gysling, J. (2005). Reforma curricular: Itinerario de una transformación cultural. In C. Cox (Ed.), *Políticas educacionales en el cambio de siglo. La reforma del sistema escolar de Chile* (pp. 213–252). Estudios.

Haddad, W. (1987). *Diversified secondary curriculum projects: A review of World Bank experience 1963–1979*. Discussion Paper. The World Bank. http://www-wds.worldbank.org/external/default/WDSContentServer/WDSP/IB/2013/06/10/000333037_20130610121836/Rendered/PDF/EDT570Box377330experience0196301979.pdf

Hall, P. A. (2010). Historical institutionalism in rationalist and sociological perspective. In J. Mahoney & K. Thelen (Eds.), *Explaining institutional change: Ambiguity, agency, and power*. Cambridge University Press.

Hanson, M. (1986). *Educational reform and administrative development: The cases of Colombia and Venezuela.* Hoover Press.

Hanson, M. (1996). Educational change under autocratic and democratic governments: The case of Argentina. *Comparative Education, 32*(3), 303–318.

Hedström, P. (2010). Causal mechanisms in the social sciences. 36, 49–67.

Heiss, C., & Navia, P. (2007). You win some, you lose some: Constitutional reforms in Chile's transition to democracy. *Latin American Politics & Society, 49*(3), 163–190.

Helg, A. (1987). *La educación en Colombia, 1918–1957: Una historia social, económica y política.* CEREC.

Helg, A. (1998). La educación en Colombia 1958–1980. In A. Tirado, J. Jaramillo, & J. Melo (Eds.), *Nueva Historia de Colombia: Vol. IV* (pp. 135–158). Planeta.

Henao, D. (1956). Veintiún Planes de Bachillerato. *Revista Javeriana, 45*(221), 14.

Hennessy, A. (2014). The sources of pension reforms in Western Europe: Domestic factors, Policy diffusion, or common shock? *International Interactions, 40*(4), 477–505.

Herbst, J. (2006). *School Choice and School Governance.* Palgrave Macmillan.

Heyneman, S. (2003). Positioning secondary-school education in developing countries: Expansion and curriculum by Donald B. Holsinger and Richard N. Cowell—Review. *Comparative Education Review, 47*(4), 506–508.

Heyneman, S. (2012). When models became monopolies: The making of education policy at the World Bank. In A. W. Wiseman & C. S. Collins (Eds.), *Education strategy in the developing world: Revising the World Bank's education policy* (pp. 43–62). Emerald Group Publishing.

Himmel, E. (1997). Impacto social de los sistemas de evaluación del rendimiento escolar: El caso de Chile. In B. Alvarez & M. Ruiz-Casares (Eds.), *Evaluación y reforma educativa: Opciones de política* (pp. 125–157). PREAL.

Hira, A. (1998). *Ideas and economic policy in Latin America: Regional, national, and organizational case studies.* Praeger.

Hsieh, C. T., & Urquiola, M. (2006). The effects of generalized school choice on achievement and stratification: Evidence from Chile's voucher program. *Journal of Public Economics, 90*(8–9), 1477–1503.

Hunter, W. (1997). Continuity or change? Civil-military relations in democratic Argentina, Chile, and Peru. *Political Science Quarterly, 112*(3), 453–475. https://doi.org/10.2307/2657566

IADB. (1999). *New school system program: Reform of education management and participation* (Loan Proposal CO-0142). IADB. http://www.iadb.org/en/projects/project-description-title,1303.html?id=co0142#doc

ILO, & UNESCO. (1963). *Some aspects of the role of manpower planning in economic planning.* UNESCO. http://unesdoc.unesco.org/images/0015/001576/157635eb.pdf

Informe sobre Escuela Nacional Unificada (ENU), Febrero 1973. (2014). *Cuadernos Chilenos de historia de la educación*, 2, 154–172.

Jakobi, A. P., Martens, K., & Wolf, K. D. (2009). *Education in political science: Discovering a neglected field*. Routledge.

Jofré, G. (1988). *El sistema de subvenciones en educación: La experiencia chilena*. Centro de Estudios Públicos.

Jordana, J., & Levi-Faur, D. (2005). The diffusion of regulatory capitalism in Latin America: Sectoral and national channels in the making of a new order. *Annals of the American Academy of Political and Social Science*, 598, 102–124.

Jules, T. D. (2012). *Neither world polity nor local or national societies: Regionalization in the Global South—the Caribbean community*. Peter Lang.

Jungck, S., & Kajornsin, B. (2003). "Thai wisdom" and GloCalization: Negotiating the global and the local in Thailand's national education reform. In K. Anderson-Levitt (Ed.), *Local meanings, global schooling: Anthropology and world culture theory* (pp. 27–50). Palgrave Macmillan.

Kaasch, A. (2013). Contesting contestation: Global social policy prescriptions on pensions and health systems. *Global Social Policy*, 13(1), 45–65.

Kamens, D. H. (1996). Worldwide patterns in academic secondary education curricula. *Comparative Education Review*, 40(2), 116–138.

Kamens, D. H., & Benavot, A. (2011). National, regional and international learning assessments: Trends among developing countries, 1960–2009. *Globalisation, Societies and Education*, 9(2), 285–300.

Kamens, D. H., & McNeely, C. L. (2010). Globalization and the growth of international educational testing and national assessment. *Comparative Education Review*, 54(1), 5–25.

Kerckhoff, A. C. (2001). Education and social stratification processes in comparative perspective. *Sociology of Education*, 74, 3–18.

King, E., Rawlings, L., Gutierrez, M., Pardo, C., & Torres, C. (1997). *Colombia's targeted education voucher program: Features, coverage, and participation* (Working Paper No. 3; Series on Impact Evaluation of Education Reforms, Development Economics Research Group, p. 43). World Bank.

King, G., Keohane, R. O., & Verba, S. (1994). *Designing social inquiry: Scientific inference in qualitative research*. Princeton University Press.

Kisilevsky, M. (1990). *La relación entre la nación y las provincias a partir de la transferencia de servicios nacionales a las provincias del año 1978*. Consejo Federal de Inversiones.

Larroulet, C., & Montt, P. (2010). Políticas educativas de largo plazo y acuerdo amplio en educación: El caso Chileno. In S. Martinic & G. Elacqua (Eds.), *¿Fin de ciclo?: Cambios en la gobernanza del sistema educativo* (pp. 19–53). UNESCO-Pontificia Universidad Católica de Chile.

Latorre, C., Nuñez, I., González, L., & Hevia, R. (1991). *La municipalización de la educación: Una mirada desde los administradores del sistema*. PIIE.

Leal Vásquez, B. (2014). Una mirada sobre la evolución histórica de la inspección escolar en Chile. *Revista de Derecho Público Iberoamericano, 5*(1), 87–110.

Lebot, I. (1971). *El sistema escolar colombiano.* DANE.

Lemaitre María José, J., Cerri, M., Cox, C., & Cristóbal, R. (2005). La reforma de la educación media. In *Políticas educacionales en el cambio de siglo. La reforma del sistema escolar de Chile* (pp. 317–418). Estudios.

Lemus Barahona, L. N. (2021). De la unidad popular al gremialismo: Paradojas del sindicalismo docente en la Guatemala del ajuste estructural. *Revista Latinoamericana de Antropología del Trabajo, 5*(10), 1–30. https://www.redalyc.org/journal/6680/668070945016/html/

Levitsky, S., & Murillo, M. V. (2008). Argentina: From Kirchner to Kirchner. *Journal of Democracy, 19*(2), 16–30.

Levy, D. (2006). How private higher education's growth challenges the new institutionalism. In H.-D. Meyer & B. Rowan (Eds.), *The new institutionalism in education* (pp. 143–162). SUNY Press.

Lewy, A. (1977). *Planning of School Curriculum* (No. 23; Fundamentals of Educational Planning). IIEP-UNESCO. http://unesdoc.unesco.org/images/0007/000771/077171eo.pdf

Ley 43, Diario Oficial de la República de Colombia 34.471, December 11, 1975. http://www.mineducacion.gov.co/1621/articles-104796_archivo_pdf.pdf

Ley 60, Diario Oficial de la República de Colombia 40.987, August 12, 1993. http://www.mineducacion.gov.co/1759/articles-85889_archivo_pdf.pdf

Ley 715, Diario Oficial de La República de Colombia, 44.654, December 21, 2001. http://www.secretariasenado.gov.co/senado/basedoc/ley_0715_2001.html

Ley 20.248 Subvención escolar Preferencial, Diario Oficial de la República de Chile, February 1, 2008. https://www.bcn.cl/leychile/navegar?idNorma=269001

Ley 20.845 Inclusión escolar, Diario Oficial de la República de Chile, May 29, 2015. https://www.bcn.cl/leychile/navegar?idNorma=1078172

Ley de financiamiento educativo No. 26075, Diario de Asuntos del Honorable Congreso de la República de Argentina, December 21, 2005. http://infoleg.mecon.gov.ar/infolegInternet/anexos/110000-114999/112976/norma.htm

Ley Federal de Educación No. 24.195, Diario de Asuntos del Honorable Congreso de la República de Argentina, April 14, 1993. http://infoleg.mecon.gov.ar/infolegInternet/anexos/110000-114999/112976/norma.htm

Ley General de Educación 115, Diario Oficial de la República de Colombia 41.214, February 8, 1994. https://www.mineducacion.gov.co/1621/articles-85906_archivo_pdf.pdf

Ley 16.617 Escala de Categorias, Grados y Sueldos de los Funcionarios, January 27, 1967. https://www.bcn.cl/leychile/navegar?idNorma=28580

Ley No. 17.398 Estatuto de Garantías Constitucionales, Diario Oficial de la República de Chile, December 30, 1970. http://www.salvador-allende.cl/Unidad_Popular/Estatuto%20de%20garantias%20democraticas.pdf

Ley No. 18.962, Orgánica Constitucional de Enseñanza, Diario Oficial de la República de Chile, March 10, 1990. http://bcn.cl/1uzde

Ley No. 20.529, Diario Oficial de la República de Chile, August 11, 2011. http://bcn.cl/1uv5c

Leyton, M. (1970). *La experiencia chilena. La reforma educacional 1965–1970.* CPEIP.

Leyton, M. (2010). Los inicios del Centro de Perfeccionamiento, Experimentación e Investigaciones Pedagógicas (CPEIP). *Docencia, 40,* 85–91.

Lijphart, A. (1969). Consociational democracy. *World Politics, 21*(2), 207–225. https://doi.org/10.2307/2009820

Llerena, J. (1998). *Libertad de enseñanza y defensa de la escuela pública.* Fundación BankBoston.

Locke, R. M., & Thelen, K. (1995). Apples and oranges revisited: Contextualized comparisons and the study of comparative labor politics. *Politics & Society, 23*(3), 337–367.

López Díez, J. C. (2017). 1992: El año en que se nos fueron las luces. *Revista Gestión & Región, 23*(Jan–Jun), 9–24.

López, J. O. (2002). Gabriel Betancur Mejía el gran reformador de la educación Colombiana en el Siglo XX. *Revista Historia de la Educación Colombiana, 5*(5), 15.

López, M. M. (2001). *Pluralidad en la manera de hacer política educativa: Reforma de descentralización de la educación.* Fundación Corona.

López, M. M. (2008). *Sindicatos docentes y reformas educativas en América Latina. Colombia.* Fundación Konrad Adenauer. http://www.kas.de/wf/doc/6792-1442-4-30.pdf

Lowden, P. (2004). Education reform in Colombia: The elusive quest for effectiveness. In R. R. Kaufman & J. M. Nelson (Eds.), *Crucial needs, weak incentives: Social sector reform, democratization, and globalization in Latin America* (pp. 315–349). Woodrow Wilson Center Press; Johns Hopkins University Press.

Mahoney, J. (2000). Path dependence in historical sociology. *Theory and Society, 29*(4), 507–548. https://doi.org/10.1023/A:1007113830879

Mahoney, J. (2001). Beyond correlational analysis: Recent innovations in theory and method. *Sociological Forum, 16*(3), 575–593.

Mahoney, J., & Rueschemeyer, D. (2003). *Comparative historical analysis in the social sciences.* Cambridge University Press.

Mahoney, J., & Thelen, K. (2010). *Explaining institutional change: Ambiguity, agency, and power.* Cambridge University Press.

Maroy, C. (2009). Convergences and hybridization of educational policies around 'post-bureaucratic' models of regulation. *Compare, 39*(1), 71–84.

Maroy, C. (2012). Towards post-bureaucratic modes of governance: A European perspective. In *World yearbook of education 2012.* https://doi.org/10.4324/9780203137628-12

Maroy, C., Pons, X., & Dupuy, C. (2017). Vernacular globalisations: Neo-statist accountability policies in France and Quebec education. *Journal of Education Policy*, *32*(1), 100–122.

Martinez, A., Ramírez, C. E. N., & Villarraga, J. O. C. (2011). *Currículo y modernización: Cuatro décadas de educación en Colombia.* Cooperativa Editorial Magisterio.

Maurer, M. (2012). Structural elaboration of technical and vocational education and training systems in developing countries: The cases of Sri Lanka and Bangladesh. *Comparative Education*, *48*(4), 487–503. https://doi.org/10.10 80/03050068.2012.702011

McGinn, N., & Welsh, T. (1999). *Decentralization of education: Why, when, what and how?* (No. 64; Fundamentals of Educational Planning). UNESCO. http://unesdoc.unesco.org/images/0012/001202/120275e.pdf

McNeely, C. L. (1995). Prescribing national education policies: The role of international organizations. *Comparative Education Review*, *39*(4), 483–507.

Melo, L. (2005). Impacto de la descentralización fiscal sobre la educación pública colombiana. *Borradores de Economía*, *350*.

Melo, M. (2004). Institutional choice and the diffusion of policy paradigms: Brazil and the second wave of pension reform. *International Political Science Review*, *25*(3), 320–341.

Meyer, H.-D., & Benavot, A. (Eds.). (2013). *PISA, power, and policy: The emergence of global educational governance.* Symposium Books.

Meyer, H.-D., & Rowan, B. (2006a). Institutional analysis and the study of education. In *The New Institutionalism in Education* (pp. 1–13). SUNY Press.

Meyer, H.-D., & Rowan, B. (2006b). *The new institutionalism in education.* SUNY Press.

Meyer, J. W. (1977). The world educational revolution, 1950–1970. *Sociology of Education*, *50*(4), 242–258.

Meyer, J. W. (2000). Globalization: Sources and effects on national states and societies. *International Sociology*, *15*(2), 233–248. https://doi.org/10.1177/ 0268580900015002006

Meyer, J. W. (2010). World society, institutional theories, and the actor. *Annual Review of Sociology*, *36*, 1–20. https://doi.org/10.1146/annurev.soc.012809. 102506

Meyer, J. W., & Hannan, M. T. (1979). *National development and the world system: Educational, economic, and political change, 1950–1970.* University of Chicago Press.

Meyer, J. W., & Rowan, B. (1977). Institutionalized organizations: Formal structure as myth and ceremony. *The American Journal of Sociology*, *83*(2), 340–363.

Meyer, J. W., & Rowan, B. (1978). The structure of educational organizations. In M. W. Meyer (Ed.), *Environments and organizations.* Jossey-Bass.

Meyer, J. W., & Rowan, B. (1991). Institutionalized organizations: Formal structure as myth and ceremony. In W. R. Scott & J. W. Meyer (Eds.), *Organizational Environments: Ritual and Rationality* (Updated ed.). SAGE.

Miñana, C. (2010). Políticas neoliberales y neoinstitucionales en un marco constitucional adverso. Reformas educativas en Colombia 1991–2010. *Propuesta Educativa, 19*(2), 37–52.

Mineduc anuncia eliminación de nueve especialidades en liceos técnicos. (2013, August 25). *La Tercera*. https://www.latercera.com/noticia/mineduc-anuncia-eliminacion-de-nueve-especialidades-en-liceos-tecnicos/

Ministerio de Educación Nacional. (1957). *Informe del proyecto para el I plan quinquenal.* MEN.

Ministerio de Educación Nacional. (1971). *La Educación ante el Congreso.* MEN.

Ministerio de Educación Nacional. (1974). *Programa Colombia PNUD-UNESCO.* MEN.

Ministerio de Educación Nacional. (1976). *Política educativa nacional: Reforma educativa, 1976.* MEN.

Ministerio de Educación Nacional. (2000). *Educación para todos: Evaluación en el año 2000. Informe nacional—Colombia.* UNESCO.

Ministerio de Educación Nacional. (2006). *Estándares básicos de competencias en lenguaje, matemáticas, ciencias y ciudadanas.* MEN. https://www.mineducacion.gov.co/1621/articles-340021_recurso_1.pdf

Ministerio de Educación Nacional, & Departamento Nacional de Planeación. (1991). *Plan de Apertura Educativa 1991–1994.* MEN-DNP.

Ministerio de Educación y Cultura. (1969). *La reforma educativa. Bases.* Ministerio de Educación y Cultura.

Minteguiaga, A. (2009). *Lo público de la educación pública: La reforma educativa de los noventa en Argentina.* FLACSO.

Mintrom, M., & Vergari, S. (1996). Advocacy coalitions, policy entrepreneurs, and policy change. *Policy Studies Journal, 24*(3), 420–434.

Mizala, A. (2007). *La economía política de la reforma educacional en Chile* (No. 36; Serie Estudios Socio-Económicos). CIEPLAN.

Mizala, A., & Romaguera, P. (2000). *Sistemas de Incentivos en la Educación y la experiencia del SNED en Chile.* Universidad de Chile. http://ww2.educarchile.cl/UserFiles/P0001%5CFile%5Csistemas%20de%20incentivos%20SNED.pdf

Mizala, A., & Torche, F. (2012). Bringing the schools back in: The stratification of educational achievement in the Chilean voucher system. *International Journal of Educational Development, 32*(1), 132–144.

Moe, T. M., & Wiborg, S. (Eds.). (2017). *The comparative politics of education: Teachers unions and education systems around the world.* Cambridge University Press.

Molano, M. (2011). Carlos Eduardo Vasco Uribe. Biographical history of a Colombian intellectual: A look at the curriculum reforms in the country. *Revista Colombiana de Educación*, *61*, 161–198.

Molina Rodríguez, C. A. (2012). FUN-Ascún, 1958–1968, un acontecimiento en el sistema universitario colombiano: Gremios, políticas y estado. *Aula: Revista de pedagogía de la Universidad de Salamanca*, *18*, 229–247. https://doi.org/10.14201/8883

Montanari, I. (2013). Social service decline and convergence: How does health-care fare? *Journal of European Social Policy*, *23*(1), 102–116.

Montecinos, V., & Markoff, J. (2010). *Economists in the Americas*. Edward Elgar Publishing.

Montenegro, A. (1995). *An incomplete reform: The case of Colombia* (Human Capital Development & Operations Policy. Working Papers.). The World Bank.

Morales Ulloa, R., & Magalhães, A. M. (2013). Visiones, tensiones y resultados. La nueva gobernanza de la educación en Honduras. *Education Policy Analysis Archives*, *21*, 3. https://doi.org/10.14507/epaa.v21n3.2013

Morduchowicz, A. (2000). *Estudio sobre la educación privada en la Argentina: Historia, regulaciones y asignación de recursos públicos*. Fundación Gobierno y Sociedad.

Morduchowicz, A. (2002). *El financiamiento educativo en Argentina*. IIEP-UNESCO Buenos Aires.

Moschetti, M. C., & Verger, A. (2020). Opting for private education: Public subsidy programs and school choice in disadvantaged contexts. *Educational Policy*, *34*(1), 65–90. https://doi.org/10.1177/0895904819881151

Movimiento Estudiantil Reconoció Tardío Retiro del Consejo Asesor. (2007, December 6). *El Mercurio*. https://www.emol.com/noticias/nacional/2006/12/07/238283/movimiento-estudiantil-reconocio-tardio-retiro-del-consejo-asesor.html

Munck, R. (1985). The "modern" military dictatorship in Latin America. *Latin American Perspectives*, *12*(4), 41–74.

Mundy, K., & Menashy, F. (2014). The World Bank and private provision of schooling: A look through the lens of sociological theories of organizational hypocrisy. *Comparative Education Review*, *58*(3), 401–427.

Mundy, K., & Verger, A. (2015). The World Bank and the global governance of education in a changing world order. *International Journal of Educational Development*, *40*, 9–18. https://doi.org/10.1016/j.ijedudev.2014.11.021

Muñoz, G., & Weinstein, J. (2019). Redefining the rules of the game for subsidized private education. In C. Ornelas (Ed.), *Politics of education in Latin America* (pp. 72–100). Brill.

Muñoz, V. (2011). *El derecho a la educación: Una mirada comparativa*. UNESCO. http://portal.unesco.org/geography/es/files/15017/13230888961Estudio-comparativo-

UNESCO-Vernor-Munoz.pdf/Estudio-comparativo-UNESCO-Vernor-Munoz.pdf

Murillo, F. J., & Garrido, C. M. (2017). Segregación social en las escuelas públicas y privadas en América Latina. *Educação & Sociedade, 38,* 727–750. https://doi.org/10.1590/ES0101-73302017167714

Murillo, M. V. (2013). Cambio y continuidad del sindicalismo en democracia. *Revista SAAP, 7*(2), 339–348.

Nardacchione, G. (2011a). La reforma educativa bajo el gobierno de Menem: Una intervención técnico-experta frente a una resistencia político sindical. In G. Vommaro & S. Morresi (Eds.), *Saber lo que se hace. Expertos y política en Argentina.* Prometeo - Universidad General Sarmiento.

Nardacchione, G. (2011b). Las maniobras gubernamentales frente a la protesta: El conflicto educativo de 1992. *Trabajo y Sociedad, 15*(17), 139–154.

Nardacchione, G. (2012). Las crisis provinciales y la nacionalización docente (1993–1997). *Revista Pilquen, 15,* 16.

Nardacchione, G. (2015). Crisis y protestas durante la provincialización del sistema educativo (1993–1997). *Cuadernos de la Facultad de Humanidades y Ciencias Sociales—Universidad de Jujuy, 47,* 24.

Narodowski, M. (2008). School Choice and Quasi-State Monopoly Education Systems in Latin America: The case of Argentina. In M. Forsey, S. Davies, & G. Walford (Eds.), *The globalisation of school choice?* (pp. 131–144). Symposium Books.

Narodowski, M., & Andrada, M. (2001). The privatization of education in Argentina. *Journal of Education Policy, 16*(6), 585–595.

Narodowski, M., & Andrada, M. (2004). Monopolio estatal y descentralización educativa: Una exploración en América Latina. *Revista de Educación, 333,* 197–222.

Narodowski, M., Catri, G., & Nistal, M. (2023). *Lo prometido es deuda educativa. La impotencia para alcanzar el 6 por ciento del PBI para educacion.* Observatorio Argentinos por la Educación. https://argentinosporlaeducacion.org/wp-content/uploads/2023/02/Lo-prometido-es-deuda-educativa.-La-impotencia-para-alcanzar-el-6-por-ciento-del-PBI-para-educacion.pdf

Narodowski, M., & Nores, M. (2002). Socio-economic segregation with (without) competitive education policies. A comparative analysis of Argentina and Chile. *Comparative Education, 38*(4), 429–451. https://www.jstor.org/stable/3099545

Natalucci, A. (2018). Entre la democratización y la república. Revisitando el ciclo de movilización en el último gobierno kirchnerista (Argentina, 2012–2015). *Estudios de Derecho, 75*(166), 30–50. https://doi.org/10.17533/udea.esde.v75n166a02

Neidhöfer, G., Serrano, J., & Gasparini, L. (2018). Educational inequality and intergenerational mobility in Latin America: A new database. *Journal of*

Development Economics, 134, 329–349. https://doi.org/10.1016/j.jdeveco. 2018.05.016

Newland, C. (1994). The estado docente and its expansion: Spanish American elementary education, 1900–1950. *Journal of Latin American Studies, 26*(2), 449–467.

Nores, M. (2002). *El sistema nacional de evaluación de la Calidad—SINEC.* Fundación Gobierno y Sociedad.

Novaro, M. (2002). *El derrumbe político: En el ocaso de la convertibilidad.* Grupo Editorial Norma.

Nuñez, I. (1989). *La Descentralización y las Reformas Educacionales en Chile. 1940–1973.* PIIE.

Nuñez, I. (1990). *Reformas educacionales e identidad de los docentes. Chile, 1960–1973.* PIIE.

Nuñez, I. (1993). *Planificación de a educación en países de América Latina en proceso de descentralización. El caso de Chile.* IIEP-UNESCO.

Nuñez, I. (2003). *La ENU entre dos siglos. Ensayo histórico sobre la ENU.* Centro de Investigaciones Diego Barrios-LOM.

Objetivo Nacional del Gobierno de Chile. (1975). División de comunicación Social, Ministerio Secretaría General de Gobierno.

Observatorio Argentinos por la Educación. (2022). *¿Cómo son los 16? Trayectorias escolares desiguales en la Argentina* (p. 12). Observatorio Argentinos por la Educación. https://argentinosporlaeducacion.org/wp-content/uploads/2022/05/ ¿Quiénes-son-los-16-Trayectorias-escolares-desiguales-en-la-Argentina_-1.pdf

OEA. (1963). *Tercera reunión Interamericana de ministros de educación. Acta final (Third Interamerican meeting of ministers of education. Final report).* Union Panamericana.

OECD. (2004). *Revisión de políticas nacionales de educación Chile.* OECD. http:// www.oecd-ilibrary.org/education/revision-de-politicas-nacionales-de-edu-cacion-chile_9789264021020-es;jsessionid=24b1cacf2ak3c.x-oecd-live-03

Oelsner, V. (2012). *Usos políticos de los sistemas de evaluación de la educación.* Eae Editorial Academia Española.

Oliver, C. (1991). Strategic responses to institutional processes. *The Academy of Management Review, 16*(1), 145–179.

Oliveros, A. (1978). Educación y política en Iberoamérica. *Revista de Política Internacional, 157*, 63–76.

Orloff, A. S. (1993). *Politics of pensions: A comparative analysis of Britain, Canada, and the United States, 1880–1940.* University of Wisconsin Pres.

Ortega, J. R. (1999). Seguimiento y perspectivas laborales de una muestra de bachilleres egresados de colegios oficiales y privados de Santa Fe de Bogotá entre 1993 y 1997. In SED (Ed.), *Intermedia. Encuentro Internacional de Educacion Media* (pp. 157–163). SED.

Ortiz Cáceres, I. (2012). En torno a la validez del Sistema de Medición de la Calidad de la Educación en Chile. *Estudios Pedagógicos (Valdivia)*, *38*(2), 355–373. https://doi.org/10.4067/S0718-07052012000200022

Ortiz, J. G. (2012). *El peso de la tradición: Evaluación educativa y cultura en Colombia 1900–1968* [Doctoral dissertation, Universidad Nacional de Colombia]. Repositorio institucional. https://repositorio.unal.edu.co/handle/unal/9363

Ostrom, E. (2015). *Governing the commons: The evolution of institutions for collective action*. Cambridge University Press. http://myaccess.library.uto-ronto.ca/login?url=https://doi-org.myaccess.library.utoronto.ca/10.1017/CBO9781316423936

Owen-Smith, J., & Powell, W. W. (2008). Networks and institutions. In R. Greenwood, C. Oliver, R. Suddaby, & K. Sahlin-Andersson (Eds.), *The SAGE handbook of organizational institutionalism* (pp. 594–621). SAGE.

Pache, A.-C., & Santos, F. (2010). When worlds collide: The internal dynamics of organizational Responses to conflicting institutional demands. *The Academy of Management Review*, *35*(3), 455–476. https://doi.org/10.5465/AMR.2010.51142368

Pacheco, J. (2013). Attitudinal policy feedback and public opinion: The impact of smoking bans on attitudes towards smokers, secondhand smoke, and antismoking policies. *Public Opinion Quarterly*, *77*(3), 714–734. https://doi.org/10.1093/poq/nft027

Palamidessi, M., & Feldman, D. (1994). Viejos y nuevos planes: El curriculum como texto normativo. *Propuesta Educativa*, *5*(11).

Parcerisa, L., & Falabella, A. (2017). The consolidation of the evaluative state through accountability policies: Trajectory, enactment and tensions in the Chilean education system. *Education Policy Analysis Archives*, *25*, 89. https://doi.org/10.14507/epaa.25.3177

Parra, J. D. (2017). El reto de la descentralización educativa: Reflexiones desde la mirada de actores nacionales y subnacionales en el caso del departamento del Atlántico. *Papel Político*, *22*(2), Article 2. https://doi.org/10.11144/Javeriana.papo22-2.rder

Patrinos, H. (2015). School autonomy and accountability in Thailand: Does the gap between policy intent and implementation matter? *Prospects*, *45*(4), 429–445.

Patrinos, H., Barrera-Osorio, F., & Guáqueta, J. (2009). *The role and impact of public-private partnerships in Education*. The World Bank.

Patrinos, H., & Lakshmanan, D. (1997). *Decentralization of education. Demand-side financing* (Directions in Development). The World Bank.

Peña, M. (2008). El examen de Estado de educación media en Colombia. Evolución y tensiones que han marcado su desarrollo. *Revista Internacional Magisterio*, *6*(36), 3–6.

Perassi, Z. (2017). El Sistema Nacional de Evaluación en la República Argentina. Políticas y concepciones. *Contextos de Educación*, *22*, 1–9.

Pérez Villamil, X. (2014, June 13). Los privados se agrupan y arman frente gremial para resistir la reforma de Eyzaguirre. *El Mostrador*. https://www.elmostrador.cl/noticias/pais/2014/06/13/los-privados-se-agrupan-y-arman-frente-gremial-para-resistir-la-reforma-de-eyzaguirre/

Persiste la incertidumbre alrededor del futuro de las Pruebas Saber. (2018). *Semana*. https://www.semana.com/educacion/articulo/no-se-realizara-la-prueba-saber-para-los-cursos-3-5-y-9/562181

Petitti, E. (2013). La educación estatal en Argentina durante el peronismo. El caso de la provincia de Buenos Aires (1946–1955). *Trabajos y Comunicaciones*, *2*(39).

Phillips, D., & Ochs, K. (2003). Processes of policy borrowing in education: Some explanatory and analytical devices. *Comparative Education*, *39*(4), 451–461.

Picazo, M. I. (2013). *Las políticas escolares de la Concertación durante la transición democrática*. Universidad Diego Portales.

Pierson, P. (2000a). Increasing returns, path dependence, and the study of politics. *The American Political Science Review*, *94*(2), 251–267.

Pierson, P. (2000b). The limits of design: Explaining institutional origins and change. *Governance*, *13*(4), 475–499. https://doi.org/10.1111/0952-1895.00142

Pierson, P. (2004). *Politics in time: History, institutions, and social analysis*. Princeton University Press.

PIIE. (1984). *Las transformaciones de la educación bajo el régimen militar* (Vol. 1). Programa Interdisciplinario de Investigaciones en Educación.

PIIE. (1989). *Educación y transición democrática: Propuestas de políticas educativas*. Programa Interdisciplinario de Investigaciones en Educación.

Pineau, P. (2003). La vergüenza de haber sido y el dolor de ya no ser: Los avatares de la educación técnica entre 1955 y 1983. In A. Puiggrós (Ed.), *Dictaduras y utopías en la historia reciente de la educación argentina (1955–1983)*. Historia de la Educación en la Argentina (Vol. 8, pp. 379–400). Galerna.

Pineau, P. (2004). Peronism, secondary schooling and work (Argentina, 1944–1955): An approach through cultural hierarchies. *Paedagogica Historica*, *40*(1–2), 183–191.

Planes y Programas de Educación Media. (1985). *Revista de Educación*, *4*.

PNUD. (1998). *Informe de desarrollo humano en Chile. Las paradojas de la dodernización*. PNUD.

Pollitt, C. (2007). Decentralization: A central concept in contemporary public management. In E. Ferlie, L. E. Lynn, & C. Pollitt (Eds.), *The Oxford handbook of public management* (pp. 371–397). Oxford University Press.

Pollitt, C., & Bouckaert, G. (2011). *Public management reform: A comparative analysis—new public management, governance, and the neo-Weberian state* (3rd ed.). Oxford University Press.

Pozo, J., Martín, E., & Pérez, M. P. (2002). La educación secundaria para todos. Una nueva frontera educativa. In UNESCO/OREALC (Ed.), *¿Qué educación secundaria para el siglo XXI?* UNESCO/OREALC.

Prawda, J. (1993). Educational decentralization in Latin America: Lessons learned. *International Journal of Educational Development, 13*(3), 253–264.

Presidencia de la República. (1999). *Plan nacional de desarrollo. Bases 1998–2002. Cambio para Construir la Paz.* DNP.

Pribble, J. (2006). Women and welfare: The politics of coping with new social risks in Chile and Uruguay. *Latin American Research Review, 41*(2), 84–111.

Pribble, J. (2013). *Welfare and party politics in Latin America.* Cambridge University Press.

Prieto, A. (1983). *La modernización educacional.* Universidad Católica de Chile.

Prieto, P. C. (1996). Los procesos de gestión educativa en el marco de la descentralización. *Revista Colombiana de Educación, 33,* Article 33. https://doi.org/10.17227/01203916.5398

Propuesta de Trabajo de Estudiantes Secundarios de la R.M. (2005). http://www.opech.cl/movisociales/propuestas/propuesta_secundarios_rm_05.pdf

Proyecto de ley 44, *Ley General de Educación,* Gaceta Oficial del Congreso 7, 1992.

Proyecto de ley 715, Normas Orgánicas en Materia de recursos y Competencias, Gaceta del Congreso 294, 2000. http://www.alcaldiabogota.gov.co/sisjur/normas/Norma1.jsp?i=7147

Psacharopoulos, G. (1972). Rates of return to investment in education around the world. *Comparative Education Review, 16*(1), 54–67.

Psacharopoulos, G. (1981a). Returns to education: An updated international comparison. *Comparative Education, 17*(3), 321–341.

Psacharopoulos, G. (1981b). The World Bank in the world of education: Some policy changes and some remnants. *Comparative Education, 17*(2), 141–146.

Psacharopoulos, G. (1986). The planning of education: Where do we stand? *Comparative Education Review, 30*(4), 560–573.

Psacharopoulos, G. (2006). World Bank policy on education: A personal account. *International Journal of Educational Development, 26*(3), 329–338.

Psacharopoulos, G., & Hinchliffe, K. (1973). *Returns to education: An international comparison.* Jossey-Bass.

Psacharopoulos, G., & Loxley, W. A. (1985). *Diversified secondary education and development: Evidence from Colombia and Tanzania.* Johns Hopkins University Press/The World Bank.

Puiggrós, A. (2003). *Qué pasó en la educación Argentina: Breve historia desde la conquista hasta el presente.* Editorial Galerna.

Puiggrós, A., & Gagliano, R. (2004). *La fábrica del conocimiento: Los Saberes Socialmente Productivos en América Latina.* Homo Sapiens.

Queisser, M. (2000). Pension reform and international organizations: From conflict to convergence. *International Social Security Review, 53*(2), 31–45.

Ragin, C. C. (1989). *The comparative method: Moving beyond qualitative and quantitative strategies.* University of California Press.

Rambla, X. (2014). A complex web of education policy borrowing and transfer: Education for All and the Plan for the Development of Education in Brazil. *Comparative Education, 50*(4), 417–432. https://doi.org/10.1080/03 050068.2014.907644

Ramírez, F. (2012). The world society perspective: Concepts, assumptions, and strategies. *Comparative Education, 48*(4), 423–439.

Ramírez, F., & Boli, J. (1987). The political construction of mass schooling: European origins and worldwide institutionalization. *Sociology of Education, 60*(1), 2–17.

Rees, C. J. (2010). Perspectives on decentralization and local governance in developing and transitional countries. *International Journal of Public Administration, 33*(12–13), 581–587.

Rein, M. (1998). *Politics and education in Argentina, 1946–1962.* M. E. Sharpe.

Repetto, F. (2001). *Transferencia educativa hacia las provincias en los años 90: Un estudio comparado.* Centro de Estudios para el Desarrollo Institucional-Fundación Gobierno y Sociedad-Fundación Grupo Sophia.

República de Colombia. (2006). Resolución 5360. *Diario Oficial de La República de Colombia, 46.481.*

Resnik, J. (2006). International organizations, the "education-economic growth" black box, and the development of world education culture, *50*(2), 173–195.

Resolución No. 84 Lineamientos políticos y estratégicos de la educación secundaria obligatoria, Consejo Federal de Educación de Argentina, October 9, 2009. http://portal.educacion.gov.ar/files/2009/12/84-09-anexo01.pdf

Riddell, A., & Niño-Zarazúa, M. (2016). The effectiveness of foreign aid to education. *International Journal of Educational Development, 48,* 23–36. https://doi.org/10.1016/j.ijedudev.2015.11.013

Rifo, M. (2013). Movimiento estudiantil, sistema educativo y crisis política actual en Chile. *Polis (Santiago), 12*(36), 223–240. https://doi.org/10.4067/ S0718-65682013000300010

Rivas, A. (2004). *Gobernar la educación: Estudio comparado sobre el poder y la educación en las provincias argentinas.* Ediciones Granica S.A.

Rivas, A. (2010). *Radiografía de la educación argentina.* CIPPEC-Arcor-Noble/ Clarin.

Rivas, A. (2015). *América Latina después de PISA: lecciones aprendidas de la educación en siete países 2000–2015.* Fundación CIPPEC.

Rivas, A., & Dborkin, D. (2018). *¿Qué cambió en el financiamiento educativo en Argentina?* (Documento de Trabajo No. 162, p. 57). Grupo Compromiso con el Financiamiento Educativo.

Rizvi, F., & Lingard, B. (2010). *Globalizing education policy.* Routledge.

Robertson, S. (2005). Re-imagining and rescripting the future of education: Global knowledge economy discourses and the challenge to education systems. *Comparative Education, 41*(2), 151–170. https://doi.org/10.2307/30044529

Robertson, S., & Dale, R. (2015). Towards a 'critical cultural political economy' account of the globalising of education. *13*(1), 149–170. https://doi.org/10.1080/14767724.2014.967502

Robertson, S., Mundy, K., & Verger, A. (2012). *Public private partnerships in education: New actors and modes of governance in a globalizing world.* Edward Elgar Publishing.

Rodriguez, A. (2001). Educación y constitución diez años después. *Revista Foro, 41,* 67–76.

Rodríguez, L. (2008). La escuela intermedia revisitada: racionalización y revisión curricular en la provincia de Buenos Aires durante la última dictadura militar. *Trabajos y Comunicaciones, 34,* 35–61.

Rodríguez, L. (2013). Los católicos desarrollistas en Argentina. Educación y planeamiento en los años de 1960. *Diálogos, 17*(1), 155–164.

Rodríguez, L. (2015). Iglesia y educación en la Argentina durante la segunda mitad del siglo XX. *Cadernos de história da Educação, 14*(1), 263–278.

Rondinelli, D. A. (1981). Government decentralization in comparative perspective theory and practice in developing countries. *International Review of Administrative Sciences, 47*(2), 133–145. https://doi.org/10.1177/002085238004700205

Rondinelli, D. A., & Nellis, J. (1986). Assessing decentralization policies in developing countries: The case for cautious optimism. *Development Policy Review, 4*(1), 3–23.

Rosenau, J. (2004). Strong demand, huge supply: Governance in an emerging epoch. In I. Bache & M. Flinders (Eds.), *Multi-level governance.* Oxford University Press.

Ruiz Berrio, J. (2006). Las reformas históricas de la enseñanza secundaria en España. *Encounters on Education, 7*(Fall), 95–112.

Ruiz, M. C., & Schoo, S. (2014). La obligatoriedad de la educación secundaria en América Latina. Convergencias y divergencias en cinco países. *Foro de Educación, 12*(16), 71–98. https://doi.org/10.14516/fde.2014.012.016.003

Ruiz Schneider, C. (1994). Educación, desarrollo y modernización. *Revista de Sociología, 9,* 83–93.

Sahlin, K. (2008). Circulating ideas: Imitation, translation and editing. In R. Greenwood, C. Oliver, & R. Suddaby (Eds.), *The SAGE handbook of organizational institutionalism* (pp. 218–242). SAGE.

Saldarriaga, O. (2003). *Del oficio de Maestro. Prácticas y teorías de la pedagogía moderna en Colombia.* Magisterio.

Salonia, A. (1981). *Educación y Política Nacional.* Docencia.

Samoff, J. (2007). Institutionalizing international influence. In R. Arnove & C. A. Torres (Eds.), *Comparative Education: The dialectic of the global and the local* (pp. 47–78). Rowman & Littlefield Publishers.

Sarmiento, A. (1998). La descentralización de los servicios de educación y salud en Colombia. In E. di Gropello & R. Cominetti (Eds.), *La descentralización de la educación y la salud: Un análisis comparativo de la experiencia latinoamericana* (pp. 165–186). CEPAL.

Schiefelbein, E. (1974). *Diagnóstico del sistema educacional chileno en 1964*. Universidad de Chile—Departamento de Economía.

Schiefelbein, E. (1976). Reforma de la educación chilena en 1964–1970. *Educación hoy: perspectivas Latinoamericanas*, 6(33–34), 3–24.

Schiefelbein, E. (2003). From screening to improving quality: The case of Latin America. *Assessment in Education: Principles, Policy & Practice*, 10(2), 141–159.

Schiefelbein, E., & Davis, R. (1974). *Development of educational planning models and application in the Chilean school reform*. Lexington Books.

Schneider, B. R. (2022). Teacher unions, political machines, and the thorny politics of education reform in Latin America. *Politics & Society*, 50(1), 84–116. https://doi.org/10.1177/00323292211002788

Schneider, B. R., Estarellas, P. C., & Bruns, B. (2019). The politics of transforming education in Ecuador: Confrontation and continuity, 2006–2017. *Comparative Education Review*, 63(2), 259–280. https://doi.org/10.1086/702609

Schneider, M., Elacqua, G., & Buckley, J. (2006). School choice in Chile: Is it class or the classroom? *Journal of Policy Analysis and Management*, 25(3), 577–601. https://doi.org/10.1002/pam.20192

Schriewer, J. (2003). Globalisation in education: Process and discourse. *Policy Futures in Education*, 1(2), 271–283. https://doi.org/10.2304/pfie.2003.1.2.6

Schriewer, J. (2012). Editorial: Meaning constellations in the world society. *Comparative Education*, 48(4), 411–422.

Schulte, B. (2012). World culture with Chinese characteristics: When global models go native. *Comparative Education*, 48(4), 473–486. https://doi.org/10.1080/03050068.2012.726064

Schwinn, T. (2012). Globalisation and regional variety: Problems of theorisation. *Comparative Education*, 48(4), 525–543. https://doi.org/10.1080/03050068.2012.728048

Scott, W. R., Meyer, J. W., Strang, D., & Creighton, A. (1994). Bureaucratization without centralization. Changes in the organizational system of U.S. public education, 1940–1980. In *Institutional environments and organizations: Structural complexity and individualism*. SAGE.

Serrano, S., Ponce de León, M., & Rengifo, F. (2012). *Historia de la educación Chilena (1810–2010)* (Vol. 2). Taurus.

Serrano, S., Ponce de León, M., & Rengifo, F. (2018). *Historia de la educación Chilena (1810–2010)* (Vol. 3). Taurus.

Sevilla, M. (2012). *Educación técnica profesional en Chile. Antecedentes y claves de diagnóstico*. Mineduc.

Sigafoos, R. A. (1962). Argentina, economic barometer of the Alliance for Progress. *California Management Review, 5*(1), 43–56.

Silova, I. (2005). Traveling policies: Hijacked in Central Asia. *European Educational Research Journal, 4*(1), 50–59.

Silova, I. (2009). Global norms and local politics: Uses and abuses of education gender quotas in Tajikistan. *Globalisation, Societies and Education, 7*(3), 357–376.

Silova, I. (2013). Contested meanings of educational borrowing. In G. Steiner-Khamsi & F. Waldow (Eds.), *World yearbook of education 2012: Policy borrowing and lending in education* (pp. 229–245). Routledge.

Silva, B. (2009). *La Revolucion Pinguina y el Cambio Cultural en Chile*. CLACSO. http://rgdoi.net/10.13140/RG.2.2.33550.72001

Simmons, B. A., Dobbin, F., & Garrett, G. (2008). *The global diffusion of markets and democracy*. Cambridge University Press.

Sironi, M. (2018). Democratizar el gobierno de la educación. Historia reciente y coyunturas críticas del subsistema educativo en Santa Fe. *Revista de la Escuela de Ciencias de la Educación, 2*(12). https://doi.org/10.35305/rece.v2i12.312

Skocpol, T. (1995). *Protecting soldiers and mothers: The political origins of social policy in the United States*. Belknap Press.

Smith, W. C. (2014). The global transformation toward testing for accountability. *Education Policy Analysis Archives, 22*(116), 1–34. https://doi.org/10.14507/epaa.v22.1571

Southwell, M. (1997). Algunas características de la formación docente en la historia educativa reciente. El legado del espiritualismo y el tecnocratismo (1955–76). In M. Amuchástegui & A. Puiggrós (Eds.), *Dictaduras y utopías en la historia reciente de la educación argentina (1955–1983)* (pp. 105–155). Editorial Galerna.

Southwell, M., & Manzione, M. A. (2011). Elevo a la superioridad: Un estado de la cuestión sobre la historia de los inspectores en Argentina. *Historia de La Educación—Anuario, 12*(1). http://www.scielo.org.ar/scielo.php?script=sci_arttext&pid=S2313-92772011000100008&lng=es&nrm=iso&tlng=es

Spreen, C. (2004). Appropriating borrowed policies: Outcomes-based education in South Africa. In G. Steiner-Khamsi (Ed.), *The global politics of educational borrowing and lending* (pp. 101–113). Teachers College Press.

Staricco, J. I. (2017). Putting culture in its place? A critical engagement with cultural political economy. *New Political Economy, 22*(3), 328–341. https://doi.org/10.1080/13563467.2016.1195345

Steiner-Khamsi, G. (2004). *The global politics of educational borrowing and lending.* Teachers College Press.

Steiner-Khamsi, G. (2012). The global/local nexus in comparative policy studies: Analysing the triple bonus system in Mongolia over time. *Comparative Education, 48*(4), 455–471.

Steiner-Khamsi, G. (2014). Cross-national policy borrowing: Understanding reception and translation. *Asia Pacific Journal of Education, 34*(2), 153–167.

Steiner-Khamsi, G., Silova, I., & Johnson, E. M. (2006). Neoliberalism liberally applied. In *World yearbook of education 2006: Education, research and policy: Steering the knowledge-based economy* (pp. 217–245). Routledge.

Steiner-Khamsi, G., & Waldow, F. (Eds.). (2013). *World yearbook of education 2012: Policy borrowing and lending in education.* Routledge.

Suasnábar, C. (2014). *Intelectuales, exilios y educación. Producción intelectual e innovaciones teóricas en educación durante la última dictadura.* Prohistoria Ediciones.

Suasnábar, C. (2018). Campo académico y políticas educativas en la historia reciente: A propósito del 30 aniversario de la revista Propuesta Educativa. *Propuesta Educativa, 2*(50), 39–72.

Suasnábar, C., & Merodo, A. (2007). Los centros de investigación privados. In M. Palamidessi, C. Suasnábar, & D. Galarza (Eds.), *Educación, conocimiento y política: Argentina, 1983–2003* (pp. 149–160). FLACSO—Manantial.

Sugiyama, N. B. (2011). The diffusion of conditional cash transfer programs in the Americas. *Global Social Policy, 11*(2–3), 250–278. https://doi.org/10.1177/1468018111421295

Superintendencia de Educación. (1966). *Sinopsis del Programa de Educación 1965–1970 (versión preliminar).* Ministerio de Educación Pública.

Taffet, J. (2012). *Foreign aid as foreign policy: The Alliance for Progress in Latin America.* Routledge.

Takayama, K. (2012). Exploring the interweaving of contrary currents: Transnational policy enactment and path-dependent policy implementation in Australia and Japan. *Comparative Education, 48*(4), 505–523. https://doi.org/10.1080/03050068.2012.721631

Takayama, K. (2013). Untangling the global-distant-local knot: The politics of national academic achievement testing in Japan. *Journal of Education Policy, 28*(5), 657–675. https://doi.org/10.1080/02680939.2012.758833

Tarazona, A. (2015). Educación, reformas y movimientos universitarios en Colombia: Apuestas y frustraciones por un proyecto modernizador en el siglo XX. *Revista de Estudios Sociales, 53,* 102–111.

Tedesco, J. C. (1980). La educación en Argentina (1930–1955). In J. Schvarzer (Ed.), *Civiles y militares: Las diez presidencias: Historia integral Argentina.* Centro Editor de América Latina.

Tedesco, J. C. (1986). *Educación y sociedad en la Argentina: (1880–1945)*. Siglo Veintiuno de Argentina Editores.

Tedesco, J. C. (1989). The role of the state in education. *Prospects, 19*(72), 455–478.

Tedesco, J. C., & Aguerrondo, I. (2005). *Cómo superar la desigualdad y la fragmentación del sistema educativo argentino?* IIPE-Unesco, Sede Regional Buenos Aires.

Tedesco, J. C., Braslavsky, C., & Carciofi, R. (1983). *El Proyecto Educativo Autoritario: Argentina, 1976–1982*. FLACSO.

Tedesco, J. C., & Tenti, E. (2004). La reforma educativa en la Argentina. Semejanzas y particularidades. In BID, Ministerio de Educación Argentina, Ministerio de Educación Chile, & Ministerio de Educación Uruguay (Eds.), *Las Reformas Educativas en la Década de 1990* (pp. 21–72). BID.

Teichman, J. A. (2001). *The politics of freeing markets in Latin America: Chile, Argentina, and Mexico*. University of North Carolina Press.

Teichman, J. A. (2004). The World Bank and policy reform in Mexico and Argentina. *Latin American Politics and Society, 46*(1), 39–74.

Téllez Rico, S. M., & Ramírez Guevara, R. (2016). Una relectura de estadísticas sobre la educación superior en Colombia. *Revista de Investigaciones UCM, 16*(28), Article 28. https://doi.org/10.22383/ri.v16i2.76

Tenti, E. (2003). *Educación media para todos. Los desafíos de la democratización del acceso*. Altamira.

Terigi, F. (2008). Los cambios en el formato de la escuela secundaria argentina: Por qué son necesarios, por qué son tan difíciles. *Propuesta Educativa, 15*(29), 63–71.

The World Bank. (1971). *Education sector working paper*. The World Bank. http://www-wds.worldbank.org/external/default/WDSContentServer/WDSP/IB/2012/10/01/000386194_20121001020449/Rendered/PDF/729770WP0 0PUBL0ector0working0papers.pdf

The World Bank. (1974). *Education sector working paper*. The World Bank. http://www-wds.worldbank.org/external/default/WDSContentServer/WDSP/IB/19 74/12/01/000009265_3961003052734/Rendered/PDF/multi_page.pdf

The World Bank. (1980). *Education sector policy paper*. The World Bank. http://documents.worldbank.org/curated/en/366981468182955979/Education-sector-policy

The World Bank. (1982). *Colombia—subsector project for rural basic education* (No. 3896; pp. 1–71). The World Bank. http://documents.worldbank.org/curated/en/1982/07/725715/colombia-subsector-project-rural-basic-education

The World Bank. (1988). *Colombia—second subsector project for primary education* (No. 7265; pp. 1–101). The World Bank. http://documents.worldbank.org/curated/en/1988/11/738861/colombia-second-subsector-project-primary-education

The World Bank. (1994a). *Argentina—decentralization and improvement of secondary education project* (No. 12993; pp. 1–223). The World Bank. http://documents.worldbank.org/curated/en/1994/08/698074/argentina-decentralization-improvement-secondary-education-project

The World Bank. (1994b). *Conformed copy—L3683—secondary education project—loan agreement.* The World Bank. http://documents.worldbank.org/curated/en/1994/08/5079560/conformed-copy-l3683-secondary-education-project-loan-agreement

The World Bank. (1995). *Priorities and strategies for education. A World Bank review.* The World Bank. http://documents.worldbank.org/curated/en/1995/08/697136/priorities-strategies-education-world-bank-review

The World Bank. (1999). *Educational change in Latin America and the Caribbean* (Human Development Network). The World Bank. http://documents.worldbank.org/curated/en/1999/01/437909/educational-change-latin-america-caribbean

The World Bank. (2001a). *Implementation completion report on a loan for secondary education—Chile.* The World Bank. http://www.worldbank.org/en/country/chile/projects/operational-documents?docty_exact=Implementation+Completion+and+Results+Report&qterm=&lang_exact=English

The World Bank. (2001b). *Secondary education project. Implementation Completion Report No. 22017.* The World Bank. http://documents.worldbank.org/curated/en/653081474631358049/Colombia-Secondary-Education

The World Bank. (2004). *World development report 2004: Making services work for poor people.* World Bank Publications. http://web.worldbank.org/WBSITE/EXTERNAL/EXTDEC/EXTRESEARCH/EXTWDRS/0,,contentMDK:23062333~pagePK:478093~piPK:477627~theSitePK:477624,00.html

The World Bank. (2007). *Chile-Institutional Design for an Effective Education Quality Assurance.* The World Bank. http://documents.worldbank.org/curated/en/2007/08/8420003/chile-institutional-design-effective-education-quality-assurance

The World Bank. (2008). *Colombia—structural fiscal adjustment; And first, second, and third programmatic fiscal and institutional adjustment loan projects* (No. 43357; pp. 1–74). The World Bank. http://documents.worldbank.org/curated/en/2008/04/9581944/colombia-structural-fiscal-adjustment-project-first-programmatic-fiscal-institutional-adjustment-loan-second-programmatic-fiscal-institutional-structural-adjustment-loan-third-programmatic-fiscal-institutional-structural-adjustment-loan-colombia-structural-fiscal-adjustment-project

The World Bank. (2011). *Learning for all: Investing in people's knowledge and skills to promote development.* The World Bank.

Thelen, K. (2004). *How institutions evolve: The political economy of skills in Germany, Britain, the United States, and Japan.* Cambridge University Press.

Thelen, K. (2014). *Varieties of liberalization and the new politics of social solidarity.* Cambridge University Press.

Tiramonti, G. (2001). *Sindicalismo docente y reforma educativa en la América Latina de los '90* (No. 19). PREAL. http://www.ub.edu/obipd/docs/sindicalismo_docente_tiramontig.pdf

Tiramonti, G. (2003). Estado, educación y sociedad civil: Una relación cambiante. In E. Tenti (Ed.), *Educación media para todos. Los desafíos de la democratización del acceso* (pp. 85–104). Fundación OSDE—IIPE UNESCO Buenos Aires—Altamira.

Tolofari, S. (2005). New Public Management and Education. *Policy Futures in Education, 3*(1), 75–89. https://doi.org/10.2304/pfie.2005.3.1.11

Torres, A. (2011). La crisis colombiana de finales del siglo XX: ¿Un choque real o financiero? *Perfil de Coyuntura Económica, 18,* 79–96.

Torres, G. (2014). Catholic church, education and laicity in Argentinean history. *História Da Educação, 18*(44), 165–185. https://doi.org/10.1590/S2236-34592014000300010

Torres, M. (2006). *Fernando Fajnzylber: Una visión renovadora del desarrollo en América Latina.* CEPAL.

Trumbull, G. (2012). *Strength in numbers: The political power of weak interests.* Harvard University Press.

UNESCO. (1971). *World survey of education. Educational policy, legislation, and administration.* UNESCO.

UNESCO. (1989). *Major Project of Education in Latin America and the Caribbean. Progress Made, Obstacles Encountered and Priorities for the Future.* UNESCO. http://unesdoc.unesco.org/images/0008/000827/082721eb.pdf

UNESCO. (2000). *Dakar framework for education. Education for All: Meeting our collective commitments.* UNESCO. http://www.unesco.at/bildung/basis dokumente/dakar_aktionsplan.pdf

UNESCO. (2005a). *Decentralization in education: National policies and practices.* UNESCO.

UNESCO. (2005b). *Secondary education reform. Towards a convergence of knowledge acquisition and skills development* (ED-2005/WS/37). UNESCO. http://unesdoc.unesco.org/images/0014/001424/142463e.pdf

UNESCO/OREALC. (2002). *¿Qué educación secundaria para el siglo XXI?* UNESCO/OREALC.

UNESCO/OREALC. (2013). *Situación educativa para América Latina y el Caribe: Hacia una educación de calidad para todos al 2015.* UNESCO/OREALC. http://www.unesco.org/new/fileadmin/MULTIMEDIA/FIELD/Santiago/images/SITIED-espanol.pdf

UNICEF. (2014). *La voz del movimiento estudiantil 2011: Educación pública, gratuita y de calidad*. UNICEF. https://www.unicef.org/chile/media/1446/file/la_voz_del_movimiento_estudiantil_2011.pdf

Unidad Popular. (1969). *Programa básico de gobierno de la Unidad Popular*. Unidad Popular. http://www.memoriachilena.cl/602/w3-article-7738.html

Uribe, C. (2014). The positioning of economic rationality in Colombia. *Bulletin of Latin American Research, 33*(1), 46–59.

Valenzuela, A. (1995). The military in power: The consolidation of one-man rule. In P. W. Drake & I. Jaksic (Eds.), *The struggle for democracy in Chile* (pp. 21–72). University of Nebraska Press.

Van Gelderen, A. (1963). *La contribución de la iniciativa privada a la educación en los países latinoamericanos*. Unión Panamericana.

Vargas Castro, T. R. (2020). *The political origins of education decentralization in Latin America* [University of Minnesota]. https://conservancy.umn.edu/bitstream/handle/11299/216812/VargasCastro_umn_0130E_21641.pdf?sequence=1&isAllowed=y

Vargas Castro, T. R. (2022). Decentralization as a political weapon: Education politics in El Salvador and Paraguay. *Comparative Politics, 55*(1), 23–45. https://doi.org/10.5129/001041522X16382201562711

Vassiliades, A. (2006). Enseñar durante la última dictadura militar en la provincia de Buenos Aires: Acerca de nuevos (y perdurables) sentidos para la escuela y los docentes. *Historia de La Educación - Anuario, 7*, 263–290.

Vegas, E., & Petrow, J. (2008). *Raising student learning in Latin America: The challenge for the 21st century*. World Bank Publications.

Velasco Peña, G. C. (2018). Las reformas al currículo oficial: La configuración de Las ciencias sociales escolares en la educación secundaria en Colombia (1939–1974). *UNIPLURIVERSIDAD, 18*(1), 78–93. https://doi.org/10.17533/udea.unipluri.18.1.08

Vélez, E. (1996). La regulación de precios y 1 calidad de la educación privada en Colombia: Posibilidades y limitaciones. *Borradores de Economía, 63*.

Vélez, E., & Psacharopoulos, G. (1987). The external efficiency of diversified secondary schools in Colombia. *Economics of Education Review, 6*(2), 99–110.

Vera, R., & Nuñez, I. (1983). *Elementos para repensar el cambio del sistema educativo en un proceso de democratización*. PIIE, Academia de Humanismo Cristiano.

Vergara, C. H., & Simpson, M. (2001). Evaluación de la descentralización municipal en Colombia. Estudio general sobre antecedentes, diseño, avances y resultados sector educativo. In *Archivos de EconomÃa* (No. 002627; Archivos de Economía). Departamento Nacional de Planeación. https://ideas.repec.org/p/col/000118/002627.html

Verger, A. (2014). New public management as a global education policy: Its adoption and re-contextualization in a Southern European setting. *Critical Studies in Education, 55*(3), 253–271.

Verger, A., Fontdevila, C., & Zancajo, A. (2016). *The privatization of education: A political economy of global education reform*. Teachers College Press.

Verger, A., Fontdevila, C., & Zancajo, A. (2017). Multiple paths towards education privatization in a globalizing world: A cultural political economy review. *Journal of Education Policy, 32*(6), 757–787.

Verger, A., Moschetti, M., & Fontdevila, C. (2017). *La Privatización Educativa en América Latina*. Universidad Autónoma de Barcelona—Education International.

Verger, A., Parcerisa, L., & Fontdevila, C. (2019). The growth and spread of large-scale assessments and test-based accountabilities: A political sociology of global education reforms. *Educational Review, 71*(1), 5–30. https://doi.org/10.1080/00131911.2019.1522045

Villa, L., & Duarte, J. (2002). Nuevas experiencias de gestión escolar pública en Colombia. In *Educación privada y política pública en América Latina* (pp. 371–413). PREAL.

Villalobos, C. (2016). El campo educativo en Chile post-dictadura (1990–2013). Continuidad y ruptura en la implementación del neoliberalismo en educación. In A. Pinol (Ed.), *Democracia versus neoliberalismo. 25 años de neoliberalismo en Chile* (pp. 160–178). Fundación Rosa Luxemburgo-ICAL.

Villalobos, C. (2019). *Los conflictos sociales en el campo educativo en el Chile Post-Dictadura (1990–2014). Análisis de su evolución, principales características y factores relacionados* [Universidad de Chile]. https://repositorio.uchile.cl/handle/2250/173279

Villaverde, A. (Ed.). (1971). *La escuela intermedia en debate*. Humanitas.

Vior, S., & Rodríguez, L. (2012). La privatización de la educación en Argentina: Un proceso largo de naturalización y expansión. *Pro-Posições, 23*(2(68)), 91–104.

Walford, G. (1996). *School Choice and the Quasi-market*. Symposium Books Ltd.

Weinberg, D. (1967). *La enseñanza técnica industrial en la Argentina, 1936–1965*. Instituto Torcuato di Tella.

Weinberg, G. (1982). *El descontento y la promesa. Ensayos de educación y cultura*. Editorial de Belgrano.

Weir, M., & Skocpol, T. (1985). State structures and the possibilities for "Keynesian" responses to the Great Depression in Sweden, Britain, and the United States. In P. B. Evans, D. Rueschemeyer, & T. Skocpol (Eds.), *Bringing the state back in* (pp. 107–164). Cambridge University Press.

Weyland, K. (2005). Theories of policy diffusion: Lessons from Latin American pension reform. *World Politics, 57*(2), 262–295.

White, J. (2011). *The invention of the secondary curriculum*. Springer.

Whitty, G. (1997). Creating quasi-markets in education: A review of recent research on parental choice and school autonomy in three countries. *Review of Research in Education, 22*, 3–47. JSTOR. https://doi.org/10.2307/1167373

Wiesner, E. (1995). *La descentralización, el gasto social y la gobernabilidad en Colombia* (Archivos de Economía). DNP-ANIF.

Williams, J. H., & Cummings, W. K. (2005). *Policy-making for education reform in developing countries: Contexts and processes.* R&L Education.

Windzio, M., Sackmann, R., & Martens, K. (2005). *Types of governance in education: A quantitative analysis* (TransState Working Papers No. 25). University of Bremen. https://www.econstor.eu/bitstream/10419/28275/1/501321926.PDF

Wiseman, A. W. (2010). The uses of evidence for educational policymaking: Global contexts and international trends. *Review of Research in Education, 34*(1), 1–24. https://doi.org/10.3102/0091732X09350472

Wiseman, A. W., & Baker, D. P. (2006). The symbiotic relationship between empirical comparative research on education and neo-institutional theory. In D. P. Baker & A. W. Wiseman (Eds.), *The Impact of Comparative Education Research on Institutional Theory* (pp. 1–26). Emerald Group Publishing.

Woessmann, L. (2007). International evidence on school competition, autonomy, and accountability: A review. *Peabody Journal of Education, 82*(2–3), 473–497.

Woessmann, L., Luedemann, E., & Schuetz, G. (2009). *School accountability, autonomy and choice around the world.* Edward Elgar Publishing.

Wolf, A. (2002). *Does education matter? Myths about education and economic growth.* Penguin.

Wolff, L., & De Moura Castro, C. (2000). *Secondary education in Latin America and the Caribbean: The challenge of growth and reform* (373 C28–dc21; Sustainable Development Dept Technical Papers Series). IADB. https://publications.iadb.org/handle/11319/4732?locale-attribute=en

Zelaznik, J. (2014). El comportamiento legislativo del Peronismo durante el Menemismo y el Kirchnerismo: Cambio de agenda y adaptación partidaria. *Desarrollo Económico, 54*(213), 203–230.

Zuñiga, M. (1979). Neutralidad ideológica o determinación social en la planeación educativa? *Revista Colombiana de Educación, 3.*

Index

Note: References in *italic* and **bold** refer to figures and tables.

accountability ideas, **169**; in Argentina, 155, 156, **156**; in Chilean education, **137**, **146**; in Colombia, **160**, **168**. *See also* test-based accountability
ACES. *See* Asamblea Nacional de Estudiantes Secundarios
active-state advocates, 126, 128; in Argentina, 108–11, 113, 127, 149–54; in Chile, 92–96, 101; Church and, conflicts between, 105–8; conversion of, 92–96; divisions within, 99; from FLACSO and UNESCO, 134; market-oriented advocates and, 108–1, 148
active-state ideas: accommodation of, 96–103; in Argentina's secondary education, 147–57; Argentinean overlapping of, 104–16; with centralized curriculum, 113; Chilean, 89–103, 126; curriculum recommendations, 26, 96, 103, 104, 113, 127; decentralized curriculum, 113; education policy, influenced, 88; education provision, decentralization of, 86; evaluation recommendations, 101, 128; to

governance of secondary education, 85–88; provision recommendations, 26; sequential translation of, 89–103

Alessandri, Jorge, 50
Alfonsín, Raúl, 108
Allende, Salvador, 56, 93, 179; Escuela Nacional Unificada, 51–53; left party coalition, 53; reform by policy area, MEP-inspired, **54**; supporters of, 90
Alliance for Progress, 44–45, 57
ANDERCOP. *See* Asociación Nacional de Rectores de Colegios Privados
anthropological scholarship, 15–17
Argentina, 3; active-state and statist advocates in, 149–52; active-state recommendations, 180; authoritarian regime, 105–8; avoidance and compromise of MEP ideas, 62–65; centralized inspection system, 68; coalitions' actors and activities in, 63, **112**; coercion in, 84, **88**, 180; democratic transition in, **107**; distribution of power, 60, 106, **107**, **149**; educational

Argentina *(continued)*
planners between Peronists and
Church, 59–62; EFA-inspired
education reforms, 152–57, **153**;
EFA recommendations, 147–48,
151; enrollment in private schools,
20; Escuela Intermedia, 64; Factory
Schools, 58, 59, 65; failures of
1990s reforms, 27, 147–48; gross
enrollment ratio in secondary
education in, *19*; local training
programs, 45–46; MEP ideas,
shift away from, 56–66; MEP
recommendations, 46; military
regime, 2, 105–8; mimesis or
mimetic pressures in, 84, 87,
88, 180; National Pedagogical
Congress, 108; policy legacies,
57–59, **60**, 105–8, 147–48, **149**;
political instability, 150; quasi-state
monopoly, 21; recentralization
of authority, 157; right-wing
governments in, 182; secondary
education, expansion of, 59, 64–65;
secondary education governance
in, changes in, **21**; shifts toward
avoidance and defiance, 41;
standardized exams in, 12; state-
managed secondary education
models, 20; state-retrenchment
ideas, failure of, 27; translation
of EFA, **156**; translation of MEP
ideas in, **66**; translation of state-
retrenchment ideas in, **115**;
vocational education, 58; White
Tent, 148
Arizmendi, Octavio, 71
Asamblea Nacional de Estudiantes
Secundarios (ACES), 138, 139
Asociación Nacional de Rectores de
Colegios Privados (ANDERCOP),
69

Association of Chilean Private
Schools, 98, 135, 136
avoidance, 27, **31**, **39**, 40, **104**,
127, **169**; Argentina shifts toward,
41, 46; of Argentinian MEP
ideas, 56–57, 62–65, **66**, **79**; of
Colombian market-oriented ideas,
121–25; of Colombian MEP ideas,
72–76, **77**, **79**; of curriculum, **66**,
79, **104**, **115**, **127**; definition, 38;
education reforms in Argentina,
173; EFA and accountability ideas
in Colombia, **168**; of evaluation,
77, **79**, **115**, 124, **125**, **127**,
168, **169**; of provision, 65, **66**,
77, **79**; of retrenchment ideas in
Argentina, 111–16, **115**; state-
retrenchment ideas in Colombia,
125; of VOCSED, 125, **125**

Bachelet, Michelle, 140; invited
leaders of Stop SIMCE Movement,
145–46; regain of presidency
in 2014, 145; reversed market-
oriented policy, 2; student
mobilization, impact of, 139
Betancourt, Gabriel, 69–71, 76
Bosch, Rodrigo, 136
Brunner Commission, 101, 102

Catholic Centre for Educational
Research and Development, 50, 55
Catholic Church, 26, 40, 78–80;
accommodation of interests in
Chile, 51; alliance with policy
elites against MEP ideas of
Colombia, 69–72; appointed staff,
62; Argentinian state advocates
and, conflicts between, 105–8;
educational planners between
Peronists and, 59–62; education
governance in Argentina and,

58; education policymaking of Chile, 47–53; Frei-Montalva's government, alliance with, 46, 63; Frondizi's administration and, 61–62, 64; VOCSED schools in Colombia, 67

Catholic University of Chile, 100

CDP. *See* Christian Democratic Party

Center for Improvement, Experimentation and Pedagogical Research, 50, 55, 74

centralized curriculum, 10, 173; active-state ideas with, 113; consensus-based, 103; demands of new communities, 33; planning, 72; recentralization of authority, 131; school competition and vouchers for, 83; selective recruitment of students in, 6; tradition in Argentina, 155

Centro de Investigación y Desarrollo de la Educación (CIDE), 50, 55

Centro de Perfeccionamiento, Experimentación e Investigación Pedagógica (CPEIP), 50, 55, 74

CEPAL. *See* United Nations' Economic Commission for Latin America

Chicago Boys, 85, 89, 91, 173, 181; funding arrangement for schools, 98–99; influence of, 180; Pinochet's alliance with, 92–96, 98, 126

Chicago School of Economics, 84

Chile: active-state advocates, conversion of, 92–96; active-state recommendations, 180; Alliance for Progress provided to, 45; authoritarian regime, 3; centralized governance, difficulties of, 89–91; centralized inspection system, 68; coalitions in, 49–53, 52, 54, 92–96, 138–42, 143; coercion in, 13, 45, 46, 84; compromise of education quasi-market in, 142–46; education model, external legitimacy of, 141; education reforms, 133, 143; enrollment in private schools, 20; General Education Law, 144; gross enrollment ratio in secondary education in, 19; Inclusion Law, 145; initiated school transfers, 1; leftist indoctrination, fear of, 89–91, 102; market-based and active-state ideas, 89–103; MEP recommendations, 46, 180; mimesis or mimetic pressures in, 46, 84, 87, 88; New Majority coalition, 141–42; normative pressures, 46, 87, 88; Penguin Revolution, 139, 140, 144; policy elites, 169; policy legacies, 26, 47–48, 49, 89–91, 135–38; Preferential School Voucher, 144; Presidential Advisory Council for Education Quality, 139–40; quasi-market of education, 9, 20, 21, 27, 98, 99, 134–47, 169, 170, 173, 178, 185; right to education, 37, 40, 138, 141; secondary education governance in, changes in, 21; shifts toward conformity and compromise, 40; standardized exams in, 12; state-managed secondary education models, 20; state-retrenchment ideas in, 104; Stop SIMCE Movement, 142, 145–46; student mobilization/movement, 138–41; student movement, 37; test-based accountability and, conformity to, 142–46; transition to democracy,

Chile (*continued*)
93–94, **97**, 101; voucher
system, 35; WB loan, 13; Youth
Parliament, 138
Christian Democratic Party (CDP),
55, 57, 96, 136
CIDE. *See* Centro de Investigación y
Desarrollo de la Educación
coalitions (political): active-state,
138–42; in Argentina, 59–62,
60, **63**, 108–11, **112**, 149–50;
in Chile, 49–53, **52**, **54**, 92–96,
138–42, **143**; in Colombia, 69–72,
73, 117–21, **122**, 161–63, **164**;
domestic, 34–38, 181; findings
and implications, 177–79; market-
oriented, **97**, 138–42
Colegio de Profesores, 93, 96, **97**,
135, 139, **143**
Colegios Particulares de Chile
(CONACEP), 98, 135, 136
Colombia, 2–3, 132; advocates for
stronger state, rise of, 117–21;
Alliance for Progress provided
to, 45; coalitions, 69–72, **73**,
117–21, **122**, 161–63, **164**;
coercion in, 45, 46, 69, 76,
84, **88**, 132, 133, 166, 180;
compatibility of policy legacies
with EFA, **160**; curricular reform,
180; Curricular Renovation,
75; curricular standardization,
165–66, 167; curriculum autonomy,
37; decentralization, 161–62;
Decentralization Bill, 121, 123,
125; defiance and avoidance of
MEP ideas, 72–76; education
governance, stronger small state
for, 163–68; education privatization
in, levels of, 68–69; education
system, centralization of, 2; foreign

aid in, 45; General Education Bill,
123, 124; gross enrollment ratio in
secondary education in, *19*; Law
715, 166; market-based reforms,
favorable environment for, 157–68;
market-oriented ideas, modification
of, 116–25, 127; MEP ideas and
domestic policy, rift between,
66–77; MEP recommendations,
46; mimesis or mimetic pressures
in, 84, 87, **88**, 132, 180; minimal
state, beliefs of, 116–17; National
Front, 71, 72, 117, **118**; National
Planning Department, 69, 119,
120; national schools, transfer
of, 2; National Testing Service,
76, 117; normative pressures, 87,
88, 132, 166; policy elites and
Church against MEP, alliance
between, 69–72; policy legacies,
26, 67–69, 116–17, 157–60, **160**;
power distribution, inherited,
117; pressures received in 2000s,
132, 133; previous reforms, failure
of, 157–60; private schools,
enrollment in, *20*; recentralized
curriculum in 2001, 2–3; right-
wing governments in, 182;
Scholastic Aptitude Test, 71;
secondary education governance
in, changes in, **21**; Servicio
Nacional de Aprendizaje, 124;
standardized exams in, 12; state-
coordinated secondary education
provision, 75; teachers' influence,
decline of, 157–60; teacher unions,
35, 71–72; teaching state, 21; test-
based accountability, avoidance
of, 166; translation of MEP ideas
in, **77**; translation outcomes, 41;
VOCSED, elimination of, 119,

120, 125, 162–63; weakened
opposition to small and controlling
state, 161–63
Colombian Federation of Teachers.
See Federación Colombiana de
Educadores (FECODE)
Colombian Institute for Education
Assessment. *See* Instituto
Colombiano de Fomento de la
Educación Superior (ICFES)
Colombian Institute for the
Promotion of Higher Education.
See Instituto Colombiano de
Fomento de la Educación Superior
(ICFES)
Colombian Pedagogical Institute, 74
compromise: Chilean education
quasi-market, 134–57; of
Colombian market-oriented ideas,
121–25; definition, 38; education
reforms in Argentina, 173; of MEP
ideas in Argentina, 62–65; of
retrenchment ideas in Argentina,
111–16
CONACED. *See* Confederación
Nacional de Centros Docentes
CONACEP. *See* Colegios Particulares
de Chile
CONADE. *See* Consejo Nacional de
Desarrollo
Concertación, 93, 95, 140; allies, 136;
education reforms proposed by, 103;
New Majority coalition, 141–42;
proposed new job regulations, 99;
shared funding, 100
CONES. *See* Coordinadora Nacional
de Estudiantes Secundarios
CONET. *See* Consejo Nacional de
Educación Técnica
Confederación de Trabajadores de
la Educación de la República

Argentina (CTERA), 109–10, 111,
127, 150, 154, 169
Confederación Nacional de Centros
Docentes (CONACED), 69
Confederation of Education Workers
of Argentina, 109–10, 111, 127,
150, 154, 169
conformity, 40, 173; Chilean MEP
ideas, 46–56; definition, 38;
market-oriented ideas, 96–103; to
test-based accountability in Chile,
142–46
Consejo Nacional de Desarrollo
(CONADE), 63–64, 74
Consejo Nacional de Educación
Técnica (CONET), 65
controlled decentralization, 27;
in Argentina, 148, 174; EFA's
recommendations in Chile, 170; in
secondary education provision, 152
Coordinadora Nacional de
Estudiantes Secundarios (CONES),
138, 139
Coordination Assembly of Secondary
Students. *See* Asamblea Nacional
de Estudiantes Secundarios
CPEIP. *See* Centro de
Perfeccionamiento,
Experimentación e Investigación
Pedagógica
CTERA. *See* Confederación de
Trabajadores de la Educación de la
República Argentina
curricular autonomy, 10, 103,
105, 129, 131; Chicago Boys
recommended, 92–93; in Chile,
127; in Colombia, 12, 119,
121, 124; criticism of, 129–30;
foreign prescriptions, 33; "freedom
of education," 102; grassroots
education movements and, 22;

curricular autonomy *(continued)*
heterogeneous interpretation, 133;
perceived as problems, 158. *See
also* curriculum
curricular governance, 5–6
Curricular Renovation, 75
curriculum, 21, 45, 130; Argentina,
60, 63, 66, 107, 149, 156;
autonomy, 96; centralized *(See*
centralized curriculum); changes in,
6–7; Chile, 49, 52, 55, 91, 94,
134, 143; Colombia, 69, 70, 71,
73, 77, 118, 122, 160, 164, 168;
decentralization/decentralized, 26,
86, 113; distribution of authority
over, 7; encyclopedic, 43, 44, 65;
FECODE on, influence of, 75; for
FEL, 113; scientific planning of,
65; secondary school, governance
of, 5–6; standardization *(See*
curriculum standardization); state-
retrenchment ideas in Chile, 104
curriculum standardization, 10;
in Argentina, 155; in Chile,
142, 144, 145; in Colombia, 41,
157, 163, 165–66, 167; General
Education Law and, 144

decentralization, 7; authority, 110;
controlled, 27; curriculum, 26,
86, 110; education system of
Argentina, 105, 106, 108, 110,
111; provision, 26, 86; social
services, 89–90
Decibe, Susana, 110
decision-making (policy), 34;
accessing, 36, 37; Argentinean,
134; compromise on global ideas
and, 40
defiance: Argentina shifts toward,
41; Colombian MEP ideas, 72–76;
definition, 38

Departamento Nacional de
Planeación (DNP), 69, 119, 120
Direction of Religious Education, 59
DNP. *See* Departamento Nacional de
Planeación
domestic coalitions, 34–38; cross-class
coalitions, 35–36; literature on, 35;
of losers of existing policies, 35,
37; power resources, mobilization
of, 37; translation of global ideas,
influence on, 36–37
domestic policy: agendas, 84;
coalitions of losers of existing, 35;
Colombia's rift between MEP ideas
and, 66–77; decisions, 23–24, 32,
88; elites, 13, 173; legacies, 26, 38,
78, 82, 176, 183; path-dependent
pattern of, 34
dualist system, 8, 185; Colombia and,
79, 116, 174

educational planning, 19; foreign-
trained specialists in, 57;
manpower, 26; MEP, 57; rise of
manpower, 26; state-led/state-based,
19, 29, 40, 50; state's responsibility
in, 1
Educational Testing Service (ETS), 71
Education Budget Law, 152

Education for All (EFA), 171, 174;
Chilean education quasi-market
and, 134–35, 141; country-
monitoring reports, 133; Dakar
framework, 130; education
reforms in Argentina, 152–57,
153; market-oriented version
of recommendations by, 169;
policy legacies in Colombia
with, compatibility of, 160;
policy legacies of Chile with,
compatibility of, 137; promotion

of, 130; recommendations
for Argentina, 147–48, 151;
recommendations in Chile, 170;
right to education, 134, 141, 150,
169, 178; translation in Argentina,
156; translation in Chile, 146
education governance: changes in,
current explanations of, 10–17; in
Colombia, 163–68; coordination
of, 86; cross-national variation
of, 18–23; curricular governance,
5–6; distribution of authority,
7; evaluation governance, 6;
Latin America, 5–10; periods of
ideas on, 19; policy alternatives
in, 8; policy-borrowing and
anthropological scholarship,
15–17; political economy,
12–15; provision, curriculum,
and evaluation, changes in, 6–7;
secondary, changes in, 21; state-
centered, 43; world society theory,
11–12
education-planning specialists:
alliance with Church, 50;
international organizations and,
44–45
education policy, 13; Catholic
Church and, 47–50; collective
bargaining of, 37; convergence
and variation, 17; design, 156;
experts, 22; global forces and, 3;
globalization, 4–5, 10, 11, 15, 23,
25, 27, 38, 180; globally diffused
ideas, 3; outcomes, 35; politicizing,
162; public schools and, 36;
scholarship on, 6; secondary,
24, 168, 181–82; teachers and
community participation in, 51;
teacher unions, influence of, 34
education system, 15; Chilean, 50–
51; Colombian, 2, 71–72; disrupted

power distribution, 90–91; global
norms, 12; new communities,
demands of, 33; recommendations
on, 172; stakeholders in, 6–7;
state-centered, 58; state-run, 112;
world society theory and, 11, 12
EFA. See Education for All
El Cordobazo, 105
elitist model of secondary education,
45
encyclopedic curriculum, 43, 44, 65
Escuela Intermedia, 64
Escuela Nacional Unificada (ENU),
51–53; MEP ideas and, 51–52;
opponents, 53; protests against, 53
ETS. See Educational Testing Service
evaluation, 21, 44, 45, 80, 130;
Argentina, 57, 60, 107, 149, 156;
centralized, 21, 62; changes in,
6–7; Chile, 48, 49, 52, 55, 91,
94, 134, 143; Colombia, 70, 73,
77, 118, 122, 160, 164, 168;
distribution of authority over, 7;
governance, 6; state-retrenchment
ideas in Chile, 104
evaluator state, 8, 148
externalization, 15, 16

Factory Schools, 58, 59, 65
Facultad Latinoamericana de
Ciencias Sociales (FLACSO), 45,
110; active-state advocates from,
134
FECODE. See Federación
Colombiana de Educadores
Federación Colombiana de
Educadores (FECODE), 72, 75,
120–21, 157; Congress without
direct participation of, 161;
Gaviria's government and, 120;
General Education Bill and, 123;
municipal councils proposed by,

Federación Colombiana de
Educadores (FECODE) (continued)
123; opposes decentralization
reforms, 162; opposition, 128,
165; organizational capacity, 121;
Pedagogical Movement within,
members of, 121; supported school
autonomy, 124
Federación de Estudiantes
Secundarios de Santiago (FESES),
138
Federación de Institutos de
Educación Secundaria (FIDE),
47–48; capacity in educational
planning, 50
Federal Education Council, 110
Federal Education Law (FEL):
abolition of, 148; negotiations in
curriculum for, 113
Federation of Secondary Schools.
See Federación de Institutos de
Educación Secundaria (FIDE)
FEL. See Federal Education Law (FEL)
Fernández, Alberto, 157
Fernández, Cristina, 2
FESES. See Federación de Estudiantes
Secundarios de Santiago
FIDE. See Federación de Institutos de
Educación Secundaria
FIEL. See Fundación de
Investigaciones Económicas
Latinoamericanas
Filmus, Daniel, 134
FLACSO. See Facultad Latino-
americana de Ciencias Sociales
Ford Foundation, 61, 71, 85
Foundation for Latin American
Economic Research, 108–9
Frei-Montalva, Eduardo, 93;
coalitions supporting and opposing
reforms of, 52; education reforms,
51, 54–56 (See also MEP ideas);

foreign- and domestic-trained
experts during, 50; government,
46; MEP-inspired reform by
policy area, 52; public secondary
schooling, expanded, 54
Frondizi, Arturo, 59; administration,
61–62, 64, 65, 110; assisted
by CEPAL, 61; encyclopedic
curriculum, preserved, 65; National
Council for Technical Education,
65; National Development
Council, 63–64, 74; National
Office for Private Education, 62;
secret endorsement from Perón, 61
Fundación de Investigaciones
Económicas Latinoamericanas
(FIEL), 108–9

Gaviria, Cesar, 2, 120
GEL. See General Education Law

General Education Law (GEL), 124,
144
global ideas, 12, 20, 78, 169, 171;
actors modifying, 3; adoption
of, policy legacies facilitate,
22–23; changes in, 45, 132;
cultural political economy
and, 14; curricular autonomy
and standardized exams, 22;
domestic policy decisions, 23–24;
incompatibility with policy
legacies, 39–40; institutionalization
of, 19; legitimacy of, 34;
policy-borrowing and, 15–17;
reinterpretation, 3–4, 10, 17,
22; scholarship describes, 11;
translation of, 24, 25, 35; by world
society theory, 16
globalization of education policy:
domestic actors in, role of, 15
global market-oriented ideas, 3–4

glocalization, 16
governance: areas of, 22; bureaucratic model of, 7; centralized, 79, 89–91, 120, 127; curricular, 5–6; definition, 5; evaluation, 6
Guido, Jose María, 61

Hasbún, Alejandro, 136
hybridization, 16

IADB. See Inter-American Development Bank
ICFES. See Instituto Colombiano de Fomento de la Educación Superior
ICOLPE. See Instituto Colombiano de Pedagogía
IIEP-UNESCO, 150, 151
ILARI. See Instituto Latinoamericano de Relaciones Internacionales
Illia, Arturo, 61
ILO. See International Labor Organization
IMF. See International Monetary Fund
INEM schools, 76. See also vocational secondary school
inspiration, 16
Instituto Colombiano de Fomento de la Educación Superior (ICFES), 76, 85, 125, 166
Instituto Colombiano de Pedagogía (ICOLPE), 74
Instituto Latinoamericano de Relaciones Internacionales (ILARI), 61
Inter-American Development Bank (IADB), 13, 132
International Institute for Educational Planning, UNESCO Buenos Aires, 150, 151
International Labor Organization (ILO), 65

International Monetary Fund (IMF), 13, 83, 109, 132. See also World Bank

juxtaposition, 16

Ketterer, Rodrigo, 136
Kirchner, Cristina Fernández de, 150, 151–52
Kirchner, Nestor, 2; government (2003–2007), 150–52; staff from FLACSO and IIEP-UNESCO, 150

Laboratorio Latinoamericano de Evaluación de la Calidad de la Educación (LLECE), 87
Latin America: combinations and sequences of reforms by, 10; education governance in, 5–10; education systems, stakeholders role in, 6–7; gross enrollment ratio in, 8, 9; loans and financial and technical assistance, 13; secondary education in, 8, 43
Latin American Faculty of Social Sciences. See Facultad Latinoamericana de Ciencias Sociales (FLACSO)
Latin American Institute for International Relations, 61
Latin American Laboratory for Assessment of Education Quality, 87
Leigh, Gustavo, 90, 92, 93
LEN. See Ley Nacional de Educación
LETP. See Ley de Educación Técnico-Profesional
Ley de Educación Técnico-Profesional (LETP), 152
Ley Federal de educación: 113, 148
Ley de Financiamiento Educativo (LFE), 152

Ley General de Educación 124, 144
Ley Nacional de Educación (LEN), 152, 155
Ley Orgánica Constitucional de Enseñanza (LOCE), 95, 98, 101, 102–4; demonstrations for abolition of, 138–39; promulgation of, 102; Superior Education Council, 102–3
Leyton, Mario, 50
LFE. See Ley de Financiamiento Educativo
LLECE. See Laboratorio Latinoamericano de Evaluación de la Calidad de la Educación
LOCE. See Ley Orgánica Constitucional de Enseñanza
Los Andes University, 85

Macri, Mauricio, 2, 152; test-based accountability during, 156–57
Major Project of Education, 87, 180
Manpower Educational Planning (MEP), 43; curriculum recommendations, 80; ideas (See MEP ideas); promoted employment, 44; provision recommendation, 80; recommendations, 44, 46, 48, 58, 75, 78; reforms by liberal governments, 79; state-centered recommendations, 81
MAPU. See Movimiento de Acción Popular Unitaria
market-based approach/market-oriented ideas: Argentinean overlapping of, 104–16; boom of, 84; Chilean, 41, 89–103, 91, 135–38; compromise and avoidance of, 121–25; conformity to, 96–103; curriculum recommendations, 26, 27, 90, 91, 179; disseminated in Latin America, 83; education

inequality and predominance in Chile, 135–38; education policy, influenced, 88; evaluation recommendations, 90, 91, 100, 116; governance of secondary education, 82–85; modification in Colombia, 116–25; policy legacies of Colombia with, compatibility of, 118; predominance of, 173; provision recommendations, 90, 91; reforms in evaluation, 100; relative incompatibility of Chilean policy legacies with, 91; sequential translation of, 89–103; supporters of, policy legacies and, 40
market-oriented coalition, 95, 97, 125, 162, 163; decision-making and, 120; education reforms proposed by, 93; municipal councils proposed by FECODE and, 123; negotiations with, 99; Transference Law of 1991 and, 112; voucher system and, 92; weaknesses of, 124
market-oriented education policies, 12
MECE-media, 99
Mediterranean Regional Project, 64
Menem, Carlos, 2, 108–9; administration/government, 109, 112, 150; appointed Jorge Rodríguez, 110; economic policies, failure of, 149–50; education reforms, 148; popularity, decline in, 147
MEP. See Manpower Educational Planning
MEP ideas, 89; Argentina's shift away from, 56–66; Chilean conformity to, 46–56; Chile's education problems, solve, 48; Colombia's rift between domestic policy and, 66–77; disseminated in Latin America,

44; inefficiency of, 84; translation outcomes by country and policy area, **79**
Milla, Juan Gomez, 50
Movimiento de Acción Popular Unitaria (MAPU), 53

NAP. *See* Núcleos de Aprendizaje Prioritario
National Association of Private School Principals, 69
National Commission for the Modernization of Education, 101, 102
National Committee for Secondary Students, 138, 139
National Confederation of Teaching Centres, 69
National Council for Technical Education, 65
national curriculum, 33, 57, 103, 131; development of, 48; "encyclopedic," 43; for primary education, 29; schools followed, 57; for secondary education, 80, 117
National Development Council, 63–64, 74
National Education Council, 51
National Education Law, 152, 155
National Office for Private Education, 62
National Pedagogical Congress (NPC), 108
National Planning Department, 69, 119, 120
National System for Education Quality Assessment, 114, 115
National System for Performance Assessment, 101, 136, 142
National University of Colombia, 46

New Majority coalition, 141–42
New Public Management (NPM), 29–30; coalition supporting policies, 41; proposals, 82; recommendations, 41
NM. *See* New Majority coalition
NPM. *See* New Public Management
Núcleos de Aprendizaje Prioritario (NAP), 155
Nueva Mayoría, 141–42

OAS. *See* Organization of American States
OECD. *See* Organization for Economic Cooperation and Development
Oliva, Walter, 136
Onganía, Juan Carlos, 61
Organic Constitutional Education Law. *See* Ley Orgánica Constitucional de Enseñanza (LOCE)
Organization for Economic Cooperation and Development (OECD), 13, 133
Organization of American States (OAS), 11, 44, 65
organizational capability, 25, 36, 37, 50

PACES, 120, 123
Pastrana, Andres: fiscal imbalances, addresses, 161; reform in 2001 under, 2; school municipalization and demand-driven funding, 161
Penguin Revolution, 139, 140, 144
Perón, Juan Domingo, 61; anti-secular trend by administration of, 58–59; civilian-military coup in 1955, 59–60; Direction of Religious Education, 59; Factory Schools, 58, 59, 65; national

Perón, Juan Domingo (*continued*)
school curriculum, 59; teacher
unions, elimination of, 62
Peronism, 174; banned from electoral
competition, 59, 61; Frondizi's
administration and, 61–62;
legacies, 65; regained office in
2019, 157; secondary public school,
expansion of, 177; "stamping out,"
61; support for, 58–59
Peronists, **63**; access to decision-
making, 61; alliances, 61; coalition
of, 150–51; educational planners
between Church, 59–62; learning
content, abolishing, 62
Piñera, Sebastian, 140, 145
Pinochet, Augusto, 90, 181; alliance
with Chicago Boys, 92–96, 98,
126; Constitution of 1980, 95, 102;
education policies, 89; initiated
school transfers, 1; regime, 26, 96,
100, 101; shared-funding system,
99–100; VOCSED schools and, 98;
voucher system during, 35
policy-borrowing, 15–17; external
references, 15–16; scholarship, 18;
translation of global ideas, 16
policy legacies, 18, 19, 172;
Argentinian, 57–59, **60**, 105–8,
147–48, **149**; Chilean, 26,
47–48, **49**, 89–91, **91**, 135–38;
Colombian, 26, 67–69, 116–17,
157–60, **160**; domestic, 26, 38, 78,
82, 176, 183; domestic conflicts
and, 25, 32–34; findings and
implications, 175–76; global norms
and domestic, 32; incompatibility
with global ideas, 39–40;
legitimacy of, 34; path-dependent
dynamics, 34; power distribution,
structure of, 33–34; role of, 32–34
Polimodal, 113, 114

political economy, 12–15; cultural,
14, 15, 16, 17, 33, 180; traditional,
13
Popular Unitary Action Movement,
53
Popular Unity, 53
post-bureaucratic form: of
governance, 6; of managing school
system, 18–19
postsecondary education, 131, 167;
Chile, 52; enrollment in, 162;
National Workers University
(Argentina), 58; technical, 163
power resources, mobilization of, 37,
39
Preferential School Voucher, 144
Presidential Advisory Council for
Education Quality, 139–40
primary education, 56, 71, 116;
curricular renovation, 75;
expansion of, 47, 68, 72;
governance in Chile, 48; national
curriculum for, 29; reorientation of
funding to, 84; universalization of,
89, 175
Priority Learning Cores, 155
private school, 57, 69; Allende's
proposal to nationalize, 55;
Arizmendi and, 71; autonomy,
53; Catholic, 47–48; compete for
funding, 1; elite, 51; enrollment in,
20; expansion of, 64; governance
of, 62; growth of, 10; nationalizing,
in Chile, 52; nationalizing, in
Colombia, 74; receiving financial
resources, 75; regularizing subsidies
in Argentina, 58; support for
Peronism, 58–59
private voucher schools, 98, 99,
135; Inclusion Law and, 145;
preferential voucher to, 144;
shared funding in, 100, 136

Program for Performance Assessment, 100
Project Chile, 85
provision, 21, 45, 64; Argentina, 60, 63, 66, 107, 149, 156; avoidance, 65; changes in, 6–7; Chile, 49, 52, 55, 91, 94, 134, 143; Colombia, 69, 70, 72, 73, 77, 118, 122, 160, 164, 168; decentralization, 26, 86; distribution of authority over, 7; state-retrenchment ideas in Chile, 104
public-private partnerships (PPPs), 130, 133, 165, 172

quasi-market of education, 10, 126; Chile, 9, 20, 21, 27, 98, 99, 134–47, 169, 170, 173, 178, 185; coalition supporting, 141; emergence of, 172–73; Gaviria helped in implementation, 177; Inclusion Law and, 145; inequality of, 135; negative consequences, 138
quasi-state monopoly, 7, 8, 193n1; Argentina, 20, 185; Latin American countries adopted, 9

Regional Comparative and Explanatory Studies of the Quality of Education, 85
reinforcement of domestic institutions, 16
result-based incentives, 81, 115
Rockefeller Foundation, 46, 61, 85
Rodríguez, Jorge, 110, 113

Salonia, Antonio, 110
Samper, Ernesto, 123, 161
Santiago's Federation of Secondary Students, 138
Scholastic Aptitude Test, 71

secondary education, 43; Argentina, active state in, 147–57; curricular orientation for, 44; curriculum goals in, 24; expansion in Argentina, 59, 64–65; expansion of, 26; governance, changes in, 20, 21; gross enrollment ratio in, 19; humanistic, 44; Latin America, 8; massification of, 29; policy, 24; policy, 24, 168, 181–82; privatized, 68; reproduces pervasive educational inequality, 186; weak state of governance in Colombia, 67–69
secondary education provision, 44, 154; centralization of, 178; controlled decentralization in, 152; controlled expansion in Colombia, 71; recommendations on, 130; reinterpreted global ideas on, 172; state-coordinated, 75
SENA. See Servicio Nacional de Aprendizaje
Servicio Nacional de Aprendizaje (SENA), 124; Articulation, 163; Uribe's administration and, 162; VOCSED curriculum to, 167–68
shared-funding system, 99–100; abolition of, 139; in private voucher schools, 100, 136
SIMCE. See Sistema de Evaluación de la Calidad Educativa
SINEC. See Sistema Nacional de la Evaluación de la Calidad
Sistema de Evaluación de la Calidad Educativa (SIMCE), 100–101, 133, 139; socioeconomic variables from reports of, 140; standardized assessments, 135, 137; Stop SIMCE Movement, 142, 145–46
Sistema Nacional de Evaluación del Desempeño (SNED), 101, 136, 142

Sistema Nacional de la Evaluación
de la Calidad (SINEC), 114, 115
SNED. *See* Sistema Nacional de
Evaluación del Desempeño
SNEP. *See* Superintendencia
Nacional de la Enseñanza Privada
standardized exams/assessments, 26,
151, 165; active-state experts
and, 96; Argentina, 2, 115;
Chilean, 84, 100, 139, 144–45;
Colombian, 125, 128; developing
countries, incentives for, 13;
development of, 83; expansion
of, 130; implementation of, 10,
22; institutionalization of, 12;
large-scale, 1; occasional, 44, 48;
SIMCE's, 135, 139; technical
expertise in, absence of, 155
state retrenchment ideas, 19, 95;
Argentina, 104–16, **107**, **115**,
126; in Chile, 89–103, **104**, 126,
127, 128; diffusion channels and
timing of, **88**; education and
diffusion channels, varieties in,
87; failure in Argentina, 37;
market-based approach, 82–85;
recommendations, criticisms to,
130
Stop SIMCE Movement, 142, 145–46
student evaluation. *See* evaluation
Superintendencia Nacional de la
Enseñanza Privada (SNEP), 62
System for Measurement of
Education Quality. *See* Sistema de
Evaluación de la Calidad Educativa
(SIMCE)

teacher unions, 34, 51, 62; Colegio
de Profesores, 93, 96, **97**, 135,
139, **143**; Colombian, 35, 71–72;
Confederación de Trabajadores

de la Educación de la República
Argentina, 109–10, 111, 127, 150,
154, 169; Federación Colombiana
de Educadores, 72, 75, 120–21,
123, 124, 128, 157, 161, 162, 165
teaching state, 7, **8**, 79
Tedesco, Juan Carlos, 134
tertiary education, 24
test-based accountability, 6; in
Argentina, 13, 41, 134, 156–57;
in Chile, 134, 136, 138, 142; in
Colombia, 2, 134, 166; during
Macri's government, 156–57. *See
also* accountability ideas
TIMMS. *See* Trends in International
Mathematics and Science Study
Transference Law, 112
translation of global ideas: domestic
actors in, 31; entities and
activities involved in, 30; foreign
recommendations, 34; mechanisms,
26, 30–32, **31**; of MEP ideas in
Chile, **55**; outcomes of, 38–40, **39**;
overview, 29–32
Trends in International Mathematics
and Science Study (TIMMS), 85

UNDP. *See* United Nations
Development Program
UNESCO. *See* United Nations
Educational Scientific and Cultural
Organization
UNICEF, 130, 141, 152
Unidad Popular (UP), 53
Unified National School. *See* Escuela
Nacional Unificada
United Nations Development
Program (UNDP), 45, 74
United Nations' Economic
Commission for Latin America
(CEPAL), 11, **44**, 45, 85–88, 96;

assisted Frondizi, 61; "Education and Knowledge: Basic Pillars of Changing Production Patterns with Social Equity," 88; promoted decentralization, 85

United Nations Educational Scientific and Cultural Organization (UNESCO), 44, 86–88, 96; active-state advocates from, 134; aid to Colombia, 73, 74; courses and in-service training in Colombia, 71; educational policy ideas, 11; "Education and Knowledge: Basic Pillars of Changing Production Patterns with Social Equity," 88; EFA framework, promotion of, 130; Latin American Laboratory for Assessment of Education Quality, 87; local graduate educational planning programs, 45; Major Project of Education, 87, 180; MEP ideas of Colombia, 69; National University of Colombia, rejection of financial support to, 46; planning networks, 62; promoted decentralization, 85; recommendations, 86; Regional Comparative and Explanatory Studies of the Quality of Education, 85; state-led educational planning, 29; students' protests and, 141

United States Agency for International Development (USAID), 11; aid to Colombia, 73, 74; conditional aid, 44; grants and financial aid program, 84; Project Chile, 85; Project Cuyo, support to, 85; testing educational innovations of, 45

University of Chile, 45, 50

Uribe, Alvaro, 162

USAID. See United States Agency for International Development

vocational education, 56; in Argentina, 58, 182; Chicago Boys and, 92–93; in Chile, 56, 103; in Colombia, 69, 134, 182; expansion of, 182. See also vocational secondary school

Vocational Education Law, 152

vocational secondary school (VOCSED), 44, 98, 129; Argentinian, 57, 61, **63**, **66**, 150, 151; Chilean, 55, 56, 139; Colombian, 67, **70**, **73**, 75–76, **77**, **118**, 119, 121, **122**, 124, 158, 159, **160**, **164**, 167–68, **168**; elimination of, 119, 120, 125, 126, 132, 162–63, 167; transformation of, 126; vocational specializations, 102; WB loans to Colombia, 84; World Bank's technical reports on, 180

World Bank (WB), 11, 13, 109, 114; coercion, 84; Colombian Pedagogical Institute, 74; Colombian VOCSED schools, loans for, 84; conditional aid, 44; EFA framework, promotion of, 130; international education aid, 83–84; loan to Colombia, 76, 132; MECE-media, loans for, 99; PACES, assistance for, 120, 123; recommendation, 83, 167; reports on VOCSED schools, 180; technical assistance to Colombia, 133; testing educational innovations of, 45

world society theory, 11–12

Youth Parliament, 138

www.ingramcontent.com/pod-product-compliance
Lightning Source LLC
Chambersburg PA
CBHW020343270326
41926CB00007B/295